DIVINE BEAUTY

Divine Beauty

THE AESTHETICS
OF CHARLES HARTSHORNE

Daniel A. Dombrowski

Vanderbilt University Press
NASHVILLE

Library of Congress Cataloging-in-Publication Data

Dombrowski, Daniel A.
Divine beauty : the aesthetics of Charles Hartshorne /
by Daniel A. Dombrowski.—1st ed.
p. cm.—(The Vanderbilt library of American philosophy)
    Includes bibliographical references and index.
ISBN 0–8265–1440–5 (alk. paper)
    1. Hartshorne, Charles, 1897–2000—Aesthetics. 2.
Aesthetics, Modern—20th century. I. Title. II. Series.
B945.H354D645 2004
111.'85'092—dc22

                                    2003017643

Contents

Acknowledgments

I would like to thank the two Vanderbilt University Press reviewers who read two quite different versions of my manuscript and who made many helpful suggestions for improvement of the work. One of these readers was Donald Viney and the other remains anonymous. It is an understatement to say that I have benefited greatly from their efforts.

Abbreviations of Works
by Charles Hartshorne

Introduction

CHARLES HARTSHORNE WAS BORN in the nineteenth century and lived to philosophize in the twenty-first. Perhaps the most neglected aspect of his extensive and highly nuanced thought is his aesthetics, a discipline within philosophy to which he contributed as early as the 1920s in his Harvard doctoral dissertation (he minored in English literature at Harvard). His efforts in aesthetics quite incredibly lasted into the 1990s, over half a century after he cofounded the American Society for Aesthetics (and its associated journal, *The Journal of Aesthetics and Art Criticism*) in 1942 (HL, 49).

The purpose of the present book is both to explicate in detail his theory of aesthetics for the first time and to use this theory to show the superiority of neoclassical or process theism over the classical theism defended by traditionalist Jews, Christians, and Muslim believers. The parenthetical citations throughout the book alert the reader to the sources from Hartshorne that I have used rather liberally. Hartshorne's own sources in aesthetics were myriad, as his extensive collection of books in art, art criticism, and aesthetics (now housed at the Center for Process Studies at the Claremont School of Theology) indicate. These sources will be cited throughout the book.

A generation ago Whitehead's aesthetics received definitive exploration by Donald Sherburne.[1] But the present work is quite different from Sherburne's magisterial book for at least three reasons. First, Hartshorne's philosophy is theocentric in a way that Whitehead's is not. Despite the fact that Sherburne's atheistic interpretation of Whitehead (developed after his book on Whitehead's aesthetics) is, from my point of view, unpersuasive for many reasons, it is nonetheless clear that his interpretation of Whitehead is at least plausible and must be taken seriously. But even Sherburne would seem to agree that it is not even remotely plausible to interpret Hartshorne's thought along non-religious lines. That is, Hartshorne's philosophy is God-intoxicated, an inebriation (ironic in light of Hartshorne's lifelong abstinence from alcohol) that affects his aesthetics at every turn, as we will see. Second, Hartshorne's aesthetics, unlike Whitehead's, appeals to an idiosyncratic but extremely interesting study of birdsong. And third, Hartshorne's aesthetics, in contrast to Whitehead's, relies heavily on the claim that sensation is a type of aesthetic feeling (at least Hartshorne uses different terminology from Whitehead's). Indeed, the Greek word *aesthesis* originally meant nothing other than feeling or what we today might call experience; only later did it refer to a disciplined feeling for beauty. This etymology fits in nicely with the panpsychist view of Hartshorne.

In this regard I would like to emphasize that the word "aesthetic" will be used in two different senses in this book. In the broad sense it refers to feeling, in general, as in the aforementioned Greek sense of the term, or to the sensory "feel" of things. But there is also a narrower sense of the term that refers to an experience of, or to a quality inherent in, a work of art, in particular. Context should indicate clearly which sense of the term I have in mind.

We will see, however, that the issue is complicated by the fact that the broad sense of the term helps us to better understand our experience of specific works of art just as certain experiences we have of works of art illuminate aesthetic experience in general. That is, artistic creation (or appreciation) is, as Sherburne puts it in Whiteheadian terms, "simply a more concentrated, sophisticated version of an activity common to all actual occasions."[2] Again, context will help the reader determine which sense of the term I have in mind in a particular discussion. It is also interesting to note, especially because of Hartshorne's fascinating treatments of panpsychism and of sensation as a type of feeling, that the broad meaning of "aesthetic" was the dominant one well into the nineteenth century. That is, the identification of "aesthetics" with the arts in particular, is a relatively recent phenomenon.[3]

Hartshorne himself tells us of his interest in the aesthetics of birdsong as early as 1920, the courses he taught in aesthetics at the University of Chicago and elsewhere as early as 1928, and his careful study of the aesthetics of birdsong under the auspices of the University of Michigan (and of the remarkable window the aesthetics of birdsong provides for aesthetics in general) in 1953. He is the first philosopher since Aristotle to be equally serious about what he sees as the most important branch of philosophy—metaphysics—and ornithology. He, like Dvořák, sees birdsong as musical, and he sees it as illustrating the thesis that physical tones are, as Beethoven implied, the primordial feelings of nature. Kandinsky expresses a similar idea about color that supports Hartshorne's view. Further, we will see that Hartshorne was a pioneer in the heroic effort (continued by Langer and others)[4] to defend opposition to aesthetic relativism; it is not the case that "anything goes," given our biological inheritance that lies behind our aesthetic sensibilities (WM, 106, 109; ZF, 43–44, 211; PC, 125).

The remainder of this introduction summarizes the salient features of the view of God that will be assumed throughout the book.

Hartshorne fully accepts the goal of the traditional religious philosophers, i.e., to use logical analysis in the service of a higher end. But he holds that the classical conception of God is internally incoherent. One of his major complaints about classical theism (in philosophy and theology, as opposed to biblical theism) is that it either explicitly or implicitly identifies God as active and not passive. St. Thomas Aquinas' unmoved mover is the most obvious example of this tendency, but in general, classical Judaic, Christian, and Islamic theists see God as a timeless, supernatural being that does not change. The classical theist's inconsistency lies in also claiming that God knows and loves and aesthetically appreciates the world. For example, if God knows, God must be a subject analogous to human subjects, and if God is a subject who knows, God must be affected by, be passive with respect to, the object known.

It will be to our advantage to get as clear as we can on what we mean by the term "God." In this book the term refers to the supremely excellent or all-worshipful being. As is well known, Hartshorne has been the most important recent defender of St. Anselm's ontological argument, and his debt to St. Anselm is evident in this preliminary definition. It closely resembles St. Anselm's "that than which no greater can be conceived." Yet the ontological argument is not what is at stake here. Even if the argument fails, which Hartshorne doubts, the preliminary definition of God as the supremely excellent being, the all-worshipful being, the most beautiful being, and the greatest conceivable being seems unobjectionable. To say that God can be defined in these ways still leaves open the possibility that God is even more excellent or worshipful or beautiful than our ability to conceive, as St. Anselm himself admits (*Proslogium,* Chapter 15) when he says that God is even greater than can be conceived.[5] This allows us to avoid objections from mystics who fear that by defining God we are limiting God to merely human language. All Hartshorne is suggesting is that when we think of God we must be thinking of a being who surpasses all others or we are not thinking of God. Even the atheist or agnostic would admit this much. When the atheist says, "There is no God," it is a denial that a supremely excellent, all-worshipful, most beautiful, greatest conceivable being exists.

The excellent-inferior contrast is the truly invidious contrast when applied to God. If to be invidious is to be injurious, then this contrast is most invidious when applied to God because God is only excellent. God is inferior in no way. Period. To suggest that God is in some small way inferior to some other being is to no longer speak about God but about some being that is not supremely excellent, all-worshipful, the most beautiful, or the greatest conceivable. Hartshorne's major criticism of classical theism is that it assumes that all contrasts, or most of them, when applied to God are invidious. Let us assume that God exists. What attributes does God possess? Consider the following two columns of attributes in polar contrast to each other:

oneness	plurality
being	becoming
activity	passivity
permanence	change
necessity	contingency
self-sufficiency	dependency
actuality	potentiality
absoluteness	relativity
abstractness	concreteness

Classical theism tends toward oversimplification. It is comparatively easy to say, "God is strong rather than weak, so in all relations God is active, not passive." In each case, the classical theist decides which member of the contrasting pair is good (on the left) and then attributes it to God, wholly denying the contrasting term (on the right). Hence, God is one and not many, permanent and not changing. This leads to what Hartshorne called the monopolar prejudice. Monopolarity is common to both classical theism and pantheism; the major difference between the two is that classical theism admits the reality of plurality, potentiality, and becoming as a secondary form of existence outside God (on the right), whereas in pantheism God includes all reality. Common to both classical theism and pantheism is the belief that the above categorical contrasts are invidious. The dilemma these two positions face is that either the deity is only one constituent of the whole (classical theism) or else the alleged inferior pole in each contrast (on the right) is illusory (pantheism). Many theists believe, erroneously, Hartshorne thinks, that these two options exhaust the systematic alternatives to atheism.

This dilemma is artificial. It is produced by the assumption that excellence is found by separating and purifying one pole (on the left) and denigrating the other (on the right). That this is not the case can be seen by analyzing some of the attributes on the right side. At least since St. Augustine classical theists have been convinced that God's eternity and beauty means not that God endures through all time, but that God is outside time altogether and does not, cannot, be receptive to temporal change. Following Aristotle, the greatest predecessor to classical theism, St. Thomas Aquinas identified God as unmoved. Yet both activity and passivity can be either good or bad. Good passivity is likely to be called sensitivity, responsiveness, adaptability, sympathy, and the like. Defective or insufficiently subtle passivity is called inflexibility, stubbornness, inadaptability, unresponsiveness, and the like. To deny God passivity altogether is to deny God those aspects of passivity that are excellences and that are partially constitutive of beauty, as we will see. To deny God the ability to change avoids fickleness but at the expense of the ability to react lovingly to the sufferings of others.

The terms in the left column above have both good and bad aspects as well. Oneness can mean wholeness, but it can also mean aesthetic monotony or triviality. Actuality can mean definiteness, but it can mean nonrelatedness to others. What happens to divine love when St. Thomas Aquinas claims that God is *pure* actuality? God ends up loving the world but is intrinsically unrelated to it, whatever sort of love that may be. Self-sufficiency can, at times, be selfishness.

The task when thinking of God is to attribute to God all excellences (left *and* right sides) and not to attribute to God any inferiorities (right *and* left sides). In short, excellent-inferior and good-evil are invidious contrasts ("good-good" is a redundancy and "evil-good" is a contradiction), but one-many, being-becoming, etc., are noninvidious contrasts. Unlike classical theism and pantheism, neoclassical or process theism is dipolar. Specifically, within *each* pole of a noninvidious contrast (e.g., permanence-change) there are invidious elements (inferior permanence or inferior change) but also noninvidious, good elements (excellent permanence or excellent change). When accused of denying God's transcendence, the Hartshornian reply should be in terms of a theory of dual transcendence: we should believe in twice as much transcendence as the classical theist.

Hartshorne does not believe in two gods, one unified and the other plural. Rather, he believes that what are often thought to be contraries are really mutually interdependent correlatives: "The good as we know it is unity-in-variety, or variety-in-unity; if the variety overbalances, we have chaos or discord; if the unity, we have monotony or triviality" (PS, 3). This claim, as we will see, has profound ramifications for aesthetics. Supreme excellence, if it is truly supreme excellence, *must* somehow be able to integrate all the *complexity* there is in the world into itself as one spiritual, aesthetically valuable whole. The word "must" indicates divine necessity, along with God's essence, which is to necessarily exist. And the word "complexity" indicates the contingency that affects God through creaturely decisions or feelings. But in the classical theistic view, God is solely identified with the stony immobility of the absolute, implying nonrelatedness to the world. God in the abstract may in a way escape from the temporal flux, but a living God is related to the world of becoming, which entails divine becoming as well if the world in some way is internally related to God.

The classical theist's alternative to this view suggests that all relationships to God are external to divinity, once again threatening not only God's love, but also God's nobility. A dog's being behind a particular rock affects the dog in certain ways because the dog is aware of it. Thus this relation is an internal relation to this particular dog. But it does not affect the rock, whose relationship with the dog is external to the rock's nature. (We will see that the situation is somewhat different for the microscopic parts of the rock; i.e., the rock as a whole is an abstraction in relation to its more concrete constituents.) Does this not show the superiority of canine consciousness, which is aware of the rock, to rocklike existence, which is unaware of the dog? And is it not therefore peculiar that God has been described solely in rocklike terms: pure actuality, permanence, only having external relations, unmoved, being and not becoming?

In short, the divine being becomes, or the divine becoming is —God's being and becoming form a single reality, according to Hartshorne:

> There is no law of logic against attributing contrasting predicates to the same individual, provided they apply to diverse aspects of this individual. . . . God is neither being as contrasted to becoming nor becoming as contrasted to being; but categorically supreme becoming in which there is a factor of categorically supreme being, as contrasted to inferior becoming, in which there is inferior being. (ps, 14–15, 24)

Thus Hartshorne's theism can be called panentheism, which literally means "all *in* God." God is neither completely removed from the world, or unmoved by it, as in classical theism, nor completely identified with the world, as in pantheism. Rather, God is (1) world-inclusive in the sense that God cares for all the world and all feelings in the world, especially suffering feelings, are aesthetically felt by God and (2) transcendent in the sense that God is greater than any other being, especially because of God's everlasting existence and love. (As before, Hartshorne defends in DR and elsewhere a concept of "dual transcendence," wherein God excels all others with respect to the terms in both the left and the right sides of the columns above.)

There are at least four logically distinct views regarding God: (1) God is merely the *cosmos,* in all aspects inseparable from the sum or system of dependent things or effects (pantheism); (2) God is both this system and something independent of it (Hartshornian panentheism); (3) God is not the system, but is in all aspects independent (traditional or classical theism); and (4) God is not the system but is in some aspects dependent on it (as in Lequyer or Brightman).⁶ (1) and (3) are simple views; (2) is complex. (1) and (2) refer to God as "the inclusive reality," but much depends on what one means by this phrase. That (1) and (2) are not identical can be seen by the fact that for *both* (2) and (3) the error of pantheism is to deny the externality of concrete existence to the essence of deity. Note that "God is all things" (1) is not equivalent to "God includes all things" (2)—e.g., through divine omniscience and love and aesthetic appreciation. And later in the book we will see why Hartshorne rejects (4), the view that accepts divine passivity but denies panentheism and divine inclusiveness.

The differences among these views can also be seen in their relation to the ontological argument. Many theists have assented to this argument, but with different results. Spinoza, for example, confused the necessary *existence* of God (i.e., the fact *that* God must exist) with the concrete *actuality* of God (i.e., *how* God exists); hence he believes that everything relating to God is necessary.⁷ Panentheists need not deduce the necessity of *everything* from an abstract definition, even if they do accept the ontological argument. God, for panentheists like Hartshorne, is necessary or absolute or self-sufficient only in bare essence or existence but is contingent in actuality in that *how* God exists at least partially depends on other things that exist, which aesthetically enrich the divine life. The actual state of the deity is partly determined by creatures as a consequence of the social character of the divine self-decision. To be more precise, Hartshorne distinguishes among *essence* (the most abstract features of a thing), *existence* (the fact that a thing is), and *actuality* (characteristics that qualify an existing thing).

It is no wonder that theologians were shocked by Spinoza's views and that the principle of divine inclusiveness was easily mistaken for its Spinozistic, necessitarian form, so that certain thinkers (such as Coleridge and Wordsworth and other English romantic thinkers)⁸ felt compelled to retreat into classical theism at times, even if they knew there were defects in that position. But the term "pantheism" cannot be applied to all varieties of divine inclusiveness. The distinction between pantheism and panentheism is certainly no literary flourish; it is due to logical differences. Spinoza missed the truth but he had great genius, Hartshorne thinks. For example, Spinoza was correct that neither his view nor those of his classical theistic critics were to be found in scripture. Spinoza was the first to expose the skeleton in the classical theistic closet: an *exclusively* absolute and eternal God cannot be related to a contingent yet aesthetically valuable world. The essence of the divine substance, by this reasoning, determines its entire career, so that divine substance must be denied contingent predicates to preserve the absoluteness of deity. As before, the defects in Spinoza's position stem from the monopolar reasoning he inherited from classical theism. His God is an unmoved mover knowing an unmoved (or better, noncontingent) world. Nor do his geometrical analogies help him here—in Euclidean geometry, at least, necessary properties are not modifications but intrinsic properties.

A more sophisticated notion of divine containment can be developed by distinguishing among three sorts of sentiency (hereafter: S) or feeling (*aesthesis*). S1 is sentiency at the microscopic level of cells, atomic particles, and the like, where contemporary physics has partially vindicated the hylozoic position of antiquity and panpsychism. The nightmare of determinism has faded as reality in its fundamental constituents seems to have at least a partially indeterminate character of self-motion. That is, the sum total of efficient causes from the past does not supply the sufficient cause to explain the behavior of the smallest units of becoming in the world. In twentieth-century physics, universal mechanism gave way to a cosmic dance. That is, Hartshorne is both an indeterminist and a panpsychist, in contrast to Leibniz, who was a determinist and a panpsychist, and to many contemporary physicists who are indeterminists yet not panpsychists.

S2 is sentiency *per se,* sentience in the sense of feeling of feeling (or *aesthesis* of *aesthesis*). This sentience is found in animals and human beings, whereby those with central nervous systems aesthetically feel as wholes, just as their constituent parts show prefigurations of aesthetic feeling on a local level. And aesthetic feeling *is* localized: think of the pain in burning one's finger or of sexual pleasure. S2 consists in taking these local feelings and collecting them on a higher level so that an individual as a whole can feel what happens to its parts, even if the individual transcends the parts to some degree. As Hartshorne says, hurt my cells and you hurt *me*. (In contrast, a non-panpsychist would concede that if one *damages* my cells one hurts me but would not concede that one can "hurt" a cell in the sense that Hartshorne thinks is possible.)

S3 is divine sentiency. Hartshorne's view can be best understood, it seems, by the following four-term analogy:

$$S1 : S2 :: S2 : S3$$

The universe is a society or an organism of which one member (God) is preeminent yet world-inclusive, just as a human being is a society of cells of which the mental part is preeminent. Hartshorne does not, however, find the following four-term analogy an adequate tool in describing the *cosmos:*

$$S1 : \text{a table} :: S2 : \text{the "uni"verse as a concatenation of parts}$$

Or as Erazim Kohák puts the point:

> Shall we conceive of the world around us and of ourselves in it as *personal,* a meaningful whole, honoring its order as continuous with the moral law of our own being and its beings as continuous with ours, bearing its goodness—or shall we conceive of it and treat it, together with ourselves, as *impersonal,* a chance aggregate of matter propelled by a blind force and exhibiting at most the ontologically random lawlike regularities of a causal order?[9]

Hartshorne chooses the former alternative. In short, the above paragraphs indicate the conception of God that will be operative throughout this book.

The chapters are arranged in the following fashion. Chapter 1 describes the historic and thematic background for the present study.

In this chapter I also indicate some of Hartshorne's unique contributions to aesthetic theory. In Chapter 2 I introduce Hartshorne's crucial theme of beauty as a mean between two sets of extremes, a theme that is echoed throughout the book. In Chapter 3 I discuss Hartshorne's view of the aesthetic attitude, which concentrates on values that are intrinsic and immediately felt, in contrast to those (economic or moral) values that are instrumental and felt only eventually.

Chapter 4 introduces the topic of Hartshorne's aesthetics of birdsong, and Chapter 6 finishes the project of detailing the aesthetics of subhuman reality by treating his panpsychism or panexperientialism. Between these two chapters that deal with the aesthetics of subhuman reality is Chapter 5, which defends Hartshorne's claim that sensation is a species of aesthetic feeling. Aesthetic relativism is the object of criticism in Chapter 7.

Chapters 8 through 10 deal explicitly with God. In Chapter 8 I examine the religious dimensions of aesthetic experience, as Hartshorne sees them, and in Chapter 9 I explore his view of divine beauty. Hartshorne argues that divine beauty is not to be equated with absolute beauty, as we will see. Throughout these last three chapters of the book I will be exploring the implications of Hartshorne's dipolar theism, as opposed to monopolar theism, for aesthetics.[10] In Chapter 10 I will examine the place of death in an aesthetics wherein, as Hartshorne sees things, the value of our lives consists in the beauty or the intensity of experience that we contribute to the divine life.

In the following chapter (Chapter 1) I will indicate in detail the place of Hartshorne's views in twentieth century aesthetic theory. At the outset, however, I would like to alert the reader to the fact that I will be claiming that clarity and precision in aesthetic discourse can be achieved only when the major concepts involved are placed, as Hartshorne does, within a metaphysics, a theistic one at that. It is Hartshorne's belief, however, that philosophy proceeds not by way of irrefutable proofs but by tentative hypotheses amenable to criticism in terms of criteria such as internal consistency, explanatory breadth and depth, and pragmatic adequacy. Hartshorne's aesthetic theory, I will argue, clears these hurdles, in contrast to certain other (usually narrower and shallower) aesthetic theories.

These initial comments are, I hope, like the first occasion of a major theme in a symphony, a theme that can be fully appreciated only after nuanced reiteration, development, and contrast with other themes. The importance of Hartshorne for aesthetic theory is that, in an effort to give an account of reality (including divine reality) in general, he arrives at the very things that are required to give an account of aesthetic experience, in both the aforementioned broad and narrow senses of the term.[11]

Finally, I would like to note that I will avoid using male pronouns for God in order to reflect the recent rejection of male bias in traditional philosophical theology. However, in some quotations from Hartshorne's earlier years these masculine terms can be found. For example, if his *Man's Vision of God* were written a few decades later it would have been titled *Our Vision of God* (HB, 159). In any event, even in Hartshorne's early years he was well ahead of his time in the effort to avoid male bias in discourse about God.

CHAPTER ONE

Historic and Thematic Background

WHEREAS THE INTRODUCTION LAID OUT in a preliminary way the concept of God that will be assumed throughout the book, the present chapter will sketch the historic and thematic background to Hartshorne's aesthetics, concentrating on the background provided by Whitehead's aesthetics as detailed by Sherburne, as an understanding of Hartshorne's view is best facilitated via a consideration of where he agrees or disagrees with Whitehead (as well as with John Cobb, David Ray Griffin, Judith Jones, and other process thinkers). But I will also situate Hartshorne's aesthetics vis-à-vis various scholars who have concentrated on the relationship between aesthetics and thought about God in particular, as well as some of the major twentieth-century aestheticians in general who dominated the field in the mid-decades of the twentieth century, when Hartshorne did most of his work, such as Croce, Collingwood, Santayana, Vivas, and Ducasse; in later chapters I will consider the relationship between Hartshorne's aesthetics and the theories of Dewey, Langer, and others. Throughout the book I will treat those early-, mid-, and late-twentieth-century authors who most influenced Hartshorne's aesthetics or who were most influenced by it. By the end of the present chapter's treatment of the historic and thematic background to Hartshorne's aesthetics, I will be ready in the following chapter to start a careful examination of Hartshorne's own texts.

The relationship between aesthetics and philosophical/theological thought about God has a rich history in the West. In the ancient world, for example, Plato clearly linked his aesthetics with religious concerns; beauty itself was in some way connected to divinity.[1] And medieval thinkers like Saints Thomas Aquinas and Bonaventure had a developed philosophy of beauty that was closely connected to their classical theistic metaphysics of being.[2] Two twentieth-century studies of the connection between aesthetics and God are already classics: Hans Urs von Balthasar's *The Glory of the Lord: A Theological Aesthetics* and Gerardus van der Leeuw's *Sacred and Profane Beauty: The Holy in Art*.[3] In recent decades the topic has continued to elicit interest among scholars, as evidenced in the works of Jeremy Begbie, Frank Burch Brown, J. Daniel Brown, Garrett Green, Richard Harries, F. David Martin, John Navone, Aidan Nichols, Patrick Sherry, Richard Viladesau, Nicholas Wolterstorff, and others.[4]

Despite the merits of the work of these talented scholars, there is still something lacking in their treatments of the subject matter in question. Although I will not detail the work of all of these scholars, I will say a few words about Wolterstorff's and Viladesau's approaches so as to briefly indicate the need for a careful study of Hartshorne's approach. Wolterstorff, an analytic philosopher who is also a contemporary Calvinist, defends a classical theistic view of God that yields not only the most troublesome version of the theodicy problem (as Hume noted, an omnipotent God *could* eliminate evil, a God who is omniscient with respect to the future would *know how* to eliminate evil, etc.), but it also yields a predestined universe that produces the aesthetic disvalue of monotony, as we will see in the following chapter. That is, there is an aesthetic price to pay when the concept of future contingency refers merely to our ignorance of what is already "in the cards" in the divine mind.

Although Viladesau does not, like Wolterstorff, reject (or, for the most part, ignore) the neoclassical view of God, he gives little indication of how we should assess neoclassical theism's implications for aesthetics. In fairness to Viladesau it should be noted that part of his thorough, scholarly approach to the relationship between aesthetics and thought about God involves the acknowledgment that for Whitehead (especially in *Religion in the Making*)[5] the foundation of the world is in aesthetic rather than cognitive experience, as in Kant. If theology is ultimately aesthetic rather than cognitive, Viladesau notes, the traditional problem of the inconceivability of God becomes less of an issue. (We will see that even if it is true to say, as Viladesau does, that the foundation of metaphysics/theology lies in aesthetic experience, for Hartshorne it is also true to say that these disciplines culminate in disciplined thought.) Further, by relying on both the aesthetic elements of religious experience and the religious elements in aesthetic experience, the neoclassical thinker can, according to Viladesau, defend a metaphysics that is more compatible with the biblical image of God than is the metaphysics of classical theism. Viladesau mentions in a note, but does not emphasize, that aesthetic experience calls us up short and directs our attention away from more practical considerations. *Some* experiences (religious as well as aesthetic) are to be appreciated because of their intrinsic, in contrast to instrumental, value.[6] Hartshorne, we will see, helps us to explore these matters in more depth.

It is important to remember, as we try to locate Hartshorne's aesthetics historically and thematically, that we are concerned not with art criticism but with something more general and abstract. David Ray Griffin, in his recent magnum opus *Reenchantment without Supernaturalism: A Process Philosophy of Religion,* indicates the level of generality and abstraction with which we must be concerned: evolutionary process is, in general, driven by some criterion of success other than mere survival; namely, it is driven by the aesthetic criterion of increase of harmonized intensity of intrinsically valuable experience. In the process view, *all* experienced order is aesthetic, consisting in the aforementioned harmonization of diverse elements from the past that are assimilated in more or less intense ways. The distinctiveness of this process view is that this ongoing patterned intensity of experience is experienced even by God; indeed it is encouraged by God in the divine lure toward higher intensities. We will see that, in Hartshorne's view, one major difference between our experience of harmonized intensity and God's is that, whereas our harmonized intensities exhibit a certain theme (as in a personality trait or a unified career) with variations that is limited both in scope and in temporal duration, God's theme-in-variations is all-inclusive and everlasting.[7]

Hartshorne's aesthetic theory, like Whitehead's, involves a process view that rationalizes the creative flux of experience that Bergson (another giant in the field of process thought) defended in such a way that he was open to the charge of anti-intellectualism. Whitehead's

famous way of refining the Bergsonian flux was to replace the traditional concept of substance or *ousia* with that of an actual occasion.
Creativity is not assigned to God (or to artists) alone, but rather to
each actual occasion with its locus of power. Each of these dynamic
drops of experience (common to Hartshorne, Whitehead, and James)[8]
is succeeded by a new one; otherwise the universe would become static
and vanish without a trace. Creativity is thus ultimate in the sense that
it constitutes the generic metaphysical character of all actualities in
the everlasting ongoingness of succeeding actual occasions. It should
be noted that for Hartshorne and Whitehead creativity itself is not so
much a thing but a principle that characterizes all concrete singulars,
as I will argue in Chapter 6. The basic rhythm of process consists in
each actual occasion drawing into a temporary unity the diverse elements that have influenced it. This unity, in turn, becomes one of the
diverse elements for future actual occasions to unify. These pulsations
of process are thus not wholly independent of each other.[9]

One of the most important differences between Whitehead and
Hartshorne concerns their respective concepts of eternal objects
(Whitehead) or universals (Hartshorne). Whitehead's eternal objects
are much more like Plato's eternal forms than Hartshorne's universals,
the latter of which are *emergent* possibilities.[10] Hence, in one sense
Hartshorne is more of a process philosopher than Whitehead. This difference has implications for aesthetics in that for Whitehead a work of
art has the ontological status of a "proposition," which, in Whitehead's
idiosyncratic use of the term, is a cross that occurs between an actual
occasion and an eternal object, specifically when the latter, as a datum
for feeling, can be felt by an actual occasion. For both Whitehead and
Hartshorne these abstract entities are "intradeical" rather than "extra-
deical"; that is, they are items in divine, psychical process rather than
free-floating entities (although Hartshorne is more consistently clear
on this point than Whitehead). And for both thinkers God lures actual
occasions toward more satisfying, more intense experiences of harmonized diversity. Indeed, perhaps the best definition of a Whiteheadian
proposition is that it is a *lure for feeling*. In effect, Whitehead militates
against the idea that a proposition is primarily a lure for intellectual
thought. By acting as a lure toward the realization of greater intensity

of experience (and hence, of value), a work of art is capable of facilitating the divine aim.[11]

In a later chapter on panpsychism or panexperientialism, we will see that Hartshorne defends the view that even biological cells are loci of aesthetic feeling. The feelings of cells are transmuted (to use Whitehead's technical term) so that a biological organism as a whole can feel what is felt by its parts, say the experience of red by optic nerve cells. A Whiteheadian proposition is a hybrid between pure potentialities or eternal objects (e.g., the eternal object red can be experienced in many different ways by many different actual occasions of experience) on the one hand and a real experience of the eternal object by some particular actual occasion on the other. A work of art, in this view, is a lure for feeling whereby simple feelings in our cells and in other microscopic existences (sounds, touches, electrical charges, etc.) are transmuted into a temporarily unified feeling on the part of the experiencing organism.[12]

Hartshorne describes his view in the following terms:

> [H]uman experience is only one form; there are the other vertebrate animals and their modes of experiencing; the lower animals and theirs—and where shall we stop? From man to molecules and atoms we have a series of modes of organization; at no point can one say, below this and there could be no experience. If atoms respond to stimuli (and they do), how else could they show that they sense or feel? And if you say, they have no sense organs, the reply is: neither do one-celled animals, yet they seem to perceive their environments. For the sake of argument at least, then, let us imagine the universe as a vast system of experiencing individuals on innumerable levels. Each such individual is in some measure free; for experiencing is a partly free act. Thus creativity, emergent novelty, is universal. In this way we perhaps understand why the physicists have had to reformulate the laws of nature as statistical, rather than absolute uniformities. (CS, 6)

By providing the historic and thematic background to Hartshorne's aesthetics through a consideration of Whitehead, I do not intend to give the impression that Hartshorne is to be seen as a student of Whitehead who merely reiterates the master's thought. I mention this because some have the mistaken idea that Hartshorne *is* Whitehead plus the ontological argument. Rather, he is a highly original thinker in his own right whose path in philosophy was already cleared by the time he became aware of Whitehead's philosophy. Therefore we should consider Whitehead's aesthetics in this chapter so as to help us to understand Hartshorne's thought throughout the remainder of the present book without necessarily assuming that the two are different stages of the same line of thought. We have seen that Whitehead's and Hartshorne's views of eternal objects and universals, respectively, are quite different. We will return to this divergence later regarding the important difference between them regarding how to deal with Hume's "missing color" in the spectrum of colors. And throughout the book we will notice Hartshorne's distaste for Whitehead's neologisms and dense prose; even devoted Whiteheadians often find many passages in Whitehead quite dark after several readings. Hartshorne is eminently clear by contrast.

Hartshorne can agree with Whitehead, however, that a work of art is a lure for feeling. In the mid-twentieth century a similar view was articulated by Rene Wellek and Austin Warren in terms of a work of art (e.g., a poem) as "a potential cause of experiences."[13] A distinction is needed here, however, between a work of art and its performance (or, in Whiteheadian terms, between a proposition and its objectification), as in the difference between a poem or a work of music on the one hand and a reading of the poem or a performance of the work of music on the other. This distinction leads us to the realization that, even if all works of art are lures for feeling, they need not all have the same ontological status. For example, a statue as a work of art *is* its performance, whereas a poem or a piece of music is not, in itself, physically real in the same way as the reading of the poem or the performance of the piece of music is. As Whitehead famously noted, philosophy is the critique of abstractions.[14]

Hartshorne could not, however, agree with the view that propositions as lures for feeling could stand on their own feet ontologically, waiting for a subject to experience them, even if he had been willing to agree with the idea that works of art are lures for aesthetic feeling (a redundancy, perhaps) more than they are lures for intellectual thought.[15] Just as beauty is, according to Santayana, objectified plea-sure, a performance of a work of art is an objectified proposition that lures us toward some harmonized intensity of experience.[16] This view of art as a proposition or as a lure for feeling has some similarities to Croce's view that art is a thing of the spirit rather than a material thing, although neither Whitehead's nor Hartshorne's views commit them to Croce's idealistic metaphysics. That is, in the process formulation of Croce's view, those who experience an objectified proposition or lure for feeling in a performance of a work of art (or who experience the work of art which *is* its performance in a nonperformance art like sculpture) reproduce the proposition or lure for feeling in their own consciousness.[17]

Many twentieth-century aestheticians have struggled with the ques-tion of the logical subject of particular arts. Music poses the greatest problem because it is so abstract. Sound waves are concrete, as are the movements of an actor on a stage playing Hamlet. And program music has contact with the world that enables us to more easily link music with the other arts. One of the advantages of the Whiteheadian theory of art as proposition or as lure for feeling (acceptable in modified form to Hartshorne, it seems) is that it can account for pure music, which often poses a problem for aestheticians because of its abstractness. Pure music, precisely because of its relative detachment from any program, acts as an *unobstructed* lure for feeling. To be specific, in this process view a musical composition is a proposition or a lure for feeling that is prehended by the composer. The notes set down on paper are not so much the work of art itself as a set of instructions to the performers to help them objectify the proposition or lure; eventually the work of art is encountered by the audience as objectified. At each stage there is the process commonplace of creative assimilation and advance: from composer to performer to audience. Similar descriptions could be of-fered for ballet and other arts.[18]

There need be nothing mysterious in thinking that behind any ar-tistic objectification there is a proposition or lure, as when conductors or music critics recognize a bull's eye as much as an archer. Aesthetic experience is thus the experience of aesthetic re-creation. If an artistic proposition is ineffective (say, by being too predictable or sloppy), then any performance of it will be unsatisfactory, no matter how polished it is technically. Obviously some philosophers will be bothered by this use of the term "proposition" by Whitehead, and perhaps it is for this reason, among others, that Hartshorne drops it. The problem is that we are conditioned to think of the term as it is used in logic, where the truth of a proposition is of primary importance. In art, however (and here Hartshorne would agree with Whitehead), what is of primary importance is that a proposition or lure for feeling be *interesting*. Later in the book I will examine both the sort of attitude that is peculiarly aesthetic, according to Hartshorne, and the sorts of aesthetic experiences that are especially interesting or beautiful.[19]

I have identified above music as an example of a performance art and sculpture as an example of a nonperformance art, or, if one prefers, as an example of an art where the work *is* the objectified proposition or lure for feeling. Obviously it is not my intent to do the work of an art critic, but merely to introduce certain distinctions from the arts that will bear on Hartshorne's aesthetics as the book proceeds. For example, the often unnoticed fact that architecture is a performance art (where the architect draws up plans for a building and the construction workers "perform" the plans) has implications for the philosophical concept of class membership and the type/token relationship. Frank Lloyd Wright's Robie House in Chicago could, in principle, be constructed (i.e., "performed") in other cities. Or again, jazz performance raises fascinating questions, illuminated by Hartshorne's views, regarding the degree to which deviation from order can still lead to aesthetic satisfaction or intensity of experience. Many jazz classics merely provide a sequence of chords for the soloist to work with, such that a melody line is simply a guide to weave the chords together. A great jazz musician, however, can objectify an artistic proposition in ways that provide a powerful lure for feeling. Or a final example: I have seen versions of da Vinci's Madonnas in London, Paris, and St. Petersburg, all of which were recognizable objectifications of the same aesthetic proposition.[20]

There is a sense in which the performance and the nonperformance arts approximate each other. For example, Mozart once remarked, or is said to have remarked, that he could hear a symphony complete in his head in an instant. Even if hyperbolic, this claim nonetheless illustrates the fact that the temporality that characterizes the performance arts (especially music) still requires the composer, the performer, and the listener to gather the discursiveness of the performance into a present unity that is analogous to that found in the largely nontemporal, non-performance arts. Because the performance arts are characterized by temporality, we can rightly suspect that there is something ephemeral about them, but buildings can last a long time before they decay (even though the pyramids are now almost in shambles and the sphinx is now barely recognizable), and recording technology enables us to hear today Rachmaninoff at the piano, albeit vicariously. We will see in due course Hartshorne pay careful attention to the connection between aesthetic feeling and time. His view can be put in the following White-headian terms, which will be dropped starting in the next chapter, where the simpler Hartshornian ones will be used: whereas a conceptual feeling is strictly general in that it is directed at an eternal object, an aesthetic feeling is less general and less abstract than a conceptual one because it is a response to a concrete or objectified proposition here and now. The eternal object "red" is indifferent to a seemingly infinite number of instantiations, but this particular shade of red experienced at this particular moment at dawn is a different thing altogether.[21]

One issue that is crucial in any aesthetic theory concerns what it means to say that an object is aesthetic. John Cobb has argued for a Whiteheadian response to this question that is useful in understanding Hartshorne's approach to the aesthetic attitude to be discussed in a later chapter. Cobb argues that there is a range of objects that are of special aesthetic interest, even if the experience of *any* object involves an aesthetic element. Further, he thinks that these objects that are of special aesthetic interest have a common distinguishing trait. It is easy to misunderstand Cobb's point here, however, because this distinguishing trait can only be discerned in the prehending subject: an aesthetic object is one that elicits more or less intense experiences of harmonized contrast in the prehending subject. That is, along with Eliseo Vivas and Curt Ducasse, process thinkers like Whitehead, Cobb, and Hartshorne can agree that any object can be seen as an aesthetic one if it is grasped in such a way as to give rise to an aesthetic experience (with "aesthetic experience" here referring to a more or less intense experience of harmonized diversity). The obvious danger here is an exaggerated subjectivism. Process thinkers want to avoid this by claiming that the reason it is so easy to adopt the aesthetic attitude (to be defined later) to objects is that the objects themselves *are* examples of harmonized diversity. Further, aesthetic objects (or at the very least their microscopic constituents) may very well themselves be experiencing subjects, as we will see in the chapter on panpsychism or panexperientialism.[22]

The process aesthetics of Whitehead, Cobb, and Hartshorne does *not* contain the view that the aesthetic first emerges in subjective prehensions and is then magically transferred to the object as one of its properties. It is precisely this sort of ontological dualism to which they are opposed, an opposition found, say, in Whitehead's critique of the legacy of seventeenth-century thought in his *Science and the Modern World*.[23] What is aesthetically prehended (once again, to use Whitehead's term) *is* the object. Hartshorne's way of putting the point, as we will see in the chapter on sensation/feeling, is that we do not first sense and then add feelings onto the sensation (the so-called tertiary qualities of modern philosophy) or transfer them to the object. Rather, sensation *is* a sort of feeling of the object. There is clearly a subjective dimension to aesthetic experience, but no process thinker would infer from this any evidence that would make either ontological dualism or reductionistic materialism viable positions, as we will see. There is indeed an internecine dispute between Cobb and Sherburne on these issues, with the latter accusing the former of excessive subjectivism in aesthetics, but presumably all process thinkers, including Cobb, could agree that the propositional character of a work of art (i.e., its ability to act as a lure for feeling) is, in fact, a character of the object that is a work of art.[24]

Sherburne does a fine job of summarizing Whitehead's view, with which I will be comparing and contrasting Hartshorne's view throughout the book:

[A]n experience is aesthetic when it is experience of an objectified proposition which lures the subjective *aim* of that occasion of experience into re-creating in its own process of self-creation the proposition objectified in the prehended performance.[25]

In other words, aesthetic experience gives a subject a vision, however dim, of what it might become because in it the normal aims of everyday life are suspended. We are all familiar, for example, with how great literature (e.g., Graham Greene's *The End of the Affair*) or a great film (e.g., *Diva*) transforms us and encourages our own creative impulse. The work of art acts as a lure; it seduces an occasion of experience into re-creating its own process of partial self-creation.[26]

We will see that the aesthetic experience of a sentient organism as a whole is made possible by the aesthetic experiences of its (at least proto-) sentient parts, like cells. Whitehead's somewhat misleading way of putting the point is to say that the human body is the instrument for the production of art in the human soul.[27] (The language of instrumentality and production plays into the hands of the modern mechanism that Whitehead would otherwise want to avoid, and the language of body in contrast to soul plays into the hands of the modern ontological dualism that Whitehead would otherwise want to avoid. Hartshorne speaks more carefully than Whitehead in this regard.) Microscopic sentiency obviously is not capable of any sophisticated intellection, although it may very well be able to respond to a lure for feeling. Many beings-in-becoming have feelings; fewer have feelings of great intensity and depth, and fewer still (the great artists) have the power to express them well in a medium and to elicit them from others.[28]

It is by no means clear whether Hartshorne would agree with Sherburne's view (shared with both Croce and R. G. Collingwood)[29] that the work of art is so much to be identified with the proposition prehended in the mind of the artist that the artifact is only a means toward the end of having those who experience it to reproduce the proposition in their own minds. From Hartshorne's point of view, this runs the risk of ignoring the intrinsic value that is the hallmark of aesthetic experience of artifacts by treating such value instrumentally, as a means toward self-improvement. The point is a tricky one to which we will return later in the book. Hartshorne is in agreement with Sherburne (and against Croce, however) in the belief that the artist is not God, although the artist presupposes God in the same way that all advance into novelty presupposes God. Croce maintains that artistic creation implies *absolute* novelty and creation *ex nihilo,* doctrines that are at odds both with Hartshorne's lifelong critique of any sort of creation *ex nihilo* and with his asymmetrical view of time wherein the past supplies necessary, but not sufficient, conditions for present partial novelty. The causal inheritance all experiencing subjects receive from the past does not make Hartshorne's view of creaturely or artistic or divine creativity excessively backward-looking in that his partial determinism is also a partial indeterminism in its dynamic thrust forward into a partially open future.[30]

To sum up what has been discovered thus far in this brief treatment of the historic and thematic background to Hartshorne's aesthetics: (1) Hartshorne's aesthetics is a clear alternative in philosophy of religion/theology to the aesthetics of classical theism. (2) This is evidenced, for example, in the fact that he avoids the aesthetic disvalue of monotony found in a universe where there is ultimately no open future, in that a God who is omniscient in the classical theistic sense of the term knows with absolute assurance and in minute detail what will happen in the future. (3) Further, if theology is ultimately based on aesthetic experience rather than on conceptual experience, then the problem of the inconceivability of God is not a worry to the extent that it has been traditionally—although it is clear that in Hartshorne's thought theology may begin in aesthetic experience, but it ends in a disciplined use of concepts. (4) Or again, if theology is ultimately based on aesthetic experience, then a concept of God can be developed that is more compatible with biblical theism than that found in classical theism. (5) Creativity is assigned not to God (or to artists) alone but to each occasion of experience in its creative assimilation of the past and advance into the future; hence there is something ultimate about creativity. (6) The criterion for success in this advance into the future involves the achievement of intense experiences of harmonized diversity, experiences that characterize the life of God as well as lives of lesser significance. (7) A work of art is a lure for feeling or a vision of what the occasion of experience that prehends it might become. And (8) sensation of works of art in particular, as well as sensation in general, *is* a type of feeling in that feelings are not attached after the fact to sensations, as is alleged by many modern philosophers.

From the above it should be clear that an understanding of Hartshorne's aesthetics will involve an explication of the beliefs that there are grades of aesthetic achievement spreading in all directions and that intrinsic value, however slight, is found at all grades. In fact, an individual existent can be seen as the felt unity of aesthetic achievement, a temporary unity that brings together former aesthetic achievements of its own and of other existents. That is, aesthetic achievement of more or less intense experiences of harmonized diversity is not so much woven into the real as it is interwoven in the real. To put the point in the strongest possible terms, these aesthetic experiences *are* the real.

The pervasiveness of tragedy in the universe, a theme to which I will return in the last chapter of the book on death, can be seen in the realization that any aesthetic achievement also involves aesthetic destruction or the elimination/cessation of certain intensities, a point that Judith Jones emphasizes. The discerning human individual is aware of both this destruction and the fact that new occasions of experience bring with them the possibility of deepened and broader intensities. We will see that these aesthetic considerations have implications for ethics in that the discerning individual recognizes both when relevant unities or diversities dominate the aesthetic field and when they dominate too much or too little. In this process view, congenial to Hartshorne but articulated by Jones, aesthetic education consists in aiding individuals first to recognize these intensities, unities, and diversities and second to discern when they lead to aesthetic disvalue, as we will see in the following chapter.[31]

The birth of any new aesthetic experience involves a *creative* process; thus the process view of Hartshorne is not to be confused with a sort of universal aestheticism wherein the rich private feelings of individuals record whatever comes on the scene. In fact, the creativity involved in aesthetic experience can act as a model for moral intuition so that we might better develop the ability to discern what we should *do* with our lives when we experience them as monotonous or cacophonous or trivial or swamped in hopeless profundity. Pure privacy is avoided because an actual occasion's unification of (or better, its incorporation of) previous intensities is *existential*. Aesthetic splendor, again to use Jones' helpful terminology, consists in our experiencing the world from our angles or perspectives so as to contribute to the beauty of the whole.[32] It is to Hartshorne's own rich concept of beauty as a mean between two sets of extremes that I will turn in the next chapter. We will see that this concept itself exhibits a mean between rationalistic criteria like unity-in-variety and empiricist (or better, phenomenological) criteria like doing justice to aesthetic phenomena *as experienced*, thereby avoiding William Dean's criticism to the effect that process aestheticians have a tendency to be too rationalistic.[33]

CHAPTER TWO

Beauty as a Mean

ARISTOTLE IS RIGHTLY FAMOUS for his view that virtue consists in a mean between extremes, the latter being vices. To cite a contemporary example, some people are kind to friends, but neglect their civic duties; others support good causes, but they are unkind to personal associates. A virtuous person knows better. But the principle of moderation applies much more generally than Aristotle supposed, according to Hartshorne. That is, it applies not only in ethics, but in aesthetics as well. I will initially assume, and then gradually indicate the argument for, the following claim from Hartshorne: beauty is a mean between two sets of extremes.

This claim rests on commonplace principles in Plato and Aristotle, although neither Plato nor Aristotle explicitly treated beauty as a moderate position between extremes. Further, although Plato offered the first great attempt to try to resolve the problem of the one and the many, it is by no means clear that he achieved a mean with respect to how this problem affects aesthetics, in that order seems to be privileged in his effort to avoid chaos. But as Hartshorne sees things, too much order and uniformity also creates an aesthetic problem, that of monotony (10, 62).

The diagram on the following page, to which I will appeal throughout the book, will help to elaborate Hartshorne's view (CS, 305; ZF, 80, 203, 205; WM, 3; BS, 7; RE, 11; SS, 86; RM, 287–88).[1]

Mechanical order that is too strict or unrelenting is not beautiful, nor is chaos or a sheer lack of order, in that with mechanism we are bored and with chaos we are confused. Beauty, it seems, is ordered diversity, as is symbolized by the imaginary vertical axis that runs through the above diagram.

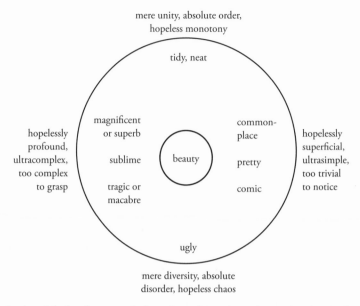

It should also be noted that there is an imaginary horizontal axis. A musical chord or a little flower is a superficial harmony, in contrast to a Mahler symphony or an old-growth forest. Deviations from beauty, however, when seen in a Hartshornian way as the central aesthetic value and as a double mean between vertical and horizontal extremes, can obviously be of great aesthetic value themselves. The simplicity of a Willa Cather novel is part of its appeal. And the profound discords in, say, Chopin's funeral march disrupt expected harmony in a way that is tragic and that challenges us to the depths. It is only those realities outside of the outer circle (if there are such) that are utterly devoid of aesthetic value. The horizontal axis should also make it clear that, as Hartshorne uses the terms, the beautiful and the pretty should not be seen as synonymous, as they often are in popular culture. That is, the vertical axis illustrates that beauty consists in *harmony or unity-in-variety*, whereas the horizontal axis illustrates that beauty requires an appropriate *intensity of experience*.

A musical chord has both unity and variety, but superficially so. One can imagine a symphony with the same proportionate balance of unity and variety as the chord, but vastly more diversity is unified in the symphony. Experiences all around the diagram, Hartshorne argues, but nonetheless within the larger circle, are valuable in themselves, quite apart from any use to which we put them. These intrinsic values are precisely what make these objects of interest from an aesthetic point of view (WM, 1–4).

Values, in general, may be seen as connected to three activities: acting morally (goodness), thinking logically (truth), and experiencing satisfyingly (beauty). It makes sense to consider the hypothesis that the last is primary. This is because if we knew what experience at its best or most beautiful consisted in, we would then better know how to act. And if thinking is a type of acting, as Peirce insisted, then logic as a normative science would be a branch of ethics. The question remains, however: what makes experiences valuable in themselves?

A start is provided by Whitehead's definition of beauty as the mutual adaptation of the elements of an experience, but mutual adaptation or harmony, although a necessary condition for beauty, is not yet sufficient, as Whitehead realized, in that some *intensity* of experience also seems to be needed, even in the case of the pretty, as is illustrated by the horizontal axis.[2] Thus, aesthetic value, according to Hartshorne, is found in diversified, intense harmonization of experience. Beauty involves not only variety of contrast, but also depth of contrast that affects the perceiver in an intense way.

Perhaps it will be objected that if beauty is at least partially defined by unity-in-variety, then *all* experiences would have aesthetic value in that each would have unity as one experience and each would have variety in terms of the parts of the experience itself and in terms of its differences from other experiences. We will see, however, that we need not be frightened away by the possibility that minimal aesthetic value is ubiquitous. In effect, sheer aesthetic failure (outside the larger circle) can quite legitimately be equated with the sheer absence of experience. To see beauty as a mean, as Hartshorne does, is to make an effort to understand aesthetic value somewhere above the bare minimum (CS, 59, 303–4).

If beauty is a balance of unity and variety, we can explain why the rhyme scheme *aaaa* is monotonous, in that it is overly weighted toward mere unity, and why *abcd* is, insofar as rhyme is concerned, mere diversity. In poetry where rhyme is not crucial, there is an analogous consideration: too much repetition of certain consonant or vowel sounds is understandably monotonous, whereas too little tends to make poetry barely distinguishable from unmusical prose. To be bored to death and to be confused to death equally leave one dead.

Deviations from the mean, however, need not leave us aesthetically dead, at least if they are not too far from the mean, according to Hartshorne. Beauty is the ideal aesthetic value, but not the only one. Some of the other aesthetic values are found in the diagram. Further, the aesthetic value of deviations along the imaginary horizontal axis varies according to the sensibilities of the perceiver: a musical chord may, in fact, be profound to a child just as a birdsong that may seem superficial to us may very well be beautiful or profound to a bird. Although there is no aesthetic value outside of the larger circle, everything inside it has aesthetic value of some sort.

The larger circle could move to the right or left, depending on various capacities to assimilate complexity, as when a bird would (probably) find a piece of chamber music hopelessly profound. The diameter of the larger circle may also vary, depending on the experiencing organism's scope of sensibility, as Hartshorne sees things. Some, for example, may have a hard time appreciating a macabre story by Poe. The diagram should also make clear that ugliness is not, strictly speaking, the opposite of beauty, but rather refers to an aesthetic value characterized by a mixture of order and discord/deformity, with the latter dominating. Not even ugliness is *pure* discord or de-formity, however, since this would lie outside the larger circle and could not be experienced as *a* case of disorder (cs, 304–5; od, 235; zf, 204–6).

Given what has been said thus far about Hartshorne's views, it is odd that some people prefer determinism (whether theological or scientific) on aesthetic grounds. Thoroughgoing determinism leads to cosmic monotony, not cosmic beauty. That is, diversity in time requires unforeseen novelty, including unpredictability regarding future scientific discoveries. If the specifics of future theories were predictable, we would have them already and there would be no need to discover them. Predictability is to a certain extent a good thing because it enables us to see the world as orderly, as a cosmos, Hartshorne thinks. But strict predictability without remainder is a negative aesthetic value;

hence from an aesthetic point of view we should be glad that we are temporal beings who enact a creative advance into the future (CS, 306).

This creative advance should not be assumed to be the special prerogative of human beings. Beauty as integrated diversity and intensity of experience, far from being anthropocentric, is, Hartshorne argues, metaphysical: it is present to some extent in any state of concrete reality, from microorganisms to God. We will see that the latter, as omnibenevolent and omnipresent, enjoys harmonized contrasts on a cosmic scale. The more sophisticated one's abilities to perceive and think, the greater one's ability to order and to diversify and to appreciate order and diversity in others. Even supposedly prosaic science can contribute to aesthetics as a means of widening the horizon of beauty. Almost everyone can see ocean waves, but only through science can we come to appreciate the "waves" governing microscopic particles (CS, 307–8).

In addition to the principle that beauty is a mean between two sets of extremes, which includes the intensity principle, we also need a principle of positive incompatibility. Aesthetic discord does not so much involve a clash of positive and negative as one between incompossible positives, in Hartshorne's view. Being a first-rate philosopher is a good thing, as is being a first-rate pianist and a first-rate second baseman, but it is seemingly impossible to be all three. The conflict of positive values is at the root of tragedy, the profound aesthetic value that tends toward discord. So as to minimize the tragedy of life, some goods must be renounced; hence we are all ascetics who must do without many good things, with the more rigorous ascetics being those who *deliberately* choose their renunciations and who choose them to a greater extent than the rest of us (CS, 311; also see AD and PD).

The beauty of friendship can also be explicated by the Hartshornian view of beauty as unity-in-difference. Friends harmonize in a concrete way felt by both parties both the commonality of interest between the two as well as the deep contrasts that are inevitable among any human beings, who are more highly individuated than members of other species. To try to explain friendship strictly in terms of the similarities between the friends fails to do justice to the friends' own intimate awareness of each other's differences; in fact, it is the latter that make the bond of friendship all the more remarkable and beautiful (cs, 313).

Because this Hartshornian view of beauty as a dual mean will be operative throughout the book, it is worthwhile to consider some of the objections to it that might be posed. John Hospers provides some useful criticisms.[3] Hospers admires Hartshorne's "heroic" effort to defend the thesis that the laws governing the entire universe are aesthetic. Strict causal necessity, as we have seen, would be monotonous, whereas sheer chance would lack unity and hence coherence. Luckily for us, the world in which we live is something of a compromise between the two. Hospers also agrees that scenes in nature and great works of art, in whatever medium, are characterized by the unity-in-variety principle. Art critics and aestheticians have been in agreement on this for over two millennia, he thinks. This is a remarkable concession to Hartshorne on Hospers' part, a concession that leads us to realize that Hartshorne is not so much imposing his view of beauty as a dual mean on the subject matter in question, but is rather, as a good phenomenologist, starting from how all of us, along with art critics and aestheticians, *experience* art.

What bothers Hospers about Hartshorne's view is that it is not clear why certain works of art are experienced as flat and uninspiring and lacking in intensity when they have as much unity-in-variety as others. Why are comparable diverse contrasts unified in two different works of art experienced differently from the perspective of intensity? A partial response to this question is provided by an appeal to the horizontal axis in the above diagram: some ordered complexities are superficial and some are deep. We will be on the lookout, especially in Chapter 10, for specificity regarding what depth means here.

Likewise, Hospers agrees that some aesthetic experiences are analogous to religious experiences, as in the exaltation found in someone listening to Handel's *Messiah* when compared to the exaltation found in a worshiper in a magnificent cathedral. But he wonders about how comparable these two experiences could really be if the object of one is a work of art whereas the object of the other is God. Further, Hospers wonders if the religious, as opposed to the aesthetic, experience really has to balance unity-in-variety. A later chapter on the religious dimensions of aesthetic experience will enable us to deal with Hospers' query here.

Hospers assumes that works of art and other objects of aesthetic experience have no intrinsic value—only the experiences of them have it. A later chapter on Hartshorne's panpsychism or panexperientialism will challenge this assumption. Further, Hospers worries that some objects possess a high degree of aesthetic value without having much diversity at all, as in a ruby or a Henryk Górecki song that consists of only a few tones. But this need not be a problem when it is realized that great aesthetic value can be achieved as a deviation in a "northerly" direction from core beauty as long as it is not outside the larger circle. Likewise, great aesthetic value can be achieved as a deviation in a "southerly" direction from core beauty—as in the jazz of John Coltrane or Ornette Coleman—as long as it is not outside the larger circle, as we saw in the previous chapter.

The key concern of Hospers, however, has to do with the place of intensity or the life of aesthetic feeling in Hartshorne's view. Piet Mondrian's arrangements of straight lines and colors hardly engage our emotional lives at all, whereas other (especially romantic) works of art are specifically designed to appeal to our feelings. The symmetries of the above diagram, he thinks, do not help us to understand our emotional response to aesthetic objects. For example, strip mining is ugly, but not solely, or even primarily, because it is too diverse. Or again, a view of the Grand Canyon is sublime, but not primarily because it is complex. A later chapter on the relationship between sensation and feeling will help us to respond to Hospers' quite legitimate concern for aesthetic feeling.

The hope is that each of these promissory notes can be paid. In any event, Hospers' questions and criticisms of Hartshorne serve the useful purpose of holding in check the tendency to have the above bold diagram fall into overstatement. That is, an aesthetician should try to have theory fit our aesthetic judgments, rather than the other way around. When some judgments can be fit into the theory only with a shoehorn, this fact should be noted. The hazard of hasty generalization, however, real enough as it is, should not be viewed as equivalent to the more egregious problems created by an aggressive aesthetic relativism, as we will see. In any event, as a result of this second chapter I am in a position to explicate later in the book the Hartshornian view that Frederick Ferré calls "kalogenesis" (from the Greek *kalos*—beauty— and *genesis*—creation): the central value in religion is the generation of beauty in experience as a contribution to the divine life.[4]

Hartshorne sums up his own view in the following way:

> The essential point of the seemingly so empty formula "unity in variety," is thus that while the ideal of success is single, the possibilities of failure are dual, and opposite to one another. This is the old Aristotelian principle of the golden mean: in the middle is the desirable quality, undesirable are the two extremes—e.g., rashness and timidity, compared to courage. So in aesthetic value. For each level of complexity there is a balance of unity and diversity which is ideally satisfying. What we spontaneously call beautiful exhibits this balance. Discord, diversity not integrated by unifying factors, is not very good; but a too tame harmony or unity, not sufficiently diversified with contrasting aspects, is not very good either. And at the extreme limit, one form of aesthetic failure is as bad as the other; for in either case experience becomes impossible. To be bored to death is no better than to be shocked to death. And both can happen, as probably most doctors would admit. Though beauty is the ideal aesthetic value, it is not the only one. For deviations from the mean still have value if they are not hopelessly far from the mean. (CS, 304)

Virgil Aldrich is correct to alert us to the fact that most contemporary aestheticians have discarded beauty in their theories. The main liability to beauty is that it is not, as Aldrich sees things, relevant to contemporary discussions in aesthetics. His fear seems to be that concentration on beauty will lead us to say, with Jacques Maritain in his classical theistic aesthetics, that beauty descends to irradiate the objects of the senses with the glory of the forms. But clearly Hartshorne does not speak of beauty in these terms both because he does not, like Whitehead or Maritain, defend a theory of eternal objects or Platonic forms and because he is much more interested in the phenomenology of aesthetic experience, in how we aesthetically experience the world in general and works of art in particular, than is Maritain in his classical theistic view. In fact, the concerns that Aldrich thinks are crucial in talk about art by educated viewers and listeners (unity, balance, incongruity, dynamic contrast, etc.) *are precisely those* used by Hartshorne in his discussion of beauty as a dual mean. That is, despite the "revolt against beauty" in aesthetics (to use Arthur Danto's phrase), there is still room in contemporary philosophy for Hartshorne's particular approach to beauty, to how we aesthetically experience the world in general and a work of art in particular.[5]

Hartshorne's concept of beauty, once carefully defined as a mean between two sets of extremes, can be brought within the mainstream of contemporary aesthetics. That is, it is still possible to get a hearing for Hartshorne's idea (related, as we have seen, to Santayana's) that beauty is objectified pleasure. However, Hartshorne's idea that the central value in religion is the generation of beauty, which is then contributed to the divine life, is probably too redolent of his systematic metaphysics for most contemporary aestheticians. There is no escaping the fact that Hartshorne is primarily a metaphysician or a philosopher of religion; hence his aesthetics will primarily be of interest to those who are open both to these branches of philosophy and to the long history of a close association between aesthetic experience and religious experience. For example, Patrick Sherry reminds us that the God of the Hebrew Bible is often referred to in aesthetic terms like sweetness *(no am)*, splendor or majesty *(hah-dahr)*, and glory *(tiphahrah)*.[6] Hartshorne would take such terms seriously as convenient starting points in the effort to re-think the logic of perfection.

Obviously a definition of beauty is not the whole of aesthetic theory, as we will see in subsequent chapters. Although Hartshorne does not follow some ancient and medieval views that suggest that beauty is the *sole* concern of what we today call aesthetics, he does believe that beauty has a *central* place in aesthetics. One of the standard reasons for refusing to give to the concept of beauty either the sole or a central place in aesthetics is the contemporary awareness of the great diversity and scope of the phenomena aesthetics has to investigate, many of which do not seem "beautiful" as this term is often used, as Thomas Munro emphasizes. That is, the single concept of the beautiful cannot do all of the intellectual work that needs to be done in aesthetics. The

Hartshornian response to Munro should be the same as that given above to Aldrich: Hartshorne's concept of beauty as a mean between two sets of extremes is explicitly designed to be reticulative in scope so as to help us understand the place of unity *and* diversity in aesthetics. It is explicitly designed to handle objections like those from Aldrich and Munro.[7] As Whitehead puts the Hartshornian point, even discord—in itself destructive—contributes to beauty by rescuing aesthetic value from sheer "tameness of outworn perfection."[8] And we have seen that even the ugly or the horrible can be experienced aesthetically, as in Shakespeare's *Richard III* or in Pieter Breughel's painting *The Blind Leading the Blind.*

Maintaining an aesthetically satisfactory unity-in-diversity is no easy task, as Hartshorne realizes. For example, imagine a painting that expresses as a lure for feeling the loneliness of a deserted dock in early morning with three boats tied down; the satisfactory unity of the composition can be compromised in any number of ways, and, as a result, in Hartshorne's language it would lose beauty even if it still retained aesthetic value of some sort. Likewise, as Hartshorne emphasizes, we fatigue easily with respect to paintings that are too unified or predictable. We also experience fatigue with respect to a masterpiece through constant exposure to it. This is one reason to be concerned with the commercialization of great art, where Verdi is played in elevators and the *Mona Lisa* is used to sell candy bars. Even sophisticated aesthetic sensibilities can be eroded or lulled to sleep by overexposure. But it is not possible to specify the boundaries of art in a strict way, for example by stipulating *a priori* how much unity or diversity is allowable. Ravel's *Boléro* stretched the concept of repetition more than we might have supposed allowable before the fact, just as bebop stretched, at the other end, the already wide range of diverse possibilities given to jazz musicians. Philosophers should be especially wary when they try to impose their abstractions from above, as when Hegel gave the philosophical reason why there *had to be* seven planets just a short while before the eighth was discovered.[9]

What can be stated with confidence, according to Hartshorne, again on the evidence of judgments made by artists themselves and art critics and aestheticians for centuries, is that there is something basic about the aesthetic tension of unity within contrast. However, there are problems in each art that are beyond the ability of philosophy to solve. For example, music has contrast built into it with its constant succession of various notes—how to appropriately struggle to attain unity? Architecture, by way of contrast, has unity built into it in that the architect is usually commissioned to draw up plans for *a* building that must be structurally integral—how to appropriately struggle to attain contrast? The philosopher can nonetheless know that the problem for both the composer and the architect is to create a form that gives lasting aesthetic satisfaction. To object that it is not illuminating to claim that beauty involves unity-in-diversity, because such a claim lacks specificity, is, in effect, to prohibit metaphysical statements at the outset. It is true that the question as to what *specifically* constitutes satisfying unity, diversity, harmony, balance, and contrast is, for the most part, to be answered by artists themselves and art critics. But the claim *that* beauty involves unity and variety of some sort, precisely because it refers to any possible experience of beauty, is strictly abstract and hence metaphysical, in the Hartshornian view.[10]

Hartshorne thinks that all of us, however, and not only those who are artists or art critics, have *some* idea regarding what specifically constitutes aesthetic unity, diversity, harmony, balance, and contrast in that we are all familiar with aesthetic fatigue or monotony, as well as with aesthetic confusion or disorientation, followed by a restoration of some sort of experience of harmony or, in a word, beauty. Hartshorne's view is similar to Whitehead's in two chapters of *Adventures of Ideas:* "Beauty" and "Beauty and Truth": beauty is a quality, a way that things are felt when several factors are mutually adapted or harmonized in an intense way. It should be noted that the words "things are felt" in the previous sentence enables process thinkers like Hartshorne and Whitehead to locate beauty both in the aesthetic prehender and in the aesthetic object. Aesthetic objects exhibit mutual adaptation of several factors, and aesthetic experiences are prehensions of this harmony. Such prehensions can be explicit, if the experiencer is reflecting on a work of art, or implicit, if the experiencer is only remotely aware of the dim, massive pattern of beauty throbbing in the microcosmic realm. Regarding those aesthetic experiences that are explicitly appreciated as such, if the depth of contrast that is in the object of such experiences is great, then the depth of satisfaction in the aesthetic experiences themselves is also likely to be great.[11]

All of the discussion in this chapter, as well as in Chapter 1, regarding aesthetic feeling should not blind us to the fact that Hartshorne, partially due to his defense of the ontological argument and partially due to his use of position matrices to solve philosophical problems, is often seen as a rationalist who expects *too much* from philosophical argument. It should be noted that his aesthetic argument for the existence of God in CS (284, 287, 289–90) brings his concern for aesthetic feeling for beauty and his firm commitment to philosophical argumentation together. The argument consists in laying out the logically possible options when certain variables are considered: (a) either there is a beauty of the world as a whole or there is no such beauty; and (b) if there is such a beauty, then (i) either no one enjoys it; or (ii) only nondivine beings enjoy it; or (iii) God also (and only God adequately) enjoys it. Thus, four options are possible:

(1) There is no beauty of the world as a (de facto) whole.
(2) There is a beauty of the world as a whole, but no one enjoys it.
(3) There is a beauty of the world as a whole, but only nondivine beings enjoy it.
(4) There is a beauty of the world as a whole, and God alone adequately enjoys it. (CS, 287)

If (1) were true, Hartshorne thinks, the world would be either a chaos or a mere monotony. Neither is possible. It cannot be a chaos because a merely chaotic world is unknowable, for no knowledge could exist in it. But the world *is* knowable, hence the impossibility of (1). It cannot be a monotony because order implies a contrasting element of disorder; the two terms are correlative and neither can be understood without the other. Further, if reality is essentially active, constituted by pulses of dynamic power, then any monotony to the world would have to be secondary and artificial in the sense that it would have to be a human creation.

(2) is unconvincing because even by thinking of the world as a whole, we enjoy at least a glimpse of its beauty. That is, Hartshorne's

view is that not only every experience but also every thought yields *some* sort of aesthetic result.

The problem with (3) is that our enjoyment of the beauty in question (or the enjoyment of the whole by any localized, nondivine being), although real, is disproportionate to the cosmic, sublime beauty in question. If this disproportion obtained, then there would be a basic flaw in reality that could never be eliminated. Because God cannot exist contingently, for such an existence would be inconsistent with God's status as the greatest conceivable being, God's existence is either impossible or necessary. (3) would therefore signal the impossibility of God's existence. Thus, (3) involves a permanent ugliness or flaw to the world as a whole. This thought does not console us, but quite apart from its psychological effect, its pragmatic value seems to be to bring us to the realization that *if* the world as a whole is *really* beautiful, it could not fail to have an adequate appreciator.

Although (4) is seen by Hartshorne as true, the hypothetical character to the argument highlights the fact that this argument cannot stand alone as a convincing argument for the existence of God. Nor does it seem that Hartshorne intends to do this. Hartshorne agrees with Peirce that instead of the metaphor that suggests that a chain of argument is only as strong as its weakest link, we should view the various arguments for the existence of God (ontological, cosmological, design, the above aesthetic argument, etc.) as mutually reinforcing strands in a cable that is quite strong. Seen in this light, the above aesthetic argument provides both interesting and substantive support to the more well-known arguments for the existence of God, especially the ontological.

Donald Viney has done the best job of analyzing this argument, which Hartshorne himself sees as his most original contribution to the global argument for the existence of God, i.e., that cablelike argument that includes strands from the ontological argument, the design argument, etc. In addition to cs, this argument can be found in nt; further, preparation for this argument can be found in the aesthetic principles found in Hartshorne's most empirical works: pp and bs. Viney finds it significant that Hartshorne speaks of the world as a de facto whole in that in a process universe the world is never a completed fact. Thus the beauty of the world as a whole would have to be dynamic; it would be less like a statue and more like a theatrical performance. Later we will see that Hartshorne views theater as the highest art form, partially because of its dynamism (although Shakespeare shows in *The Winter's Tale* that even statues, in a way, can come to life).[12]

If (1) is the case, it is for one of two reasons. First, the concept of beauty might lack objective reference, a possibility that I will examine in a later chapter on the idea that beauty is merely in the eye of the beholder. The second possibility is that, in point of fact, the world as a whole lacks beauty, which, as Viney attests, is coherent diversity according to most philosophers. Consider Hartshorne's own words:

> Is the universe as a whole beautiful? Certainly it contains more contrasts than anything else, for all contrasts fall within it. And it does have unity. Physics discovers the same kinds of matter, the same laws, even in the most distant heavenly bodies. (MV, 213)

The mere presence of aesthetic value does not necessarily mean the presence of beauty, but in Hartshorne's view the world as a whole exhibits a *balance* of unity and variety. Further, the beauty of the world as a whole is not a contingent fact, in Hartshorne's view, but is necessary. This is because, if it is necessary that something exists (in that the existence of absolutely nothing is unintelligible), and if reality is defined in terms of dynamic experience, and if, further, dynamic experience is essentially aesthetic, then the something that exists has beauty if the aesthetic value that necessarily exists exhibits a balance of unity and variety. And it does exhibit such a balance, given the evidence of the design argument. The necessary existence of beauty cannot be viewed with indifference, according to Hartshorne, because we can only be indifferent regarding that which we do not at all notice. That is, what we notice affects us positively or negatively, in however slight a way. Yet we cannot be negative regarding the necessary beauty of reality in that such negativity would seem to imply the urge toward the existence of absolutely nothing, which, once again, is an impossibility (GE, 28).[13]

Hartshorne is obviously not claiming that everything that now exists in the world is necessary, but rather that the fact that there be *some* world that is a balance of unity and diversity is necessary. The ontological and the aesthetic arguments together only show that *some* beautiful world has to exist, not necessarily the one that exists at present. If no one exists to appreciate this beauty, as in (2) above, then either (a) the world's beauty could be known, but it is a contingent fact that it is not known; or (b) the world's beauty could not, in principle, be known. The problem with (b), in Viney's account, is that it is vulnerable to the criticism that the only meaning that could be given to the concept of reality consists in an agreement between concept and percept. How could we know there to be a reality that is, in principle, unexperienced? And the problem with (a), in Viney's interpretation of Hartshorne, is that the only possible being who could adequately appreciate the beauty of the world as a whole is God, yet if God is possible then God exists necessarily, according to the logic of the ontological argument.[14] Hartshorne summarizes this view as follows:

> Beauty as a value is actualized only in experience. However, the concrete beauty of the cosmos . . . could not be adequately appreciated by our fragmentary kind of perception and thought. There can then be an all-inclusive beauty only if there be an all-inclusive appreciation of beauty. (NT, 15)

Viney considers the objection to Hartshorne's aesthetic argument that, if there is no appreciator of the beauty of the world as a whole, the flaw is epistemological, not aesthetic. If God does not exist to appreciate such beauty, this is not ugliness, but is rather just a fact about the world, according to this objection. But this objection is mistaken simply because we *do* normally think that it is a good thing if beauty is appreciated; on phenomenological grounds we regret it if beauty is not appreciated. However, if the beauty of the world as a whole is necessary, according to the global argument that includes both the ontological and aesthetic arguments, then this proposed necessary flaw in the world as a whole is not defensible. Just as a painting on a wall, to use Viney's helpful example, is not just covering up a blemish on the wall, but is an aesthetic object toward which one can adopt the aesthetic attitude (described in the following chapter), so also the world as a whole is an aesthetic object for us (however inadequately) and for God (adequately).[15]

David Ray Griffin provides a related argument for the existence of God from *excessive* beauty. In that Whitehead did not put much stock in arguments for the existence of God, Griffin's use of this and other arguments, along with his Hartshornian view of God's existence as a personally ordered series of occasions, indicates a great debt to Hartshorne. The key idea here is that the world's beauty is explainable only as a reflection of divine beauty. By "excessive" Griffin means that the beauty of the world is beyond that which seems explainable in neo-Darwinian, agnostic terms. *Some* of the beauty of the world is explainable in such terms, as when the bright colors of flowers are explained in terms of the selection of bees. If bees are attracted to flowers with bright colors, those flowers will be pollinated and thus have a better chance at surviving. The attractiveness to females of the otherwise dysfunctional tail of the male peacock can be explained in a similar fashion.[16]

When all such explanations have been exhausted, however, there is still much beauty that remains. As the physicist Steven Weinberg puts the point, nature seems more beautiful than is strictly necessary; it at least seems that the beauty is placed in nature for the sake of someone's aesthetic benefit.[17] That is, from a strictly utilitarian point of view, the beauty of the world is, in part and as a whole, excessive.

It may be objected, however, that the ugliness (or better, the aesthetic disvalues) of birth defects and cancer must also be taken into account. Although it is not the task of the present book to present in detail and defend the theodicy of neoclassical theism, we should at least note that Griffin's response to this objection, like Hartshorne's, would be that such a view primarily points out the severe difficulties with supernatural, classical theism, with its omnipotent God who could prevent such birth defects, but who for some strange reason chooses not to do so. The objection is not devastating to neoclassical, process theism. Griffin thus offers support for Hartshorne's belief that the fundamental order of the world is aesthetic.[18]

Viney's way to supplement the theodicies of Hartshorne and Griffin is to say that if the many instances of suffering are taken as evidence against the beauty of the world, it looks as if there is an insufficient unity in the universe. It should be noted, however, that it is, in fact, a *univ*erse and that, as Viney emphasizes, all of the joys, ecstasies, and happinesses in it count as heavily as all of the suffering. If theists seem, at times, to be callous regarding suffering, then they should be criticized for such callousness; likewise, when atheists or agnostics seem, at times, to be insensitive regarding the beauty of the world as a whole, then they should also be criticized. It is by no means obvious that suffering outbalances aesthetic delight. In any event, we have seen above that suffering, in itself, is not incompatible with beauty, as in the tragic beauty of Victor Hugo's Quasimodo.[19]

Conversely, orderliness is not to be identified with beauty. Any good machine can give us extreme orderliness, but "who cares to listen to or watch such a machine for aesthetic satisfaction alone?" (RM, 287). By distinguishing between beauty and orderliness on the one hand, and between beauty and prettiness on the other, Hartshorne has offered a model of beauty that is worthy of critical scrutiny. To use one of his own examples, Richard Nixon's looks elicited in a viewer haunting fears and thoughts about nefarious purposes, and it was precisely these features that made him aesthetically interesting. Along with Bosanquet, Hartshorne provides a service for aestheticians by insisting that ugliness is not the opposite of beauty but a deviation from it in a southerly direction.

We will see that this complex theory of beauty is integrally connected to Hartshorne's neoclassical theism when the sublimity of religious belief is considered. Astronomy shows the cosmos to be vast almost beyond comprehension, with perhaps billions of planets. This should convince us, at the very least, that the universe is not here for *us*. Replacing anthropocentrism with theocentrism is one possible way to do justice to our experience of the sublime. Religious faith is obviously not to everyone's liking, but a theistic metaphysics that enables us to appreciate the sublime beauty of the cosmos makes it easier to articulate the appropriateness of such a faith (RM, 288).

CHAPTER THREE

The Aesthetic Attitude

IN THE PRESENT CHAPTER I would like to highlight the fact that the aesthetic values treated in the previous chapter are aesthetic precisely because they are intrinsic and immediately felt. At the other extreme are what Hartshorne calls economic or ethical values, which are extrinsic (or instrumental) and eventual (as opposed to immediately felt). Most human activities, at least, contain a mixture of the two. In mathematics, for example, we usually use numbers as a means to an end, but some revel in the beauty of the mathematical relations themselves. In effect, objects (perhaps subjects, too) are suitable for the enjoyment of intrinsic, immediately felt (aesthetic) value when they exhibit certain features, such as unity-in-variety, as discussed in the previous chapter.[1]

A related goal of this chapter is to examine the following two Hartshornian claims: (a) aesthetic value is presupposed by ethical value; and (b) nonetheless ethics is not to be reduced to aesthetics. We will later see in relation to certain ethical issues in environmental ethics both that we cannot understand such issues apart from a consideration of aesthetic value and that, even with such a consideration, we cannot resolve such issues without the aid of ethical theory.

Hartshorne describes the aesthetic attitude, which is that attitude wherein we are most attentive to experience in its concreteness, in the following way:

> From usual definitions of the aesthetic attitude it follows that it is in this attitude rather than in making ethical decisions or solving practical or cognitive problems that we are most attentive to experience in its concreteness. In listening to music, for instance, at least under ideal conditions, it is the whole of what we hear that we enjoy.

Similarly, in adequate concentration upon a painting, it is the whole of what we see that is relevant. By contrast, in practical affairs, only certain features of the seen or heard count. Cognitive pursuits tend to be even more selective, even farther from the concrete in their interests. In spite of this, innumerable philosophers have discussed the content of perception almost exclusively as it appears to the pragmatic or cognitive stance, not as it is present in and for aesthetic experience. (CS, 75–76)

I should make it clear that by "intrinsic value" Hartshorne means the first of three possible meanings of this term: (1) *noninstrumental value*, or something that is valuable in itself; (2) something that is valuable in itself in the sense that it is *nonrelational*; or (3) something that is valuable in the sense that it is *independent of any valuer*. We will see that there are good reasons to be suspicious, along with Hartshorne, of these last two meanings of the term. I should also note at the outset that by the "aesthetic attitude" and "intrinsic value" Hartshorne is not necessarily wholly committed to the art-for-art's-sake position in aesthetics that was popular at the beginning of the twentieth century, as we will see later in this chapter.

Intrinsic values are those of experiences as such, even if we often live for the sake of the future. That is, aesthetic values are more basic than, and broader than, ethical or economic values. In fact, they are also more basic than, and broader than, those found in the fine arts, as we will see (CA, 99). The roots of all abstract ideas, including those in ethics, are found in concrete experiencing of some kind. Hence it is in the aesthetic attitude, rather than in the ethical one, that we are most attentive to concrete experience. In the type of selectivity associated with ethical affairs or cognitive pursuits, only certain practical or intellectual features of what we see and hear count, in contrast to what occurs when we view a painting or listen to music, where what is at issue is a different sort of selectivity that privileges intrinsic, immediately felt value. (We have seen above that Hartshorne misleadingly indicates that there is no selectivity at all in aesthetic experience; I take it that what he means is that in aesthetic experience we do not select away or ignore concrete, immediately felt value.) Thus those philosophers who discuss the content of perception almost exclusively in cognitive terms (such as Husserl) misunderstand what the aesthetic attitude is all about (CA, 99; CS, 75–76).

I would like to emphasize, however, that Hartshorne does not want to open too wide the gap between aesthetic value, on the one hand, and ethical or cognitive value, on the other, in that ethical and cognitive value ultimately rest on aesthetic value. The Hartshornian point seems to be that ethical value, say, is only one sort of value that stands in relation to other sorts of value, especially aesthetic value.[2]

The overemphasis of cognition over aesthetics is also found in the preference in certain modern philosophers for primary qualities over secondary and tertiary ones, according to Hartshorne. An abstract primary quality like extension is often seen as an emotionally neutral marker in the cognition game that precedes secondary and tertiary qualities (or better, feelings) like warm or red, respectively. In a later chapter on sensation/feeling I will argue that for Hartshorne all directly given qualities are aesthetic. This means that such qualities are *felt* or that they are experienced as emotional. As a result, the traditional secondary and tertiary qualities should be seen as the primary ones. The qualitative aspects of experience are emotionally prehended (rather than cognitively apprehended) as feelings first. We do not so much neutrally cognize the world and *then* develop feelings about it; rather, cognition is a way of understanding and evaluating what we feel.

We are given blues and sweets, joys and sufferings, broadly construed. Cognitive neutrality is, indeed, a great *achievement,* but it is definitely not a presupposed substratum. To hold that sensory qualities are initially devoid of feeling tone or aesthetic character is, at the very least, bad phenomenology (CS, 76–77).

If aesthetic value is broader than cognitive or ethical value, then it perhaps makes more sense to say that truth or goodness relies on beauty than it does to say the reverse. Hartshorne's point here is not to defend a reductionism, whereby the criteria specific to judgments regarding truth or goodness collapse into those regarding beauty as a mean between two sets of extremes. Rather, the point is a less ambitious one: the criteria involved in judgments regarding truth and goodness *presuppose* those involved in judgments regarding beauty. Beauty, once again, is the core aesthetic value of experiences in themselves. Both truth and goodness are also instrumentally valuable as we act in light of them. Seen in this way, ethics is the effort to understand how to increase the value of future aesthetic experiences for all involved, as we will see momentarily. The will that is good both enriches its own present experiences (its aesthetic character) as well as those in the future, not necessarily its own. In religious terms, the good will is devoted to God, to whom the good will contributes, on Hartshorne's view. The good will thus ironically escapes from the agonies of egoism by seeking present, aesthetically rich, peace or harmony of experience that it can contribute to the divine life. It is this peace that is the reward of virtue, as in the cliché "virtue is its own reward." So long as one's own future (rather than that of others, including God's) is seen as *the* crucial goal, there is no reward, no peace (cs, 308).

In short, since aesthetics involves the intrinsic value of experience, according to Hartshorne, and since the good will seeks to enhance the present and future likelihood of such intrinsic value (think of both the good will in deontology as well as the utilitarian preference for pleasure over pain), ethics presupposes, but is not reducible to, aesthetics. Further, the empirical fact that all animals are subject to experience aesthetic values but are not cognitively sophisticated enough to experience ethical ones, lends support to the claim that the former is more basic than the latter for rational animals like ourselves (cs, 308–9).

An aesthetic object is one that enables sentient creatures to have aesthetic experiences—that is, experiences that are intrinsically worthwhile, quite apart from any instrumental value they may possess. These aesthetic objects need not be works of art (unless, of course, nature itself is seen as the handiwork of the Supreme Artist), although works of art are specifically designed to highlight aesthetic value and to elicit in us the experience of such value. The connection between aesthetic value and ethical value becomes apparent when it is realized that some people who think themselves to be acting righteously make life miserable for those around them, to use Hartshorne's helpful example. Regarding these people we are led to ask: what exactly is the point of ethics if not to maximize interests, happiness, well-being, or purity of heart, etc., for ourselves and for those whom we affect? (zf, 203–4,

206). Virtue ethicians, deontologists, and utilitarians alike can agree, it seems, albeit in different ways, that this is precisely the point of ethics.

Likewise, religious values are ultimately aesthetic, at least if God is not construed as discharging duties in a grim, reluctant manner, as in the customs official mentioned by Bergson, who asked of those who had just been rescued in a shipwreck if they had any goods to declare.[3] It makes more sense to think, as we will see, that God *enjoys* creation, albeit in a preeminent way, as Hartshorne for decades emphasized. Creatures enjoy it as well, even subhuman ones, relative to the species-dependent mode of appreciation they have of the life around them. It will be argued in the next chapter that the aesthetic value appreciated by humans is not distinctive merely because it is aesthetic but rather because: (1) The intrinsic values appreciated by human beings can often be appreciated at a higher level of complexity than those appreciated by other creatures. That is, the typically human mode of appreciation is further "westward" in the diagram in Chapter 2 than the aesthetic appreciation of members of other species. And (2) the intrinsic (aesthetic) values appreciated by human beings provide a basis for further ethical, political, scientific, and religious values (ZF, 206–7).

Paying attention to the aesthetic attitude need not involve a denigration of ethical principles, but it does encourage a skepticism regarding a one-sided theology or philosophy that is moralistic or excessively driven by abstract principles (some, but not all, varieties of deontology are prime examples here). Once again, the point here is not to reduce ethics to aesthetics, in that the ethical search for fair decision-making procedures so as to equitably resolve our disputes is not likely to go away soon (nor should it!), but to emphasize that ethical values nonetheless presuppose aesthetic ones. That is, the intrinsic values being furthered or facilitated by our ethical duties should always be attached to our justification of these duties. Another way to put the point is to suggest that aesthetic value has both a subjective and an objective aspect. The former does not refer to relative value that is merely a matter of opinion, as in the cliché that beauty is merely in the eye of the beholder. Rather, it refers to *intrinsic* value that is actually experienced by some subject. The latter refers to the *instrumental* value associated with the experience of an aesthetic object, an instrumentality that is the lifeblood of ethics and religion (CS, 207–8).

The fact that many have at least a limited sense of the beauty of the cosmos is not unrelated to their religious belief in a God who can appreciate that beauty in its fullness. And regarding each other we only have partial glimpses into each other's feelings, but a divine being-in-becoming would feel with ideal adequacy *all* creaturely feelings. Neoclassical theism, at least, is precisely the belief that creaturely experiences add up to an overall meaning. Individual beautiful experiences come and go, but apart from our faulty memory, they perish unless there is Someone to preserve and cherish them. Traditional or classical, as opposed to process or neoclassical, theism was inadequate in part because it posited a God who was unchanged and unmoved, a God who could not be changed or moved by the aesthetic experiences of the creatures, not even by their tragic experiences (CS, 209–10). It is interesting to note that Christian and other mystics have traditionally criticized the "God of the philosophers" (i.e., classical theism) for precisely this reason.

The reasonableness of arguments for theism is not the topic of the present book, but it should be noted that along with the standard arguments there is also an aesthetic approach to God, as we saw in the previous chapter, wherein God is posited as the only one who could be the bearer of an inclusive, objective beauty for the cosmos, a beauty that many of us intuit, albeit through a glass darkly. We feel the damage done to our own cellular parts, say when intense heat rips open the walls of the cells in the tip of our forefinger when we touch a hot object. But theists (even some classical theists who are mystics, like St. John of the Cross or St. Teresa of Avila)[4] experience *themselves* as parts or cells of a mighty whole, indeed as contributors to the divine life. One should care for oneself not so much for egoistic reasons but rather because one's virtues and vices are contributions to the divine life, which suffers with our sufferings and which vicariously enjoys our joys (CS, 210–14).

The move beyond aesthetics to ethics and religion is a familiar one in philosophy, and a quite legitimate one *as long as* the aesthetic attitude itself is respected and is not viewed *solely* as preparation for something beyond itself. Once again, the point here is not to reduce truth and goodness to beauty but rather to secure the aesthetic effort to appreciate intrinsic value. The aesthetic attitude consists precisely in the effort to associate with the aesthetic object only those properties that allow the affective content of the aesthetic response to remain the focal point, rather than such as will replace it. No doubt most of us most of the time are too busy to tease out the aesthetic attitude from the instrumental purposes to which aesthetic value can be put. This "teasing out," however, is not the same as abstracting; in fact, the aesthetic aspect of experience may very well be the best clear look (or touch) we get at concrete reality (PP, 189; OD, 234, 241).

It is obviously not my intention in this chapter to develop Hartshorne's ethical theory, but rather to point out that in a process view aesthetic intensity of some sort is a significant presupposition of ethical value. Low-grade or trivial intensity yields minimal value, whereas high-grade intensity yields greater value. Although the intrinsic value of microscopic events may be minimal, the instrumental value of such events may be enormous. We have seen both that these intensities are the result of ordered contrasts and that depth of contrast increases intensity. Further, these intensities have both an intrinsic character and an instrumental one; the latter has implications for other intensities, especially the divine one. That is, narrowness of focus in an intensity as well as depth of contrast among intensities are alike in being among the significant value contributions to the divine life, which anchors the general good.

The relationship between aesthetics and ethics is thus analogous to the relationship between subjectivity of some sort, perhaps even at a very low grade, and a more sophisticated consciousness. But divine love encompasses all contributions and grades them: aesthetic, ethical, and rational. This relationship between aesthetics and ethics, as Hartshorne articulates it, perhaps shapes the way ethical issues will be viewed, but it does not necessarily resolve them, as Kant better than anyone has shown. Further theoretical considerations are called for in order to do that.

For example, consider some contemporary issues in environmental ethics that are illuminated by, but not necessarily resolved by, the necessary role aesthetic feeling plays in ethics. My treatment of these issues is intended to clarify the relationship between aesthetic value and ethics. If one had to choose *in extremis* between saving the life of a deer or that of a wildflower, but one could not save both, it is clear that the deer's experiences are much more intense than those of the cells in the wildflower. For Hartshorne, the wildflower as a whole, lacking a central nervous system, has little or no experience at all; it is, in his (and Whitehead's) language, a metaphysical democracy rather than a metaphysical monarchy.

But the issue would be a bit more complex if the wildflower in question were an extremely rare one. The complexity stems from the fact that rich experiences for us, and even more so for God, are derived from the feelings of individuals *as well as* from the patterned contrasts among individuals. Regarding the latter, the loss of variety would be a terrible thing, hence the value of the wildflower increases with its rarity. It is still not obvious that even a rare wildflower is to be valued more than a deer in an *in extremis* situation, but, once again, it is not so much my task here to resolve this issue as to point out, as Hartshorne does, the aesthetic components of any defensible resolution.

It is questionable whether Clare Palmer is correct in claiming that a Hartshornian ethics is necessarily consequentialist, although it is easy to understand why she alleges this, given Hartshorne's contribution-ism, his belief that a human being's *telos* is to contribute to God with one's whole heart and mind.[5] Palmer herself unwittingly points out the rights-based orientation to Hartshorne's view when she notes that in his view human beings have a privileged place in nature if only because they produce extremely high-grade intensities and ordered contrasts of greater depth than those of a deer or a wildflower (see SH). If we are to contribute to God, and if God values *both* our high-grade inten-sities *and* the patterned contrast among creatures in general, some of whom produce only low-grade intensities, we might end up sym-pathizing at different times with both deontologists and consequen-tialists, respectively.

The Hartshornian preference in environmental ethics is for a moral individualism that is sentient-centric (rather than anthropocentric) in character, but the main point here is that whether one accepts this view or some other view in environmental ethics, one will, in any event, require a great deal of concern for aesthetic value. Aldo Leopold is notorious for claiming in *A Sand County Almanac,* as noted by Palmer, that the land without humans is the perfect norm, so one can assume not only that he would *in extremis* choose to preserve the rare wildflower over the deer (he was, of course, a hunter), but his land ethic would require him to choose to preserve the rare wildflower over a human being, although I assume that in this instance Leopold would refuse in practice to follow his theory to its logical conclusion. From an aesthetic point of view this would seem to indicate a preference for patterned contrast over high-grade intensity, whereas anthropocentrists seem to indicate a preference for high-grade intensities over patterned contrast in nature. An ideal aesthetic spectator (God), in the Hartshornian view, would presumably prefer a balance between the two.

Those who prefer patterned contrast to high-grade intensity would presumably not be bothered by someone who burned down a school as long as there was no brush fire. As Tom Regan has pointed out, "deep" ecology can easily lead to a sort of environmental fascism where sentient individuals (high-grade intensities) are sacrificed for the ecosystem.[6] Conversely, the anthropocentrism criticized by Hartshorne is likely to make the natural world unbearably monotonous by diminishing patterned contrasts (through monoculture farming, species extinction, etc.). On aesthetic grounds it would be difficult to defend either deep ecology or anthropocentrism, at least if the former consists in an antipathy or indifference toward high-grade intensities like human beings or, to a lesser extent, deer.

In any event, it should be noted that ethicists have historically paid too little attention to aesthetics. It is one thing to say, along with deontologists, that each person is an end in itself, which can easily be accepted intellectually, and another thing to get people to *sympathize* with others as ends in themselves. The utilitarian refrain that every sentient being counts rings hollow if there is no basis in fellow *feeling* among these sentient individuals. The utilitarian tendencies in Hartshorne's ethics, as well as the Kantian tendencies wherein he emphasizes the importance of rights (again, see SH), indicate that the nuanced decision-making procedures made possible by these ethical theories are not to be denigrated, nor are they to be "reduced" to aesthetics, in Hartshorne's view.[7] One of the points to the present chapter, however, is to indicate the aesthetic component in any ethical theory, including those favored by utilitarians and Kantians.

Griffin is helpful in the effort to sort out the relationship between the aesthetic and the ethical in Hartshorne. The latter is derived from the former, or better, the former is more basic than the latter. Further, ethics requires support not only from the aesthetic values "beneath" it but also from the reticulative metaphysical vision or cosmology "above" it, as we will see. Unfortunately, some may reach the conclusion that because aesthetic value is crucial in establishing the importance of ethics, ethics is thereby denigrated. This is decidedly *not* Hartshorne's view. He only suggests that if there were not intrinsic values of some sort (that are brought to explicit attention when we adopt the aesthetic attitude, but that are nonetheless apparent implicitly in ordinary experience), the idea that we have ethical duties, whether utilitarian or Kantian, would not make much sense. Utilitarians largely *assume* that pain is intrinsically bad and that pleasure is intrinsically good; Kantians largely *assume* (although Kant himself argued for) the intrinsic value of human beings as ends in themselves. Although it is not exactly true to say that the goal of Hartshorne's ethics is to maximize aesthetic enjoyment, it is true to say that the goal of his ethics is to maximize intrinsic value as a contribution to the divine life.[8]

Hartshorne's approach to the aesthetic attitude can be better understood if seen in comparison and contrast with perhaps the two most important aestheticians of the mid-twentieth century—Dewey and Langer—as well as with other thinkers. These comparisons and contrasts will continue the work initiated in Chapter 1 to see how Hartshorne's aesthetics fits in, historically and thematically, with the discipline in general. At one extreme there is the theory of artistic detachment defended by I. A. Richards, where it is not the job of art to reveal any characteristics of things at all in that if it did try to do this it would be put in competition with science, a competition it would surely lose.[9] Other variations on this popular theory of art as detachment are defended by Edward Bulloch and José Ortega y Gasset, the latter famously holding that a spiritual distance from lived reality is required in art so as to achieve a contemplative rapport with an ethereal artistic "ultra-object."[10] At the other extreme is the view of Vernon Lee, who stresses the idea that one feels oneself into *(Einfühlung)* the object of aesthetic experience, a type of enactment whereby the activities of the self are objectified.[11]

In between these two extremes lies Dewey's view, which, with modifications, is similar to Hartshorne's. For Dewey as well as for Hartshorne, art is a kind of *experience,* as Hartshorne often notices and as the title to Dewey's famous book makes clear.[12] Hartshorne agrees with Dewey that *some* sort of break with ordinary experience is required in order to experience aesthetically, as when Hartshorne often contrasts aesthetic experience with ethical or economic affairs, but the goal of such a break is not detachment for its own sake. Rather, the goal is a heightened sort of experience of life that will better prepare us to reenter ordinary experience when the aesthetic experience is over, according to Dewey, and make us better able to contribute to God, according to Hartshorne. The aesthetic experience itself is an experience that is more intense than ordinary experience; it is what leads us at times to exclaim, "*That* was an experience!"

The aesthetic experience, or the aesthetic attitude that characterizes it, is often elicited by what Aldrich calls the phenomenon of categorical aspection, as when we can finally see the duck in Wittgenstein's famous duck-rabbit. For example, some people eat to survive, whereas the connoisseur who has adopted the aesthetic attitude toward soup will eat in such a way that the broth is finally tasted as broth; it is *really* tasted. Experiencing the aesthetic object as something other than just another thing is usually, but not always, a gradual achievement; indeed, Aldrich uses the Whiteheadian term "prehension" to describe what is eventually grasped in aesthetic categorical aspection. That is, rather than the subjectivism of Richards and others, and rather than the objectivism of Lee and others, Dewey and Hartshorne defend a view of art that emphasizes the ongoing movement from ordinary experience, to detachment, to aesthetic experience, and then to enhanced ordinary experience, and so on. The moment of detachment is not literally detachment from the world, but instead consists in detachment from things in the world seen as physical objects rather than as aesthetic ones.[13]

An understanding of Hartshorne's approach to the aesthetic attitude is also enhanced through a consideration of the aesthetics of Langer, who wrote her dissertation under Whitehead and whose relationship to process thought has been variously studied.[14] Her view of art (especially music) is that it consists in a form that expresses a feeling, and a work of art must somehow achieve a semblance of the feeling of a living organism. For example, a weeping willow cuts a drooping figure in that there is an intrinsic sadness to such a form that is there not merely by its association with human posture. Langer's view is not that art depicts particular things like willow trees that exhibit feelings but rather that the form of the feeling itself is depicted in art, as in the sad drooping figures of certain musical compositions. Of course artistic forms involve the activity of some *particular* composer, performer, or listener, such that the dynamism that characterizes the aesthetics of both Langer and Hartshorne is nonetheless compatible with the Scotist idea of particularity or *haecceitas,* as used by Gerard Manley Hopkins to explain the introspective idea of "inscape."

For example, the gap between the fiction of some *particular* author, on the one hand, and reality, on the other, is amenable to two types of distortion: postmodernist critics reduce the real to the fictional invention of some particular artist or group of artists, whereas fundamentalist critics (especially in religion) collapse (biblical) fiction into the real or the literal. A more moderate view, defended by both Langer and Hartshorne, is that *both* the form of feeling (in fiction, music, etc.) created by particular artists *and* reality are required in aesthetics in that these two are dynamically related; neither should be reduced to the other.[15]

It should be noted that the aesthetic attitude, as Hartshorne sees it, can be given both a descriptive meaning and a prescriptive one. Regarding the former, an approach or an attitude can be described as aesthetic when certain features are identified (e.g., a relative detachment from a world of things with their mediated, instrumental values and a concentration on intrinsic values as immediately felt). The prescriptive meaning comes into play when one is encouraged, or when one encourages oneself, to bring about these features intentionally. Use determines which meaning of "aesthetic attitude" is at work in some particular context. In any event, Hartshorne does not intend to give an essentialist definition, delivered *sub specie aeternitatis,* for the aesthetic attitude. Once again, he is largely functioning as a phenomenologist with respect to how we experience reality in general or a work of art in particular as aesthetic. Great works of art facilitate the shift in categorical aspection required to adopt the aesthetic attitude because these works of art are formally expressive at once of materials and subject matter that make it easy to notice the intrinsic, immediately felt values found there.[16]

Hartshorne is like Whitehead (in *The Function of Reason)*[17] in refusing to use the aesthetic attitude to defend without qualification the art-for-art's-sake stance made famous by several members of the Bloomsbury Group, including Clive Bell.[18] Both seem to agree with Dewey that art is for *life's* sake. A certain detachment or psychical distance is, however, required in order to adopt the aesthetic attitude, and herein lies the grain of truth in the art-for-art's-sake position. If such detachment were not present in viewing a play, for example, one would understandably jump on stage to prevent the knifing that takes place in a performance of Shakespeare's *Julius Caesar.* But the distance involved is not as wide as that required in Bulloch's aesthetics, as we have seen. The only distance required is the realization that the aesthetic object is, in fact, a lure for feeling. The actor playing Julius Caesar is not really murdered in the performance of the play in that his "murderers" use rubber daggers, but we nonetheless know as a result of the play what it is like to experience opposition the way Julius Caesar did. That is, the unqualified belief in art for art's sake is both bad aesthetics and bad metaphysics. It is true that overly practical approaches to a work of art (which Hartshorne refers to as ethical or economic approaches, with their concentration on instrumental values) miss the aesthetic attitude, as when an art dealer checks a painting for water damage. However, the detachment required for the categorical aspection associated with the aesthetic attitude is but a moment in the overall view of aesthetics found in process thinkers like Hartshorne, Whitehead, and Dewey.[19]

The largely subjective distinction between aesthetic and nonaesthetic attention is sometimes elucidated by, and sometimes obscured by, art critics and aestheticians. At times we adopt the aesthetic attitude in its purest form unconsciously when moments of concentrated and active attention spontaneously appear like volcanic islands amid a sea of shallow thoughts and emotions. Most of us most of the time, it seems, exhibit a mixture of the aesthetic attitude, more practical (although less concrete) concerns, and more analytical discrimination, as Stephen Pepper notices.[20] And this is a good thing if the goal of art is that it be for life's sake, or in Hartshorne's case, for the sake of (or better, a contribution to) the divine life. The goal is to live better and to contribute such creative advance to God. Somewhat paradoxically, the suspension of practical concerns found in the aesthetic attitude is ultimately for the sake of something practical in that the autonomy of the aesthetic attitude is only temporary.[21]

Hartshorne sums up the relationship between aesthetic value and ethical value in the following way:

> To enjoy music by constantly asking about one's duties is impossible. Moral discernment is never the whole of experience, but the aesthetic values of experiences are their entire intrinsic values, what makes them good simply in themselves. Moral values do add something to aesthetic values. A morally good will is a kind of harmony in experience, as ill-will is a kind of disharmony. . . . The best definition of aesthetic value is that it is intrinsic value. Extrinsic value is simply the potentiality of further intrinsic value. The value of ethical goodness, or virtue, is that besides helping to make life in the present good in itself it will tend to make life in the future good in itself. Supposedly good people whose presences or actions make life ugly for themselves or others are dubious specimens of goodness. (CD, 244)

Further, to define deity *solely* in terms of ethical goodness is to suggest that God is a mere abstraction.

CHAPTER FOUR

Birdsong

In Chapter 2 Hartshorne's model for aesthetic value was introduced; it was alleged to apply in a nonanthropocentric way. Eventually I will show in detail how it applies in the divine case; here I would like to show how it applies in a subhuman one. Both the aesthetic attitude discussed in Chapter 3 and the theme of beauty as a dual mean are exemplified in an extremely interesting way in the songs of birds.

The most notable skeptics of Hartshorne's claims made in regard to the songs of birds are behaviorists, who urge that birdsong is programmed into birds to enable them to defend territory and to mate. What the behaviorist view leaves unexplained, however, is (1) how the bird *experiences* its territorial song and (2) why it sings when territory is not threatened and when mating season is over. It should be noted that bird "cries" are primeval and unlearned, as in the alarm notes that are presumably the oldest forms of bird utterance; bird "songs," by way of contrast, are at least partially learned, either through imitation or practice, and are more musical than cries. The point here is not to challenge the principle of parsimony, whereby a simpler explanation is to be preferred *if* it has the same explanatory power as a complex one. On the basis of this principle in ethology, the science of animal behavior, a higher function should be attributed to an animal only if a lower, more primitive function will not do the job. In the case of birdsong, the behaviorist alleges, as we will see later in the chapter, the territorial and mating functions explain the phenomenon *simpliciter* (BS, xi, I, II; WS, 133–40).

Behaviorism is, in fact, a plausible form of intellectual parsimony, but as in the case of the aesthetic sensibilities of human beings, it does not adequately explain the phenomena associated with birdsong, according to Hartshorne. If one *assumes* that aesthetic value concerns only the subordinate refinements of human life, and not essential principles, one might be led to assume the same regarding birdsong. It is precisely this assumption, however, that Hartshorne challenges. It is questionable to claim that we can understand either ourselves or birds without having recourse to the view that conscious beings flee the evils associated with both extreme monotony and discord. Animal curiosity, at the very least, should lead us to consider broadly aesthetic criteria of unity and contrast. If the aesthetic sensibilities of animals are not on a par with those of humans, it does not mean that they are not aesthetic. In some cases the aesthetic sensibilities of animals actually surpass ours, as in animals, such as dogs, whose sense of smell far surpasses our own (BS, 1–2).

It makes sense to urge caution regarding the attribution of anthropomorphic tendencies to birds, but to say they have aesthetic feelings is not to say they have aesthetic thoughts; hence this caution is not violated in Hartshorne's view. From an evolutionary point of view, one assumes that birdsong favors reproductive success. But it does not follow that this behaviorist or evolutionary account exhausts the facts. It should be obvious in the human case, at least, that sexual behavior is not only a mode of acting in an evolutionary context but also a mode of feeling. If the evolutionary functions of birdsong involve territoriality and mating, this tells us little about the emotive impact of the song on the singer. Perhaps it is *because* birds enjoy singing that they have propagated their kind, Hartshorne hypothesizes. Or perhaps it is because birds *like* their territory that they sing to defend it. Finally, when territory and mating seem irrelevant, perhaps birds find a simple joy in singing (BS, 2–3).

If the function of Sousa marches is to inspire patriotism, it does not rule out the possibility that the musicians who play them actually enjoy the music. Even if the evolutionary causes of animal behavior lie deep in the past, birds and flutists live in the present with a sequence of emotions from moment to moment. In fairness to behaviorists it must be admitted that the tendency to sing is closely related to the presence of male hormones and is thus maximal at breeding season. But these physical factors might alter not only the behavior but also the feelings of the bird. To view bird feelings as epiphenomena is no more plausible than to view human feelings in this way, in the Hartshornian view (BS, 3).

The crucial question for Hartshorne is the following:

> Do birds have a primitive but still genuine musical sense, remotely analogous to our human pleasure in sound patterns? One sign of pleasure in patterns of sound is the tendency to imitate them. That there is a good deal of this in bird life we know, since it has been established that in many species, hearing adults of the species sing helps the young to learn the proper songs. Another sign of musical feeling is the tendency to make sounds of some complexity, and not just occasionally and under strong and immediate environmental stress, as in alarm cries, but persistently and for long periods. Birds do this. . . . In the nightless arctic summer, a bird has been known to sing more than twenty out of the twenty-four hours. The creatures must be deriving some satisfaction from this activity. (ZF, 44)

A profligate use of analogy no doubt leads scientific thought astray, but without analogy our thought has little explanatory power at all. By viewing bird music as analogous to our music we are able to explain certain phenomena in nature that we would not otherwise be able to explain, as we will see momentarily. Alarm calls from birds are analogous to some of our exclamatory prose, yet songs from birds are more closely analogous to our music. For example, the various parts of a birdsong do not each have a separate denotative significance, as do parts of a prose sentence, but collectively say the same evaluative thing, as in music. Valuation, in general, can be seen to have both a subjective component (as in "I like it") and an objective one (as in "I like it because of its complexity"). It seems fair to conclude, Hartshorne thinks, that some bird singers are better than, or at least exhibit greater complexity than, others—say, if members of one species have a repertoire of six distinguishable songs, whereas members of another species have comparable songs, but only two of them (BS, 4–6).

We have seen that the theory of beauty as a dual mean must be qualified by the phrase "for a given experiencing organism." What is hopelessly profound for a bird may be ultrasimple for a human being,

Hartshorne notes. But the aesthetic analogy still holds. Running up
and down the scale chromatically on a piano is neat and orderly but
not exactly beautiful. We can sympathize, therefore, with birds when
they seem to get bored with their music; even birds avoid the utmost
extremes of mechanical regularity and mere chance diversity, as well
as the ultrasimplicity found in mere chirps or squeaks. Before exam-
ining the monotony threshold in birdsong, consider the following
examples provided by other animals: a newly trapped and caged wild
animal has its impulses thwarted and hence it experiences discord to a
tragic degree (animal rightists of whatever philosophical persuasion are
united in this belief), but the same animal after a long time in captivity becomes bored, lifeless, hardly a wild animal any more. A kitten
excited by a ball of twine strikes us as comic (BS, 7–8). No doubt the
play of kittens has an evolutionary explanation in terms of its preparation for the serious business of predation. But if we consistently apply
Hartshorne's view of the songs of birds, we should not be surprised to
learn that kittens also *enjoy* their play.

Birds sing for various reasons: to signal location, to signal danger
(alarm calls), to indicate readiness to mate (courtship songs), to defend
a breeding or foraging territory (territorial song or countersinging,
where rival males sing alternately from their rival territories), etc. But
birdsong is indeed *song* and is not to be reduced to scolds or growls or
cries, as is indicated by the fact that it is subject to learning and hence
is not entirely due to sheer instinct. Further, it should be noted that
bird singers tend to use very brief sounds, crowding several times as
many distinct notes into a second as a human singer would or perhaps
could. This is understandable given the faster tempo at which birds
live (higher temperatures, faster heartbeats, swifter respiration, shorter
neural paths, etc.). Thus what may appear to be insignificant sounds
for us need not be so for birds. Because a second must seem longer
to a bird than to us, the songs of the best singers are respectably long.
The danger is not that we would overestimate their musical ability, but
underestimate it, as Hartshorne sees things (BS, 15–16, 20, 33, 36).

It is an interesting thought experiment to imagine how a human
composer would fare if subjected to the limitations of the bird's attention span; it is not obvious that the human would drastically improve

on the bird's music. And it is hard to believe that the bird sings as well as it does primarily because it is defending territory for hours on end with its song. In fact, birdsong tends to degenerate when singing becomes sharply functional, as when territorial rivalry approaches real combat or when courtship approaches real copulation. This is what we should expect, in the Hartshornian view, given what was said above regarding the aesthetic attitude. If "aesthetic" is seen in *contrast* to (rather than in *contradiction* to) "utilitarian," then as utility increases, aesthetics understandably takes a backseat. The point is a subtle one in Hartshorne. Musicality has evolutionary origins, but it flourishes only when evolutionary utility is not pressing or narrowly focused, as is exemplified in those bird species whose members sing best in late summer or fall, well beyond mating season and when mating territory is not threatened (BS, 41, 47, 53).

If there is a major difference between bird and human music, it is in the short temporal span of the former, typically three seconds or less, with an upper limit of about fifteen seconds, although only a few species have songs longer than five seconds. Like human beings, birds play with sounds in infancy, improve with age and with the luxury of momentary feelings of pleasure when partially freed from the demands of the environment. Members of a highly imitative species obviously do not improve to the degree that members of an innovative species do. The latter are especially represented among the Oscine species, and most especially among the singing Oscines. Their singing in particular includes several distinguishable kinds: simple repetition of a song pattern hundreds or thousands of times per day, repetition of the same song pattern with variations, a repertoire of distinct songs that are repeated, a repertoire with variations, and most notably, a variable sequence of songs, such as those of the seven species of Western Meadowlark, who have at least a dozen separate songs, perhaps more, in their repertoire. Unfortunately, according to Hartshorne, none of these Western Meadowlark songs has become a literary or poetic or even musical topic for a truly great human artist (BS, 56–57, 71, 90–91, 122, 245).

The amount of birdsong does not always correlate well with the biological need to sing. What seems to stimulate the singing is change, and what deadens it is sameness or persistent repetition. Even birds who are repetitive singers tend to vary the pauses between reiterations so as to avoid monotony; those that tend not to vary the length of pauses tend to vary the songs themselves. Either way, birdsong conforms to aesthetic principles as one would expect as a result of viewing beauty as a dual mean, Hartshorne thinks. The avoidance of monotony encourages the value of contrast and unexpectedness, or better, the value of unexpectedness is a balance to the correlative (rather than contradictory) value of sameness/repetition. Again, this claim especially applies to Oscines, as non-Oscines have a much greater tolerance for reiteration without appreciable pauses (BS, 38, 119, 136, 224).

The shortness of the reiterated unit patterns is largely due to the bird's limited attention span, but this in no way contradicts the bird's *interest* in sound as such, in Hartshorne's view. The evolution of organs for song in birds seems to have been accompanied by a psychological evolution toward greater interest in sounds, and hence toward delicacy, unexpectedness, etc. Most notably regarding physiology is the syrinx, the vocalizing organ in Oscines that forms the base of the windpipe and whose muscular arrangements control voice production; unlike human vocal cords, the syrinx is not a set of cords in the windpipe but in effect the windpipe itself, like a built-in flute! In this sense birds are *more* musical than we are. A harmony of sufficiently varied notes, in the Hartshornian view, seems to be what birds, along with human beings, like when they have it and long for when they do not.

Depending on the precise criteria used to define singing, there are approximately four to five thousand singing bird species, hundreds of which are threatened with extinction, a result that would make *our* world, at least, less aesthetically interesting than it would otherwise be. Primal human beings inherited these birds as parts of a magnificent environment that they appreciated, indeed that they feared and revered and divinized. Now that we no longer fear the natural world, the danger is that we would no longer be sensitive to the beauty of that world, including its avian singers. Quite ironically, Hartshorne notes, this beauty and glory are being made accessible to us by the very technology that tends to destroy it. The key for Hartshorne seems to be to develop a rational understanding of the world that preserves the best of our primal appreciation of natural beauty (BS, 225–29, 255).

To human ears, birdsong is pretty rather than sublime, but even for us it exhibits a harmonious mixture of order and disorder, a mixture of the expected and the unexpected. It may not strike us as profound, but the attentive human listener would not normally find it monotonous. Some birds have over fifty songs in their repertoire, singing *a*, then *b*, *c*, *a*, *d*, *c*, etc., in a nonrepetitive way until the repertoire is exhausted. The order is never completely predictable, especially when, among singers who do not have an extensive repertoire, the pauses between songs are considered. We have seen that for Hartshorne, lengthening pauses with the degree of repetition and shortening pauses with the degree of song variety is what the aesthetic principle of beauty as a mean calls for.

The variety involves not only the number of separate songs, but also the variety of musical elements within the songs, as Hartshorne notes: melody, rhythm, harmony (unlike most of us, birds can sing contrasting notes simultaneously), theme with variations, accelerando, rallentando, crescendo, diminuendo, change of key, change of tempo (as when some birds give a trill at half or double speed), etc. By way of contrast, insects and the batrachians do not have melody (they cannot discriminate pitch), but they do have rhythm that resembles human drumming. Although cicadas and katydids also avoid monotony by varying repetitions, their music is quite primitive compared to that of birds. Hence it is understandable why primal humans totemized bird feathers, etc., and that shamans who could imitate the songs of birds were imputed magical powers (AB, 311–15).

Given the prevalence of music in some subhuman beings, the mystery regarding human beings is not that they sing or make other music but that they talk, and talk in a sophisticated way with grammatical and logical rules to guide them. But it is hard for us to avoid anthropomorphizing birds no matter how exalted a status we think we have as rational thinkers and talkers. For example, in previous ages religious believers (in the Franciscan tradition, say) heard in birdsong sweet praises of God. But contemporary behaviorists are no less anthropomorphic when they have the bird saying, "Get away or I'll peck your eyes out!" as if birds had been raised watching violent films and television shows and had never enjoyed their songs. The older sentimentalism and the newer cynicism, Hartshorne thinks, both need to be taken with a few grains of salt (AB, 311–15).

It should be clear that the aesthetics of birdsong is compatible with, but not reducible to, an evolutionary account of the phenomena. For example, why do some birds not sing? Tanagers, which are brightly colored and avoid dense vegetation, maintain contact with other birds largely through sight; hence they have little need for vocalization. The matter can be put more forcefully, according to Hartshorne: not only is the aesthetic analogy compatible with a scientific account of birdsong, but it can be used to amplify that account by making us aware of and enabling us to explicate phenomena we would otherwise ignore, as in the aforementioned example of birds singing exuberantly when territory and mating are not at stake.

Alexander Skutch is one critic who credits Hartshorne with the discovery of the antimonotony principle in birds, whereby hypnotic repetition is avoided either through varied pauses between repetitive songs or varied songs in continuous singers. Here is a concrete example of what we will see in a later chapter to be a commitment to the belief that partial freedom or indeterminacy pervades all nature. This partial indeterminacy enables us to respond to a possible objection, which goes as follows: flowers seem to have aesthetic value to us, but we do not suppose that the flowers themselves have aesthetic sensibility; might the same be true of birdsong? Once again, however, the fact that birdsong is useful in proclaiming territory and attracting a mate only accounts for a fraction of the bird singing that goes on. How should we account for the rest? Analogously, Skutch argues, gardening and cooking are necessary for our survival, but how do we account for the activity of weeding when it serves no evolutionary purpose or buying a cookbook when it fulfills no survival need? The obvious response is that people *like* to garden and cook. That is, there is no contradiction between the claims "Birds sing to maintain territory and to attract mates" and "Birds sing for aesthetic pleasure." Birds, with central nervous systems and a concomitant affective life, are qualitatively different from flowers. The aesthetic analogy between human beings and birds is precisely meant to exorcize the specter of Cartesian animal automatism, the belief that animals are mere machines.[1]

Lucio Chiaraviglio places Hartshorne's aesthetics of birdsong into an appropriate wider context by noting three themes: (1) mentality broadly understood is an active process ultimately constituted by feelings; (2) this active process is manifested in various degrees across a full evolutionary range, with birds exhibiting an aesthetic mentality qualitatively superior to that of plant cells and largely inferior to that of most human beings; but (3) the universe is nonetheless an aesthetic continuum of unity and contrast bounded by monotony and chaos. These themes play a major role from cells to birds to humans to deity.[2]

Chiaraviglio's comparison of the different degrees of aesthetic mentality, as described by Hartshorne, enables us to see the connections among the aesthetics of birdsong, human beauty, and divine beauty. There is a distinction between the aesthetic value found in abstract ideas and that found in concrete experiences. God's abstract and necessary *existence,* the fact *that* God always exists, is of the former sort, but God's contingent *actuality*—that is, *how* God exists—is of the latter sort. God's actuality involves an enjoyment of the whole evolving cosmos, in which the contingent harmonies of birdsong and human creations are appreciated. A bird cannot adequately appreciate the aesthetic value found in a human symphony. Likewise, according to Hartshorne, although human beings can, via the ontological and other arguments for the existence of God, know *that* God exists, they cannot adequately appreciate the aesthetic value found in the concrete beauty of the cosmos, as can God. We should not exhibit hubris in our relations with birds when we realize that in our relations with God we are more like the birds than we like to admit. God cares for the fall of a sparrow even if we are of more value than many sparrows (see Matthew 10:28).

There is hardly an exception, Hartshorne thinks, to the antimonotony principle among the thousands of Oscine species; the birds who sing largely mechanically (e.g., barbets, nightjars, etc.) are non-Oscines whose self-motion is largely exhibited in areas other than singing. The evolution of singing among songbirds (Oscines), however, is toward maximizing unexpectedness. This unexpectedness is consistent with the following Hartshornian aesthetic principle: the richer the individuation of the diverse elements of an artistic unity, the higher the unity itself. Birds (not merely bird species) do have richly individuated songs and pauses in their repertoires; hence the unity of their aesthetic accomplishment is of a higher order than many imagine. How much greater, then, must be the unity of the divine aesthetic accomplishment as God brings together the contributions of *all* creaturely artists, human and nonhuman (cs, 306–7; dr, 115).

We have seen that beauty is a mixture of similarity and difference/ contrast that elicits more or less intense feeling, with the limits of tolerance for similarity and difference varying with the type of experiencing organism. This intensity of feeling is, in part, due to contrast or variety, which in its temporal form is the partially unexpected, in Hartshorne's process view. All bird species, and to a lesser extent individual birds, however, have a general singing style that is at least in general outline *somewhat* predictable. The musical sense of the bird is biologically useful, as are nests, but to admit this much is not necessarily to claim that the bird cannot enjoy either its partially unpredictable song or its contingently built nest (built contingently, that is, in that exactly which twigs will be chosen cannot be predicted in advance, for example). Aesthetic value, as opposed to religious value, is thus not peculiar to our species, Hartshorne thinks. Subhuman music is a reality, but not subhuman philosophy or theology (bh, 262–63).

Many philosophers and theologians and scientists have, over the centuries, claimed that they have sought the truth because of its beauty. But this in itself leaves divine beauty undefined. Many have supposed that it meant absolute order devoid of unexpectedness or dissonance, as in the ancient Greek worship of circularity as an aesthetic ideal. Birdsong helps us to see that this is not the case, according to Hartshorne. We live in a time when there is a tendency, to be treated later, to lean in the other direction, toward arbitrariness and lack of order, as in the music of John Cage or the novels of William Gass. But notice that we refer to Gass' relatively amorphous work *The Tunnel* as *a* novel with its own properties and peculiar structure, a fact that not only does not contradict, but indeed reinforces, Hartshorne's view of beauty discussed above in Chapter 2 (wm, 105–16; pp, 205).

In a typical case, a male bird adopts a territory and begins to sing abundantly, both to hold the territory and to attract a mate, thereby combining both evolutionary functions of birdsong. Hence it is saying, "Come here to join me!" as much as it is saying "Keep out!" Occasionally countersinging occurs with another male, the birds all the while resolving their urges more through feeling than through thinking. Life for them, as for us, is at base an aesthetic problem, although we have a need to move on to ethics and religion. In the end, however, Hartshorne thinks that even we return to aesthetics in the sense that, for religious believers at least, one's ultimate goal is to serve God with one's whole heart and mind, to contribute to the beauty of the world as spectacle for divine enjoyment. In effect, a bird's life is an aesthetic problem from beginning to middle to end, whereas, according to Hartshorne, ours is an aesthetic problem at the beginning and end, but in between we have to think (ZF, 43–47).

Birds show an interest in their own affairs; we show an interest both in our own affairs and in the affairs of other living beings; and God is the supreme form of life interested in other life. Hence birdsong offers to us a window into reality in that a bird in its curiosity has to make a decision (literally, a cutting off of certain possibilities) regarding which direction its song will take next. The task, as Hartshorne sees things, is to be generous enough concerning the psychological life of the bird to account adequately for its aesthetic achievement, on the one hand, without undue anthropomorphism in attributing self-consciousness to the bird regarding its decision-making process, on the other.

We are not being overly generous, Hartshorne thinks, in seeing the bird's task as strongly analogous to our own: the goal is to lead interesting, beautiful lives both for our own sakes and for the sakes of those (including God) whom we influence. An evolutionary account of birdsong should both predict certain behaviors as well as point out the limitations in its ability to predict. The rest is left to the birds themselves. The beauty of birdsong lies, as it apparently does for all beauty, in something unitary that exists not in spite of, but by virtue of, qualitative contrast (ZF, 47–50; MV, 260, 292).

It was noted earlier that BS and PP are Hartshorne's most empirical books. Indeed Hartshorne thinks of the former as a work in ornithology rather than in philosophy, and the latter is as much a work in psychology as it is in philosophy. In this regard it is instructive to see how contemporary ornithologists view the type of project attempted by Hartshorne's empirical study of birdsong, a project that is closely allied to the work of the great ornithologist W. H. Thorpe, who also defended the thesis that birds *enjoy* singing.[3]

Peter Slater, for example, is a scientist who confirms many of Hartshorne's claims regarding birdsong, including the facts that most singing is done by males, although duets with females also occur, as in the antiphonal singing of Australian whipbirds; that choruses among several birds occur as well; that the bird's syrinx is in contrast to our larynx; that the more than four thousand species of songbirds are mostly Oscines, which are a suborder of Passeriformes; etc. However, in the thousands of musical phrases sung by birds, Slater, accepting the behaviorist account, sees little evidence for improvisation. For example, the red-winged blackbird, which does not sing, has more intrusions into its territory than other birds. But Slater gives back with one hand what he took away with the other. Regarding birds with large repertoires, such as sedge warblers and European nightingales, Slater curiously suggests that the "main message is variety itself." This is precisely Hartshorne's point. And regarding birds with small repertoires, like chaffinches, Slater sees *eventual* variety. Once again, Hartshorne agrees. In order to "save the phenomena," Slater must partially abandon his behaviorist assumptions, but he still retains these assumptions when he asks with puzzlement, How could we possibly test the hypothesis that birds enjoy singing? Hartshorne's empirical studies regarding the monotony threshold are meant to respond to this question. In any event, despite Slater's doubts regarding our ability to access the inner feelings of birds, he does admit that there is nothing incompatible between the behaviorist view he defends and the thesis that birds enjoy their singing.[4]

In reply to Slater's skepticism, the Hartshornian response should be to emphasize, in partial agreement with Thomas Nagel, the fact that our own feeling, in general, and our consciousness, in particular, is what makes the mind-body problem really intractable from a behaviorist or reductionist point of view. Recent reductionist euphoria, of which Slater's work is but one example, still fails to explain adequately why *we* enjoy singing (as we obviously do), much less a bird's enjoyment in doing so. Reductionistic behaviorism also fails to explain how *we* can have developed inner feelings (as we obviously do). The fact that reductionistic behaviorism leaves out something significant is clear in Slater's own work when he says that the main message of sophisticated bird singers is variety. The fact that birds have shorter neural pathways and shorter attention spans than humans, a fact seemingly admitted by Slater himself, seems to indicate implicitly just how bird feelings are both different from *and similar to* our own.

We can recognize certain facts about the experiences of others (in this case, of bird others) without necessarily having a sophisticated enough language to describe those facts. As Nagel forcefully puts the point in his essay "What Is It like to Be a Bat?" (which, with modifications, could be titled "What Is It like to Be a Bird Singer?"): "If we acknowledge that a physical theory of mind must account for the subjective character of experience, we must admit that no presently available conception gives us a clue how this could be done."[5] To imagine something sympathetically, as in what it would be like to be a bird singer, we must put ourselves in an experiential state resembling the thing itself. That is, we are quite unequipped to think about the subjective character of either other human beings or of birds without relying to some extent on sympathetic imagination. Luckily, because of their aesthetic sensibilities and their central nervous systems (both of which are somewhat analogous to ours), birds make this task manageable.

Another contemporary scientist who (unwittingly) supports Hartshorne's case is Carol Whaling, who emphasizes that birds sing partly due to instinct, in that birds raised in captivity will recognize on tape songs of members of their own species, and partly due to learning, in that members of bird species that have singers must hear songs in order to gradually learn to sing on their own. This latter factor supports the process notion of creative advance and the process rejection of strict determinism.[6] This rejection of strict determinism, however, does not mean that evolution in general or birdsong in particular proceeds by way of pure chance. Chance *does* play a role in biology. Indeed, the biologist Charles Birch argues that Hartshorne points out more clearly than anyone else the fact that Darwin logically could not (due to his determinism) admit to the reality of chance, despite the obvious role he attributed to it.[7]

Hartshorne clearly likes to skip back and forth between rationalist and empiricist modes of argument. Each of these is a moment in his overall method, which can be summarized in the following terms, a summary that will help us to better understand his view of birdsong:

Three primary methodological devices or procedures are at work in Hartshorne's philosophy. First, he very often uses a model or a systematic exhaustion of theoretical options—or the development of position matrices, sometimes containing thirty-two (!) alternatives—in considering philosophical problems. This procedure is evident throughout his philosophy, including his aesthetics, with its use of the model of beauty as a mean between two sets of extremes. To take another example, he thinks it important to notice that regarding the mind-body problem there are three options available to us, not two, as is usually assumed: some form of dualism; some form of the materialist view that *psyche* is reducible to body; and some form of the panpsychist or panexperientialist view that body is in some way reducible to, or is at least always connected to, *psyche.* This last position is supported by the claim that all concrete singulars (e.g., cells or electrons) in some way show signs of self-motion or activity or aesthetic feeling.

Second, Hartshorne frequently uses the history of philosophy to see which of the logically possible options made available by position matrices, or which features made available by the abstract model, have been defended before, so as to avail ourselves of the insights of others in the effort to examine in detail the consistency of these positions or features and to assess their consequences. Among these consequences is the ability to account adequately for lived experience or for the phenomenologically given or for what is aesthetically felt. Nonetheless, those logically possible options that have not historically found support should be analyzed both in terms of internal consistency and practical ramifications. It should be noted that Hartshorne's use of the history of philosophy often involves lesser-known views of famous thinkers (like Plato's belief in God as the soul for the body of the world) as well as the thought of lesser-known thinkers (such as Jules Lequyer).[8]

Third, after a careful reading of the history of philosophy has facilitated the conceptual and pragmatic/empirical examination of all the available options made explicit by a position matrix or model, the

(Greek) principle of moderation is used by Hartshorne as a guide to negotiate the way between extreme views on either side. For example, regarding the issue of personal identity, the view of Hume (and of Bertrand Russell at one stage in his career) is that, strictly speaking, there is no personal identity, in that each event in "a person's life" is externally related to the others. This is just as disastrous, Hartshorne thinks, as Leibniz's view that all such events are internally related to the others, so that implicit in the fetus are all the experiences of the adult. This Leibnizian view relies on the classical theistic, strong notion of omniscience, wherein God knows in minute detail and with absolute assurance what will happen in the future. The Humean view fails to explain the continuity we experience in our lives, and the Leibnizian view fails to explain the indeterminateness we experience when considering the future. Further, both views produce aesthetic disvalue: the Humean stance leaves us with a cacophony of selves, and the Leibnizian stance monotonously leaves us with one undifferentiated self. The truth lies between these two extremes, Hartshorne thinks. His view of personal identity is based on a conception of time as asymmetrical in which later events in a sentient being's life are internally related to former events, but they are externally related to those that follow, thus leading to a position that is at once partially deterministic and partially indeterministic. That is, the past supplies necessary but not sufficient conditions for bird or human identity in the present, which always faces a partially indeterminate future.

Only the first of these methodological devices or procedures supports the widely held claim that Hartshorne is a rationalist. His overall method is a complex one that involves the other methods or procedures, where he does borrow from the rationalists, but also from the pragmatists, the scientists, and the Greeks. It must be admitted, however, that Hartshorne was educated in a philosophic world still heavily influenced by late-nineteenth- and early-twentieth-century idealism.

After having empirically established, to his satisfaction, the monotony threshold in birds, Hartshorne switches to his rationalist mode with the claim that even God has a monotony threshold, exhibited in the divine call for new patterns of order. If God is not viewed as a cosmic judge, he thinks, but as a cosmic artist appreciating and adding to the beauty of the universe, then an aesthetic phenomenon like the monotony threshold as applied to God makes perfect sense.[9]

There is something dangerous, however, in translating the above three methodological devices or procedures in Hartshorne into the language of rationalism and empiricism. Hartshorne, like White-head, is a critic of the legacy of seventeenth-century thought to such an extent that to emphasize his rationalist or empiricist tendencies too much would be to misinterpret his philosophy. And Hartshorne, like Whitehead, is interested in reverting to pre-seventeenth-century modes of thought.[10] That is, to refer, as Griffin does, to Hartshorne and Whitehead as constructive postmodern philosophers is to suggest that they have either gone beyond or dug beneath the split between rationalism and empiricism. Hartshorne's empirical studies of birdsong are attempts to confirm his abstract ("rationalist") model of beauty as a dual mean, which, in turn, is constructed out of the phenomenologi-cal evidence provided for centuries by artists, art critics, and aestheti-cians. His overall method is *sui generis* and should not be tarred with the brushes of Descartes, Leibniz, Locke, or Hume.

One of the salient results of Hartshorne's nuanced method is that it makes clear that the crux of the debate concerning Darwin and religion is not between evolution per se and fundamentalism (as the simpleminded bumper sticker battle between the Darwinian fish and the Christian fish would have us believe). Rather, there are at least two kinds of evolutionary theory (one of which is deterministic and reductionistic, whereas the other, more defensible, kind admits of both partial indeterminism and self-motion) and at least two kinds of theism (the fundamentalist/classical theistic view, which, for the pres-ent purpose, can be linked despite their obvious differences, and the neoclassical view). That is, religious belief need not be at odds with the evolutionary hypothesis; indeed, neoclassical theism *requires* some version of evolutionary theory (DS, 277).

CHAPTER FIVE

Sensation/Feeling

In the previous chapter I took a first step toward an understanding of Hartshorne's nonanthropocentric aesthetics by showing the intelligibility of claiming not only that birdsong can be appreciated by *us* in aesthetic terms but also that the best way we have of accounting for birdsong is in terms of both its evolutionary significance *and* the function song performs in the aesthetically rich emotional lives of birds themselves. In the following chapter I will continue the effort to understand Hartshorne's nonanthropocentric aesthetic theory by making the case for panpsychism, pushing even further "down" the scale of being-in-becoming than birds. Before showing the connection between aesthetic theory and panpsychism, however, it will be worthwhile to clarify the aesthetic dimension of human experience; then we can elaborate further on the analogy between this dimension of human experience and that of subhuman reality.

Hospers is again instructive regarding the wide net cast by Hartshorne's philosophy, dominated as it is by aesthetic principles. This domination is made possible by a "powerful" and "all-pervasive" view of the relationship between sensation and feeling, in Hosper's interpretation. The dominant philosophical tradition divides human faculties into knowing (or cognition), feeling (or emotion), and willing (or volition). But where does sensation belong in this division? Traditionally it has been seen as a type of cognition, but there are good reasons, Hartshorne thinks, to classify it as a type of feeling. It is true that through our senses we receive information regarding the world, but sensations are *experienced* as feelings rather than as thoughts. It is also true that without sensation we would not know very much, if anything at all, and no doubt this is the cause of the mischaracterization of sensation as a species of cognition. But sensing is first a kind of immediate experience, a kind of feeling, before it is information or a premise from which we can make inferences.

Some feelings (e.g., sadness or disappointment) are obviously not sensations, but this is compatible with the view that all sensations are feelings, including the crucial cases of pleasure and pain. That is, feeling is a more general category than sensation and is inclusive of it, in the Hartshornian view. Sensations are feelings because they are constantly suffused with affect; they are the sort of feelings dependent on the functioning of a sensory apparatus that localizes these feelings in phenomenal space. Intersensory similarity helps us to appreciate this effect, as when high-pitched sounds are *experienced* as bright, and when low tones are *felt* as heavy.

This account of sensation is not necessarily at odds with the account given by associationists in the tradition of Hume, but it is much wider than the associationist account, Hartshorne thinks. We are all familiar with associationist examples: a woman wears a purple dress because she associates this color with pleasant experiences she had while wearing purple as a child, or she is exhilarated by a banal song because it was played during her honeymoon, etc.[1]

These personal associations are due to the accidents of biography, but quite apart from these accidents, sensations in general have certain affective qualities, as in the feeling tones tightly *connected* with (rather than accidentally *associated* with) various sensations of color. Because these connections are found whenever the color is experienced, quite apart from accidental associations, as we will see in Chapter 7, if we misleadingly refer to them as associations we should at least call them "universal associations" so as to differentiate them from the accidental ones, as in the woman above who associates purple with pleasant childhood experiences. Despite the inadequacies of narrow Humean associationism, it should be noted that Hume himself ironically comes close to Hartshorne's view that feeling is the more inclusive category, with sensation a particular type of feeling. And despite the fact that sensations are feelings of a specialized (local) kind, we will see in Chapter 7 that they can provide iconic signs of feelings of other kinds that are not dependent on sense organs and therefore are not so localized (ZF, 211).

Aesthetically enjoyable objects tend to be more closely unified, with more extensive likenesses and interpenetrations among the parts, than objects that are not as amenable to aesthetic enjoyment, although we have noticed that this unity cannot be so rigid as to exclude variety. As is well known, the coherent diversity of an aesthetically enjoyed object can elicit in us intense concentration or absorbed attention, a concentration or attention that involves feeling. We are *moved* by the way the parts in a harmonized object reinforce rather than interfere with each other. The aesthetic object (whether a work of art, say, or an instance of natural beauty) encourages us to notice the affective character of *all* sensation, Hartshorne thinks. That is, sense data are hardly distinguishable from emotional tones; this is the whole point, it seems, to still life painting.

Perhaps the biggest mistake made in the history of modern aesthetics was to fall unwittingly into the dualistic trap set by the great thinkers of the seventeenth century. The mistake was to assume that there is an ontological separation between sensation (the "sense data" of modern philosophy) and emotional tone, with the latter a psychic addition heaped onto sensation after the fact. Hartshorne calls this view the "annex theory of value" (PP, 94). As before, however, a more plausible phenomenological or experiential account would make the secondary and tertiary qualities of modern philosophy the real primary qualities. In fact, this stance is supported by certain developments in neuroscience, as we will see detailed in the work of Ralph Ellis.[2] Careful attention to sensation would indicate that the feeling tones "associated with" sensing a particular sound, say a shriek, are not entirely or even primarily due to purely personal or accidental associations. Take the case of a person who hears a piercing sound that he has never heard before, a sound that sends a chill up the spine and elicits fear. *Later* he finds out that the shriek came from a domesticated dog who was confronted by a cougar. (I have heard such a sound myself.) In this case the sound sensation *itself* was charged with feeling, indeed with intense feeling (PP, 159–68). It should be noted here that Hartshorne's view of sensation as charged with feeling is close to the expressive function of consciousness found in Ernst Cassirer.[3]

Feelings that are associated with sensation through personal history or accident indicate a looser relationship than the tight connection between feelings and sensations that is innate to members of our species, and perhaps to other species as well. For example, the associated feelings can more easily change than the innate or biological ones. A certain pleasant song, heard first on a CD that was a gift, can later be hated if one's estimation of the giver changes. However, if there is no tight connection between sensation and feeling, but only an accidental association of feeling, then artistic creation is, strictly speaking, a gamble. The composer, in these terms, could never count on high-pitched sounds being perceived as bright, nor on low tones to be perceived as heavy, according to Hartshorne. On associationist grounds, these are purely accidental linkages. Aestheticians are certainly free to continue to defend associationism, but they make a mess of artistic creation in the process (PP, 59, 169–70), as Langer as well as Hartshorne claims.[4]

There are several objections that might be made regarding Hartshorne's views discussed in this chapter. One objection is that an emotional tonality is not really given in the sensum, that there is only an illusion of such being given, and it is this illusion that is apprehended. We can describe a thing as odious without meaning that we perceive odium in the thing, according to this objection. Likewise, to say that flowers are ebullient or that clouds are gloomy should not lead us to confuse these feelings with the objects themselves. However, according to Hartshorne and Langer it is hard to see how the subtle aesthetic qualities of the aesthetic object that appear to impart aesthetic feeling to us could not inhere in the aesthetic object itself in *some* way (PP, 170–76).

Langer's distinction between discursive and presentational symbols is helpful here. The former is the vehicle of propositional or logical thinking that makes possible science and philosophy. This is "language proper." However, the latter presents to us meaning that widens our conception of rationality. This expansion is due in part to the emotion inhering in the symbol. It is precisely this world of presentational symbols that was isolated by Bergson in his "intuition," although Hartshorne, Whitehead, and Langer insist that such symbols *expand* rationality rather than transcend it, as in Bergson. That is, we can *understand* symbols, both discursive and presentational.[5]

This inherence of feeling in sensation is, in part, conceptual. The emotional tonality that is part of the sensum, for example a sound sensum, can be conceptually abstracted from the sensum but cannot otherwise be separated from it. If it were otherwise separated from the sensum, then the sudden appearance of the emotional tone in the perceiver would be something magical. A red without emotional tone can no more be conceived than a red without spatial character. A sensum is logically saturated with both primary qualities on the one hand and secondary and tertiary ones on the other. Sensory feelings are facts precisely because aesthetic experience (a redundancy, perhaps) reports them as such. Distinctions between sensation and feeling are not so much experienced as they are brought into existence when we drop the aesthetic attitude and initiate practical or intellectual manipulation of the aesthetic object. An example is when red is taken to be a sign of danger, a related treatment of which is found in Langer. We will return to this complicated example in a later chapter (PP, 176–77).[6]

Once again, our aesthetic analyses must always be reconcilable with observed or experienced fact, and it is questionable whether we ever experience a sensum without emotional tone. In fact, "inherence" or "similarity" may be designations that are too weak to convey the tight connection between sensation and feeling, in Hartshorne's view. To say that feelings "inhere" in sensations or that sensations "imitate" or are "similar to" human feelings can be taken in such a way that a subtle dualism between sensation and feeling again reasserts itself. In Hartshorne's view, musical sounds are not simulacra of feelings but *are* feeling tones themselves. That is, there is, apart from certain dissociative states, an all-pervasive blending of aesthetic factors and sensation that obviates the need to ascribe the affectivity of sensations to any factor distinct from the sensations themselves (PP, 177–79). Once again, Hartshorne's view here is close to Langer's.[7]

In short, some feeling is connected with sensations by association, but some of the feeling simply *is* the sensations, as Hartshorne sees things. Regarding the latter, aesthetic feeling is given as pervading the object in a way that makes no sense whatsoever unless the sensations are identical with the "secondary" qualities felt (like color or sound). Our vivid enjoyment is thus, in part, identical with the sensory contact. To be explicit, in addition to its associational affectivities, a color or a sound has its own affective character. For example, I have sat in the back row of a symphony hall and *felt* my eardrums rattle when I heard the kettledrums struck violently. Or if one's hand is placed in warm water, into which extremely hot water is running, one can gradually *feel* the transition from pleasure to pain; the feelings of pleasure and pain are not to be divorced from the temperature sensations (PP, 7, 49–50).

There are sounds that are strikingly painlike in character, as in the shrieking of automobile brakes, such that we should pause, Hartshorne thinks, when we are tempted to locate pain strictly in an intrabodily locus in phenomenal space. Of course pain can be accompanied by a sense of pleasure if the pain is conceived to lead to some future pleasure or some other future good. The point Hartshorne is trying to make here, however, is that pleasure and pain can each be equally described as sensations or as feelings, as in the aforementioned example of there being no sharp distinction between temperature sensations and pleasurable/painful feelings. To cite another example, sounds such as thunder are felt as violent because they *are* violent; they are attacks on the auditory systems of the hearers. The supposed discontinuity between sensation and feeling is contradicted not only by the above considerations and examples, but also by common speech, where sounds are described as sweet and colors as warm. Usually we call these locutions "metaphors," but it may well be the case that these metaphors contain a deep insight (PP, 53, 57, 73; RM, 289).

To greater or lesser degrees we are all "synesthetic" in the sense that the aesthetic or emotional content of the given can be described in terms of different senses, as in "bitter smells." The phenomenon of synesthesia further supports the interpenetration of sensation and feeling and makes even more implausible the separation of the traditional secondary and tertiary qualities from the primary ones. (More exactly, the phenomenon of synesthesia would support the theory of affective continuum *provided that* genuine synesthetes uniformly paired the same sensory qualities. The difficulty here, as Hartshorne complains [PP, 78], is that by the 1930s psychologists still had not teased out the genuine synesthetic experiences from the rather artificial associations of persons who were not sufficiently attentive to their experiences. I get the impression, however, that Hartshorne thinks such a "teasing out" is possible.)

Equally implausible is the separation of the tertiary qualities from the secondary ones, Hartshorne thinks. If by "tertiary qualities" we mean characters of an emotional or aesthetic sort, it would be a mistake to think that these are merely leftovers when we abstract away the space-time configurations and colors/sounds (the primary and secondary qualities, respectively). In fact, secondary qualities can best be seen, according to Hartshorne, as formalized references to aesthetic feelings (i.e., to tertiary qualities). As before, aesthetic value is central in perception in that the feeling of a color or a sound is not something over and above these phenomena (PP, 81, 95, 97–98).

We have seen both that the aesthetic attitude consists in beholding just to behold and that it is only in the aesthetic attitude that we can vividly "know" by acquaintance. The Hartshornian point to be emphasized regarding the aesthetic attitude is not that we should denigrate (scientific) knowledge by description but that it is worth our while to carve out a space for (aesthetic) "knowledge" by acquaintance, or more simply, feeling. This latter sort of "knowledge" (feeling) is approximated by childish fascinated attention to certain objects, by a primal human being's interest in the immediately given environment, and by the romantic poet's (especially Wordsworth's) seeing "into the life of things." Piaget does an admirable job of helping us to connect the aesthetic attitude of the child with the present chapter's concern for the relationship between sensation and feeling: it is only with difficulty that a child can separate the (external) world from his feelings.[8] We adults have the opposite problem, Hartshorne thinks, of failing to notice that our awareness of the world only comes about through feelings: of warmth, brightness, contact with a hard surface, etc. (PP, 103–5).

The child's eventual abandonment of panpsychism (or better, of panexperientialism) is not necessarily to be welcomed as a sign of maturity. It can, conversely, be seen as a partial abandonment of the aesthetic attitude itself. Attentive study of (external) sensations by adults yields the realization that they are integrally connected to (internal) affections. Likewise, close scrutiny of (internal) affections reveals that they are not unrelated to (external) sensations. In sum, although not all feelings (e.g., nostalgia) are sensations, all sensations are feelings of some sort; hence feeling is the more generic category. In Hartshorne's view, sensations can be understood as particularized, clearly defined affections. Hence it is a confusion to think that scientific *analysis of sensation* is the same thing as sensory experience itself, which is as-suredly not devoid of aesthetic qualities. And scientists who analyze sensation can avoid aesthetic categories only as a result of a great deal of discipline and abstraction on their part (PP, 126–28).

The experience of redness is a feeling that can be pleasurable or painful, but either way it is a feeling. If an automobile brake squeals, we may legitimately doubt that the brake is in agony, but there is no reason to doubt that our auditory nerve cells are suffering. In fact, it is because they "suffer" that we suffer, Hartshorne thinks, as we will see in the following chapter (PP, 250–52).

It should now be clear that Hartshorne's view of sensation/feeling is both philosophical (in his opposition to modern philosophy's treat-ment of primary, secondary, and tertiary qualities) and empirical (in his phenomenological description of how we experience the world). Several recent studies can be used to clarify Hartshorne's stance.

For example, Natika Newton is a contemporary philosopher in consciousness research who works in the same tradition of American phenomenology as William James and Hartshorne himself. Newton puts the key issue as follows:

> Contrary to the hopes of Churchland and other reductionists, sensory phenomena seem incapable of being experienced as brain properties. Try to see the red of the book in front of you as a property of your brain! Colors are essentially visual phenomena, and we cannot (nor-mally) see our brains with our own visual mechanisms. I can learn to think about my brain when I see red, but I cannot thereby affect the phenomenology of red. Sensory properties are *not like* brain proper-ties.[9]

Newton's view, which is quite compatible with Hartshorne's, is opposed not only to the reductionism of Churchland[10] but also to the linguistic approach to (human) consciousness that is currently the dominant view. In this view, entertaining a thought is analogous to expressing a statement. But in Newton's account, the many different versions of the linguistic view have failed to explain the *experienced* properties of human perception and reasoning, which is precisely Hartshorne's view as well. Further, Newton is instructive regarding how the brain structures and central nervous system that humans share with animals allow us to extend what we know about feeling (and, more problematically, rationality) in human beings to animals. The appeal of the linguistic view is clear: human philosophy, science, literature, etc., all require language, and only human language has the combinatorial productivity that allows the elaboration of concepts on which advanced human culture depends. But these facts should not obscure the equally obvious facts of animal feeling (e.g., in Hartshorne's view, the pleasure birds have when singing) and the sophisticated signs animals use to communicate with each other.[11]

Another recent scholar in consciousness studies who supports Hartshorne's thesis that not only all sensation but all consciousness is permeated and directed by emotion is Ralph Ellis, who relies on the neurobiological investigations of Gerald Edelman and Jeffrey Gray. Ellis is also, like Hartshorne, a critic of both dualism and behaviorism as adequate responses to the mind-body problem. His view is very compatible with Hartshorne's: sensation and consciousness are *higher-order processes* that take as substrata *lower-order processes* such as electrical or chemical events. Although he calls his view "connectionism" rather than "panpsychism," it is nonetheless clear that he thinks that the best available evidence in neurobiology supports a relational view wherein it is the interactions or connections among processes that enable us to understand sensation and consciousness. Further, there is a priority of process over substratum in Ellis' view of sensation and consciousness, which he sees as thoroughly *organic phenomena* that resist any variety of psychophysiological reductionism, along with its concomitant annex theory of sensation and value.[12]

As a psychologist, Wayne Viney (father of Donald Viney) concentrates on the contributions to psychology found in PP that bear on the subject matter of the present chapter. Viney locates Hartshorne's aesthetic psychology historically by seeing him primarily as a student of Leonard Troland (Hartshorne's psychology teacher at Harvard) and in opposition to the standard view of sensation in the early decades of the twentieth century, as defended by Hermann von Helmholtz. Five theses are prominent in Hartshorne's approach: (1) there is continuity within and between sensory modalities; (2) affective tone is integral to sensory quality; (3) experience is social in the sense that "feeling of feeling" accounts for communication between and within experiencing systems; (4) sensation is closely related to adaptive behavior; and (5) sensory qualities have an evolutionary history from a common origin.[13]

Hartshorne was well ahead of his time regarding (4) and (5), Viney thinks. Few today would argue against the claim that there is a functional or adaptive nature to sensory qualities. Shapes, colors, odors, sounds, tactile sensations, and tastes, as well as the intrinsic feeling tones they contain, are incitements to adaptive action. In effect, the annex theory of sensation defended by Helmholtz and others is bad biology. It is no accident that very young humans are attracted to sweetness and avoid bitterness in that the latter is often a marker for poisonous objects. Further, the idea that the adaptive character of each sensory quality emerged all by itself is a pre-Darwinian notion that implies discontinuity with the rest of nature; continuity punctuated by differentiation and elaboration makes much more sense in evolutionary terms.

(1) and (2) have also been corroborated by psychologists (though not without opposition) since the 1920s when Hartshorne started defending these theses. The most controversial of Hartshorne's five theses in PP is his panpsychism or panexperientialism, as found in (3). This thesis will be examined in detail in the following chapter. (Troland's way of putting (3) is to say that our cells have "sciousness," whereas we have "consciousness.")

There is a complex psychological literature regarding (1), the claim that Helmholtz was wrong concerning the stance that sensory modalities operate in independence of each other, that they are isolated, irreducible, and *sui generis*. In Helmholtz's view we cannot say, according to Viney, that a sweet taste is more like the smell of lilacs than the smell of rotten eggs. That is, Helmholtz's view is indicative of a modern, atomistic approach wherein there is no analogy by which one could gain access to one quality from another. By contrast, Hartshorne's defense of intersensory continuity helps us to understand what we notice in ordinary experience and what we say in ordinary language: that sounds may be sweet, colorful, or flat; that colors can be loud or warm; that pain can be sharp or dull; and that wine can be tasted as dry or light. Hartshorne's treatment of Helen Keller in IS is indicative of his fascination with the ability of human beings to learn about one sensory modality through experience of another. And Viney is informative regarding the complex evidence regarding newly sighted persons, a topic that is also of interest to Hartshorne in PP. Finally, Helmholtz's opposition to intersensory continuity is, once again, at odds with evolutionary thought in that such continuity is adaptive.

The present chapter, however, has been primarily concerned with (2), with the affective nature of sensation. As before, the view of sensation that Hartshorne rejects is too heavily influenced by an atomism whereby bare awareness was thought to be stripped of all feeling and valuation. As Viney notes, the sensation of pain is a prime example of the primacy of affective tone in that it is almost impossible to describe such a sensation without adjectives like insistent, excruciating, throbbing, stabbing, etc. "Disinterested pain" is oxymoronic, at best, but for most people it is nothing short of a contradiction. It must be admitted that dull sensations at times appear to be devoid of affect, but Hartshorne thinks that the missing affect can be discovered if the appropriate means of observation are established (TR, 237–41).

Viney is also helpful in leading us to a defensible response to the question, Why has Hartshorne's theory of sensation not been more influential, given the fact that four of his five basic claims have been confirmed by subsequent psychological research, two of them with no current opposition whatsoever? Viney proposes three possible reasons. First, as a result of William James' antipathy to the psychology of sensation, the discipline for several decades largely moved away from this subject. This seems odd, considering that in other respects Hartshorne's views are often close to those of James. Second, throughout much of the twentieth century, behaviorism was the dominant force in American psychology, and behaviorists tended to be opposed to the affective nature of sensation. And third, the sweeping nature of Hartshorne's claims (involving philosophy, biology, psychology, physics, etc.) would have been seen as too promissory for most practicing psychologists, in Viney's reasoning.[14]

In response to the behaviorists' challenge, Hartshorne puts his case in the following terms:

> Behaviorism, in the sense of the reduction of mind to matter, has as its overt or covert premise a false report upon the nature of sensory phenomena as directly observable. And its falsity is beginning to be recognized, as introspective methods are refined and rendered more exact. The future of introspectionism is bound up, it begins to appear, with the future of the affective continuum. In general, psychology is, in its present state, decidedly more favorable to the doctrine of the affectivity of sensations than it has ever been before. All the great advances in recent times encourage the conviction that the idea of neutral, non-appreciative awareness—"bare awareness," it might be called—is a self-contradictory abstraction; that apart from factors of motive and valuation, apart from aesthetic and emotional aspects, nothing recognizable remains of consciousness or experience. (PP, 108)

We now know in hindsight that Hartshorne was a bit premature in throwing dirt on the grave of behaviorism, but many psychologists eventually came around to his view of the affectivity of sensation, as Viney shows. Further, by "introspectionism" in the above quotation, I assume that Hartshorne means the phenomenological effort to "report upon the nature of sensory phenomena as directly observable," to use Hartshorne's own words.

Perhaps the most enduring of Hartshorne's contributions to the theory of sensation, however, concerns the basic idea that sensation is *intelligible*. Before Hartshorne it was commonly assumed in philosophy and psychology that the qualities of sense experience were ineffable simples and that only complex configurations of these were describable. Hartshorne challenges this assumption in two ways. First, simple sense qualities, such as an experience of the color orange, *can* be described—say, by phrases such as "both red-like and yellow-like," or "that which is qualitatively intermediate between red and yellow." Second, the assumption that simple sense qualities are ineffable can be challenged in terms of the intersensory continuum. For example, Helen Keller inferred the characters of colors and sounds on the basis of the other experiences with which she was familiar, notably touches and smells. Keller even claimed that she was able to appreciate the changes of another person's voice by placing her hand on that person's throat so as to feel the vibrations there, a procedure that she thought indicated "the spirituality of the universe." Or again, a newly sighted person might be able to identify the red end of the color spectrum by virtue of his prior knowledge of the sound of a trumpet (IS, 161–69).

These two elements of Hartshorne's theory of sensation are connected: the affective nature of sensation and the intersensory continuum. It is *because* sensation is suffused with affect that we can appreciate different sensory modalities when they are suffused with the same affect. Feelings are not special cases of knowing, nor are they "ideas," as the British empiricists believed. They are *experienced* in several different sensory modalities. The affective nature of sensation, if not the intersensory continuum, seems to have been appreciated by several major twentieth-century philosophers, including Whitehead, Dewey, and Heidegger, the latter of whom saw the illusoriness of the notion of mere givenness *(pures Vorhandensein)* untinged with concern *(Sorge)*. But it seems to be Hartshorne's unique contribution to theory of sensation that *he alone sees the connection between the affective nature of sensation and the intersensory continuum* (IS, 170–73).

Hartshorne is prepared for some obvious objections to theses (1) and (2). For example, some will say that because we can distinguish verbally between a "sense quality" and a "feeling tone," that these expressions refer to two distinct entities. But some distinctions, he thinks, are purely verbal or logical. The sense quality (e.g., the redness) is here referred to in strictly denotative fashion, whereas the quality of feeling is connotative. Hartshorne admits that there is a logical, but not an ontological, distinction between denotation and connotation, between pointing to and feeling the quality of what is so indicated, and between "sense quality" and "feeling tone," respectively. The fact that there is no ontological distinction between the elements in these three pairs can be understood by considering the person who goes blind and misses not only the feelings associated with the lost colors but also (and primarily!) the colors themselves. As Hartshorne puts the point forcefully: "no facts, as recorded by careful observers, are necessarily incompatible with the affective theory of sensation" (IS, 183). As a result, the alleged ineffability of simple sense qualities is a dogma or an unexamined assumption, not a phenomenologically or scientifically established result (IS, 174–76, 184).

I mentioned in the introduction that the word "aesthetic" is used in two different senses in the present book. One refers to perception in general (based on the ancient Greek sense of the term), and the other refers to perception of works of art in particular. Context, I promised, would clearly indicate which of the two senses of the term was operative in any specific discussion. Thus far in the present chapter I have obviously been using the term in the former sense. But the affective nature of sensation that is of prime concern in this chapter provides the best link available for bringing together the two senses of the term. The aesthetic, affective character of concrete experience in general, provides the basis for aesthetic experience of art in particular. As Sherburne puts the point, "unless one finds something aesthetic in the concrete facts from which anyone starts . . . he will never come out at the end of his reflections with an adequate theory of art."[15] Experiencing a work of art, in particular, presupposes experience in general.

The annex theory of sensation that Hartshorne opposes implies that sense data are neutrally received and later have affect dumped on top of them. Likewise, some people think of representational art as a transparent medium through which we can neutrally see the world. Unreflective approaches to realist painting and to photography are especially prone to the adoption of this mistaken view. But not even representational art is a transparent medium, like an ideally polished piece of glass, through which we neutrally experience the world. Rather, an artistic medium is not so much a vehicle for transparent communication as it is a vehicle for the *transfiguration* of the affect found in sensation in ordinary experience.[16] (The religious import of this word in Christianity is not to be underemphasized.)

Representational art is actually constructive re-presentation of ordinary experience, with its dual properties of affect-laden sensation and intersensory continuity. A work of art *is* representational to the extent that its design requires that it be seen (or heard, etc.) *as* something, and it is nonrepresentational to the extent that it features content without any specific referent. In fact, some nonrepresentational works of art have so little content that has reference to the ordinary world that they are often characterized as purely formal, although sensation of the lines and colors of a Mondrian painting involves affect of a certain sort in that shapes and colors themselves, quite apart from any further representational content, are full of feeling tones. In any event, it would be a mistake to assume that the affective nature of sensation and the intersensory continuum were only applicable to experience in general and not to artistic experience in particular.

A link between the present chapter's concern for sense quality and feeling tone and the following chapter's concern for panexperientialism is supplied by Hartshorne's declaration that the feelings that are part and parcel of sensation are "objective" rather than "reactive." This objectivity means "that they are intuited as outside the body and as separated by a certain 'psychic distance'" (sq, 168). Hartshorne's stance here is in response to the empirical psychological research of Edward Bullough on the one hand and Myers and Valentine on the other.[17] This distance is not between sense quality and feeling tone; indeed, Hartshorne thinks that sensation *is* a sort of caring for, or valuing of, things. The idea that value is added by oneself after the fact of sensation, rather than given in sensation itself as a result of a connection with something "out there," is both bad phenomenology and bad aesthetics, he thinks. In the whine of a dog, a listener intuits a feeling tone of displeasure *in the whine itself.* Any distinction that may arise between sense quality and feeling tone is a merely verbal one. As before, such a verbal distinction is due to the difference between denotative and connotative reference: "whine" is a name for something that is recurrent in experience; the nature of the experience is given not by this name but by terms such as "pained" or "agonized" (sq, 169).

Hartshorne emphasizes the point that the old view of sensation is analogous logically to the old, materialistic physics and biology, where certain heterogeneities and separations were taken for granted: particles from waves, matter from energy, irreducible and fixed species from each other, etc. The new view of sensation he defends is consistent with evolutionary biology in the sense that lately evolved functions are seen as specializations of earlier ones. Visual and auditory sensations are late arrivals that build on the pleasurable or painful feelings that preceded them in evolutionary history, feelings that are as old as life itself. Wordsworth makes the point poetically by reference to jocund daffodils. Our present sensations preserve primitive (or childlike) animism where we *feel* what goes on in the world, a socialized feeling that Hartshorne, in his theocentrism, sees as evidence of spirituality or love pervasive in the world (SQ, 170–72).

CHAPTER SIX

Panexperientialism

IN THIS CHAPTER I WOULD LIKE TO FINISH the effort, initiated in Chapter 4, to examine Hartshorne's nonanthropocentric aesthetic as it relates to subhuman reality. We are in a more favorable position to understand panexperientialism as a result of the connection between sensation and feeling treated in Chapter 5.

Regarding the traditional mind-body problem, we have seen that it is important to notice that three—not merely two—logical alternatives are open to us: (1) dualism, the view that reality is composed of two quite different sorts of stuff, soul-spirit-mind, on the one hand, and matter, on the other; (2) materialism, the view that material reality is all there is—that is, feeling or psyche (whether translated as soul, spirit, or mind) is in some way reducible to matter; and (3) panexperientialism or panpsychism or psychicalism, the view that all concrete singulars are psyche-like or at least exhibit some slight ability to feel or experience the difference between themselves and the rest of what is. We will see that, for Hartshorne, flowers and rocks have cells or atoms that are active, experiencing singulars, but they are not metaphysical monarchies that experience as wholes; they are metaphysical democracies, to use Hartshorne's terms, borrowed from Whitehead. For a panexperientialist there is no completely inert or dead matter. (The ancient Greek word "psyche" originally meant "life" or "breath," and only later referred to "cognition" or "mind." Plato interestingly defines "psyche" in terms of self-motion—e.g., *Phaedrus* 245.)

It should also be noted that, according to Hartshorne, materialism is really temporalistic dualism, positing an ancient mindless matter from which eventually emerged minded matter, such as we find ourselves to be. Hartshorne's panexperientialism avoids both sorts of dualism: the explicit sort as well as the temporalistic sort that goes under the guise of materialism. Panexperientialism explains abstract material beings in general in terms of more concrete sentient instances of becoming. Although I have used "panexperientialism" as well as "panpsychism," I will generally use the former term, coined by David Ray Griffin, for two reasons in the effort to capture well Hartshorne's view. First, the term "psyche" often suggests to people a very high level of experience, whereas Hartshorne's view is that all concrete singulars have *some* experience; and second, the term "psyche" often suggests an enduring individual, whereas, according to Hartshorne, the ultimate units of experience are momentary (10, 159–63; ZF, 133–37; RS, 69–84).[1]

We should not assume that, because so much of the world is supposedly inert, we must choose between materialism and dualism or take an agnostic stand between these two positions. Hartshorne thinks it is a mistake to assume that we only have the flickering torches of dualism to raise against the encompassing darkness of a mechanical and aesthetically monotonous view of the world as seen through materialistic monism.

We should also avoid the assumption, easily made by those who have not read Hartshorne carefully, that panexperientialism is to be equated with Berkeley's idealism. The three options in the mind-body problem listed above—some form of dualism, some form of reductionistic materialism, and some form of panpsychism or panexperientialism—are metaphysical positions, not epistemological ones. Berkeley's idealism, however, the view that to be is to be perceived, is an epistemological stance in opposition to realism. Hartshorne thinks that in epistemology the realists have been largely correct. That is, he believes that there are real instances of active, experiencing singulars quite apart from *our* experience of them (but perhaps not apart from God's experience of them, where Berkeley's view is a bit more congenial to Hartshorne's). There is much evidence in favor of the claim that Hartshorne is a metaphysical idealist and an epistemological realist, a description that makes sense as long as by "metaphysical idealist" we do not create the mistaken, Berkeleyan impression that the physical world vanishes. The physical world does not vanish in Hartshorne in that aggregates of active, concrete singulars can be found in cancerous tumors and runaway trains: physical realities that are quite real! Hartshorne sums up his view as follows:

> My contentions are, that the realists have been largely right, and the idealists often largely wrong, concerning the epistemological question, but that *both* realists and idealists have in most cases been largely wrong as to the logical relations between this question and the ontological one. For I hold that the realistic position in epistemology is the very one from which the most cogent argument for an idealistic ontology can be derived (RS, 69; see also 70–84 and ZF, 137–50).

Hartshorne holds that feeling characterizes anything concrete—leaving out of the picture abstractions like "twoness" and collections of concrete individuals like "two cats," which may feel individually, but not collectively. Of course, tables and rocks do not feel, but that does not mean that there is no feeling *in* them. Although the table is *relatively* concrete, being more concrete than the number two, it is really a collection of more concrete singulars: subatomic particles, atoms, and molecules. As contemporary physics, chemistry, and biology have made apparent, these concrete singulars do show signs of spontaneous activity; they are always in process. This activity consists in a sensitivity to causal influence from the environment; indeed it consists in experience (however primitive) of the environment and a response to it. "Mere matter," construed as the "zero of feeling" and process, is an absolute negation whose meaning is wholly parasitic on what it denies. Nothing concrete is obviously devoid of experience; even inert rocks have active molecules, atoms, or particles. No positive meaning can be given to the negative of "sentient" because all concrete singulars react to their environments. As before, Hartshorne holds both a partial indeterminism and panexperientialism, in contrast to Leibniz, who defended the latter but not the former (ZF, 133–37; RS, 69–84).

If all concrete individuals are sentient, it might be asked if "sentient individual" loses its distinctive meaning. Not necessarily, because, as in the cases of tables or trees, many pseudoindividual entities are not really individuals at all, according to Hartshorne. Rocks as swarms have *some* degree of organization in them, but not to the extent that interpenetration and amplification of the parts leads to a monarchical whole.

Materialism groundlessly attributes the qualities of the apparent singulars (like rocks) to the generally unperceived (yet perceivable) real singulars, in Hartshorne's view. In order to describe these active units of process accurately, we must have recourse to the only active singulars we perceive as such: ourselves or other animals. The principle of change or dynamic unity in the world is soul-like or feeling-like, in that a self-moving character, or appetitive aspect, must be used to explain changes in each concrete singular.

Hartshorne can do justice to the relative difference between life and "lifeless" matter. That is, the word "sentient" does not lose its distinctive meaning, as two contrasts remain: (a) that between active singulars and comparatively inactive aggregates and (b) that between microscopic sentiency (S1) and sentiency *per se* found in the animal or human individual (S2). And a panexperientialist like Hartshorne is able to show how soul and body are related in animals and human beings. Pain is due to damaged cells; we participate in their suffering. Soul or self-motion is found on both sides of the relation, but on different levels; the gap is crossed by sympathy. Our cells can enjoy themselves or suffer; and we can, via our central nervous systems, participate in their enjoyment or suffering. So it should not be surprising that sympathy can occur in the reverse direction as well, although cells cannot be as much aware of us as we are of them.

The dynamic unity of action in a tree or in a plant as a whole is too slight to justify the attribution of sentiency (S2) to them, although there is obviously striving *in* plants, even if they do not experience pleasure and pain as wholes. As democratic, rather than monarchical, societies they exhibit *some* unity of action, Hartshorne thinks, but not nearly the unity of action exhibited by animals with S2. We should not be harsh on those who have a panexperientialist view of trees, however, in that the pathetic fallacy is no more dangerous than the "prosaic" or "apathetic" fallacy, its opposite, which assumes that reality is aesthetically monotonous along dualistic or materialistic lines (ZF, 159). The admission of contingency and partial disorder into concrete singulars removes the modern materialistic artificialities that has precluded appreciation of panexperientialism from the time of Newton to the present.

The actual things in the world are careers, or series of actual occasions. The primary concrete entities are happenings, including divine happenings, unit cases of becoming or activity, in Hartshorne's view. Because none of these events in process is *completely* determined by antecedent conditions—which would end change in all its forms—*creativity* is a universal principle for panexperientialists. A feeling (of a microscopic event or of an animal or human individual) responds to prior feelings, but it is also spontaneous, in however slight a way. We should oppose those "neat and tidy minds" who claim that indeterminacy is our lack of knowledge; indeed it seems that when quantum physics in its present form is superseded, we will move even further away from classical conceptions of substance, determinism, and insentient matter. It is not only human beings, nor only animals, who defy an absolute regularity in their actions (although statistical regularity may be present, distorted as it is by our observation of it). Even the very atoms defy such absolute regularity, as any student of contemporary physics knows.[2] One of the objections Hartshorne can raise with the positions he opposes (materialism, determinism, atheism) is that they are purely negative or derivative (denying, respectively, experience, creativity, and self-surpassing but otherwise unsurpassable experience and creativity).

Dualism, like materialism, can easily lead to the view that nature is there for us to plunder, in that reality is mostly devoid of value (whether aesthetic or ethical), except for a few minds scattered about that deserve consideration. The clearest basis of respect for nature consists in a renunciation of two different sorts of dualism: an absolute schism between psyche and matter and a near-absolute schism between the human and other forms of psyche. The fallacy of composition would be committed in inferring the sentience of stones from that of molecules, and the fallacy of division prohibits us from inferring the insentience or inactivity of molecules from that of stones (10, 294–95). It might be alleged that the fallacy of division is also apparent in inferring the sentience of cells from the sentience of the organism containing the cells. However, the experience of *localized* pleasure or pain works against this accusation in that it gives us compelling evidence of feeling (S1) on a level much more primitive than that found in whole animal organisms (S2).

In short, Hartshorne is opposed to materialism, dualism (in its various forms: experience versus nonexperience, mind versus matter, sentience versus insentience), and anthropocentric idealism (in the sense of the epistemological doctrine that finite things have no known existence apart from their being perceived by human beings). Hartshorne is also obviously opposed to the fallacy of misplaced concreteness—that is, taking abstract composites for concrete singulars.

Hartshorne employs a cautiously positive form of sentient-centric (rather than anthropocentric) argument, provided that both S1 and S2 count as types of sentiency. We should attribute to other creatures neither the duplication of, nor the total absence of, those aesthetic sensibilities exhibited in high degree, and in a refined or complex way, in us. Primitive animism is defective in many ways, but it is nonetheless more reasonable than the modern view of the world inherited from certain forms of seventeenth-, eighteenth-, and nineteenth-century science (reliant on Newton, even if Newton himself did not hold this view in that he was a panexperientialist of a stripe)[3] that the world is a machine whose parts are submachines. Machines only occur when animals, especially human animals, make them. To use Popper's terms, it is probably more accurate to say that clocks (mechanical symbols for absolutely determined regularity) are clouds (symbols for partially indeterminate reality exhibiting only statistical patterns) than it is to say that clouds are clocks. Not even machines are mere machines in their microscopic parts.[4]

We have no alternative to interpreting nonhuman nature by analogy with our own aesthetic sensibility. Our own natures are for us the basic samples of reality, Hartshorne thinks. Dialectic takes us *to* nonhuman nature, even if we can never have *concrete* nonhuman feelings. The task is to try to know how it feels to be another subject of feeling than one's own present self. This is often difficult even for one's own past selves, as an infant, say, in Hartshorne's view. Because of their familiarity and relative similarity to us, dogs make the project easier, strange as that may seem; but because of their vastly different lifestyles, the feelings of mollusks and crustaceans are much harder to imagine; those of insects are harder still; the hardest of all to imagine are those of paramecia, molecules, atoms, or particles. There is no need even to try for winds, rocks, oceans, or perhaps even plants when taken as wholes, for these are swarms or colonies of individuals rather than true individuals. A reasonable sentient-centrism or panexperientialism like Hartshorne's can move cautiously upward to more exalted and universally efficacious psyches and downward to lesser psyches. Although it is true that individuality is a matter of degree based on form of organization, Hartshorne thinks that a threshold is crossed with the presence of S2 such that for practical purposes, at the very least, he dichotomizes plants and animals because of the absence of S2 in the former (10, 248–50; cs, 49).

Materialism dies hard, however. There are those who wish to preserve the belief that reality is made of bits of stuff, substances. Hartshorne's view, on the other hand, is that every singular active agent—there are no singular inactive ones, the seemingly inactive being composites of active agents—resembles an animal in having some initiative in its activity, or spontaneous movement, or feeling. The feelings of cells would include their internal relationships and the stimuli they receive from other cells—or in nerve cells, across synaptic connections. We have direct evidence that cells *do* feel; that is, we feel pain because cellular harm is done. Our suffering is an immediate sharing in, or sympathy with, feeling in our cells.[5]

Granted, awareness of our cells is blurred, in that we cannot identify the microindividuals as such, but our experience of pain indicates cellular feeling nonetheless. Once again, notice that pain is localized, as is sexual pleasure. And where there is feeling there is valuing or mattering, and in more than an instrumental sense, as we have seen above regarding the aesthetic attitude. But this is not a night in which all cows are black. Important distinctions among the different sorts of sentient reality can be made. Mountains, trees, vegetables, winds, and rivers have feeling in them, but they are composites of active singulars. Only their invisibly small constituents have a remote analogy to our own inner life and activity. We can feel as whole individuals, and we can also, via our central nervous systems, feel the experiences of the microscopic organisms that constitute us. Later in this chapter I will return to Hartshorne's variety of American phenomenology, on which his empirical claims regarding localized pleasure and pain are based.

Although molecules within an animal body exhibit peculiarities not noticed outside an animal body, it is only persons who can have a grasp of universals, Hartshorne notices. Even human persons, however, have many bodily functions that are not completely under unifying control, such as localized pleasure and pain or the beating of the heart. Worms and jellyfish are extreme examples of decentralized, democratic societies, but even persons are a little like worms in that their personal dominance is always only partial. As before, however, although individuality is a matter of degree, a threshold is crossed when the level of individuality is such that S2 is present as a result of a central nervous system.

Although it is hard for creatures (even human creatures) to know how much creativity they have, they most definitely have it. Causal regularities mean not the absence of open possibilities but their confinement within limits, as Hartshorne emphasizes in almost all of his books. Just as the banks of a river determine where the water will go (ignoring floods) while leaving open a virtually infinite number of possibilities for each molecule of water, so also causal regularities regulate creaturely freedom. The complete determinist would have to reduce the gap between the banks to zero, but he or she would thereby eliminate the river altogether. Likewise, to eliminate creative process altogether is to eliminate life.

There is a philosophical difference between the "categories" applicable to all creatures and the "transcendentals" applicable to creatures *and* creator, as Duns Scotus argued.[6] For Hartshorne, *the* transcendental is creativity, or, in other words, response to previous instances of response. God is the form of creativity that is surpassable only by this very form in a subsequent phase; creatures are surpassable forms of creativity.[7] A reasonable indeterminism, Hartshorne thinks, holds not that some concrete events have no causes but that the exact nature of ensuing events is left unspecified by the totality of their causal conditions. Something is left for the momentary self-determination of events.

Recent physics has made materialism and dualism problematic, thereby making Hartshorne's panexperientialist view of nature more plausible than ever. It is true that quantum physics has been variously interpreted. It appears, however, that the view that physical processes are spatially and temporally continuous must be dropped, even if macroscopic objects do conform to the thesis on continuity. Atoms do not travel from one energy state to another in a smooth motion; they do so in discrete, quantum jumps, or at least our measurement of them indicates not continuity but discrete, quantum jumps. Atoms "jump" because they are subject to forces from other particles. The "free" particle (even in quantum physics) has a continuous spectrum of *possibilities* of motion, but there are no *completely* free particles. Every particle has an existence defined by its relations with others. "What *are* the 'things' that jump?" one might ask. Some physicists have argued that we are dealing merely with numbers or mathematical entities, whereas others defend a pragmatic stance in which quantum formalism does not reveal the essence of the physical world, though it does *work* in experimental situations (LP, 162–68; BH, 142–47; RS, 89–90; IO, 76–77; CA, 139).[8]

Hartshorne is very much interested in how we *experience* nature, or speaking crudely, in what *works* for us when we try to explain the world. The principle of indeterminacy led some, like Einstein, to speculate that hidden variables would be found to save absolute determinism, but these hidden variables have never been brought to light.[9] At the very least, this much must be said about the effort to speculate metaphysically on the basis of discoveries in contemporary physics: we cannot understand microscopic (or submicroscopic) events on the analogy of macroscopic objects like billiard balls, yet it is precisely these objects that give us our modern notions of inertness and determinism, notions that lead to aesthetic monotony. What is not discussed in physics is not denied.

This fact does not give us carte blanche, but it does give us the freedom to take Hartshorne's view of nature seriously. This view assumes that throughout animate nature, even plant life, there is feeling; that so-called inanimate nature is not really inanimate; and that nature as a whole expresses a unified soul-like reality, of which lesser lives are participants (as we will see in a later chapter). In our perceptions of nature we at least indirectly experience these truths, but most civilized people are not aware of them because after childhood they lose the message of experience of nature, being preoccupied with supposedly more practical concerns; these ignorant or forgetful people claim to know that most of the universe is "dead matter," whatever that means.

The view of nature of preliterate animists, children, romantic poets like Wordsworth, and at least some who are familiar with contemporary science, may win out yet. In this regard Hartshorne is very much like both Whitehead and Cassirer (ID, 80–91). Life and feeling, in many forms, pervade and constitute nature. As before, the cosmic machine of the eighteenth century has become the cosmic dance of the twentieth. Although contemporary science does not exactly prove the panexperientialist right, it cannot prove her wrong, and it does provide her with some support.[10]

Dualism, materialism, and panexperientialism each has a price. Dualism admits feelings or experiences to persons, at least, but it strikes Hartshorne as an admission of defeat in the attempt to explain animate creatures; that is, dualism leaves the psyche unintelligible or insufficiently related to body. Mere materialism not only fails to explain the mind, but it also leaves matter as an empty abstraction. Both dualism and materialism lead us unnecessarily, Hartshorne thinks, to an aesthetically deprived, monotonous view of the world. But panexperientialism's more reasonable price, he thinks, is that it makes us aware of our human or animal incapacity to share in feelings radically different from those produced for us by our central nervous systems. This price is easier to pay because of Hartshorne, whose glory is that he gives philosophical expression to one of the three options for thought, an option to which disciplined speculation now imposes fewer obstacles than it did two centuries ago.

The key issue is: are we, in part, creators of the world, further determiners of a partly indeterminate reality? The dignity of the human individual is in the power to settle, here and now, in context, what all the past, and divine power, have left unsettled. Divine creativity does not settle the details of cosmic history, in Hartshorne's view. It is only human beings, imitating God as tyrant, who try to do this. Creative freedom even in animals means a pervasive element of real chance in the world. Thus some conflict and frustration are to be expected, as we will see in more detail later.

Wordsworth's description in "Tintern Abbey" could apply as well to Hartshorne: "with an eye made quiet by the power / Of harmony, and the deep power of joy," the panexperientialist sees "into the life of things." The first human beings who emerged on earth inherited a magnificent environment, and they appreciated this fact. However, their appreciation (or better, their reverential awe) was clouded by fear. Events in nature, especially animals, were themselves deified, as I have mentioned above. Civilization has stripped, in a commendable way, human beings of this fear of nature, and of the deification of animals. But it has also stripped human beings of their sense of the inexhaustible beauty and glory of the web of life, in Hartshorne's view. Paradoxically, it is only now that beauty and glory, in their planetary totality, are being made accessible by the very industrialism that tends to destroy them. Our machines have not enabled us to find our proper place among the other natural kinds of things. Only art or philosophy or religion can help us to do this. The task is to avoid preliterate fear while still respecting nature. Panexperientialism enables us to do this.

It should be reiterated that Hartshorne distinguishes between lower organisms (for example, cells that thoughtlessly adjust to the ideal of harmony) and higher organisms. The lower organisms can be parts of "democracies," as in plants, or parts of "monarchies," as in animals or human beings, where there is a presiding occasion or a mind or soul that collects together at a higher level what is felt locally.[11] For example, in "Lines Written in Early Spring" Wordsworth says of (monarchical) birds that "Their thoughts I cannot measure:—/ But the least motion which they made, / It seemed a thrill of pleasure." But concerning (democratic) plants he says, "The budding *twigs* spread out their fan, / To catch the breezy air; / And I must think, do all I can, / That there was pleasure there" (quoted in ID, 80–91; emphasis added). I take it that these twigs stand poetically for the microscopic organisms that make up the plant.

If the key insight of Chapter 5 (that sensation is a type of feeling) is linked with the key point in the present chapter (that feeling or partial self-motion in response to the past is ubiquitous in nature), we can reach some startling results in aesthetics, including the following: (a) beauty is a sort of objectified pleasure because (b) there is no basis in experience for mind vs. mere matter dualism. Support for (b) is provided by the experiential evidence that we have that sensation is a type of feeling. That is, physical reality is not first given in aesthetically neutral terms, with aesthetic feeling later projected upon this neutral datum; rather, the given is pervasively composed of feeling. The idea of neutral material stuff is itself a rather high-level abstraction that has led us to confuse low-intensity feeling with no feeling at all (CA, 147). These points, it should be noted, are compatible with Dewey's belief in the primacy of "qualitative thought."[12]

Within a panexperientialist metaphysics like Hartshorne's, scientists would have the same predictive abilities as they are otherwise assumed to have (or slightly more of them, as we saw in Chapter 4 regarding birdsong). The real gain, however, comes in terms of reticulative vision, experiential accuracy, and an ability to explain the beauty of the world. This beauty, described as "objective" in point (a) in the previous paragraph, is not objective in the sense that our own feeling of beauty is projected onto the world, such that it is the projection itself that makes it objective.[13] Rather, the colored objects or the sounds that we encounter in sensation are themselves composed of feelings. Our sensory pleasures do not have to be objectified in that they are already given to us as objective (LP, 129; DL, 151).

If Hartshorne is accused of preserving an "animistic semblance," he need not be ashamed of this accusation if the very kernel of sensation, when not overshadowed by intellectual and practical concerns, consists in grasping (an aesthetic "prehension" rather than an intellectual apprehension) an aesthetic object that is akin to ourselves because it is vibrant. Thus, the whole tradition of *Einfühlung* or empathy or intuition in aesthetics can be easily explained on a panexperientialist basis.[14] Can materialists or dualists say the same? Hartshorne doubts that they can. In the view Hartshorne defends, aesthetic value is the key to the relation between subject and object; the latter, in fact, exhibits nascent subjectivity. It is intellect, not fidelity to experience, that makes this claim seem odd in some circles (BH, 167).

We know that both we and other monarchical animals with central nervous systems act as if our actions were influenced by feelings, desires, memories, hopes, fears, etc. (RS, 38). Panexperientialism is precisely the view that suggests that every singular active agent (once again, there are no singular inactive ones in that seemingly inactive ones are composites of active singulars) resembles an animal. Each of these has *some* sort of self-motion or initiative or unpredictability. And each also has *some* degree of self-enjoyment that contributes, perhaps largely unwittingly, to deity. Value obviously decreases when we consider very primitive active singulars, but zero value is not to be found in "mere" matter or in a "mechanical" body (the materialist and the dualist view alike), but in sheer nonexistence, assuming for the moment that such is intelligible. We have seen that there are subtle and complex relationships among contrast, intensity, and value, even for primitive active singulars that asymptotically approach zero value. The failure to achieve a great degree of value in a cell, for example, is due to the fact that there is too little contrast in a cell's life for much intensity to develop, for Hartshorne. Or in some cases, there are dramatic contrasts, but these are insufficiently integrated or unified or harmonized to produce much intensity, and *a fortiori* to produce much value. Comparatively trivial beauty we conceptualize as pretty, but where complexity and intensity are great, we have sublimity. Further, according to Hartshorne, insufficiently unified variety of contrast, when attended by low intensity, yields the comic or ridiculous, while lack of unity in a context that is nonetheless intense is tragic, etc., as we saw in Chapter 2 (WM, 121–24).

Strict determinism is completely negative in the sense that it altogether denies creativity to creatures, including the small ones that asymptotically approach zero creativity, just as they approach, but never attain, zero value. In Hartshorne's panexperientialist view, matter is positive because it contains rudimentary creativity and hence rudimentary value. It must be admitted that Hartshorne's views regarding the subject matter in question are not primarily derived from physics, as were Whitehead's, but from metaphysics and phenomenological/ aesthetic observation. Yet the metaphysical and phenomenological/ aesthetic case is not only compatible with, but is enhanced by, considerations in science concerning the apparent shift from strict determinism to causality understood in terms of the past supplying necessary but not sufficient conditions for the precise character of any occasion's reality in the present. If panexperientialism is correct—metaphysically, phenomenologically/aesthetically, scientifically—then not only can we not escape language, as contemporary philosophers are usually willing to grant, we cannot escape sensory/emotive experience. The most obvious example of our inability to escape sensory/emotive experience is when our cells suffer acutely, influencing us to do the same, unless, of course, anesthesia, paralysis, or meditative discipline intervene (ZF, 134–35, 157, 159, 162, 164–65, 170).

Panexperientialism is quite compatible with hylozoism and even with Aristotelian hylomorphism. In fact, panexperientialism can alternatively be called dynamic hylozoism or dynamic hylomorphism in that an adequate understanding of something's being temporal requires that we see it as a responsive/appetitive or body/soul complex actively assimilating past influences (or remembering them), dynamically responding to them, anticipating (however faintly) the next moment, etc. Thus the description of aesthetic experience or beauty as objective pleasure needs to be qualified by the phrase "over the course of time." It is quite common to have a highly localized pleasure, as in sweet food that initially tastes good on the tongue, that gradually merges into a pervasive joy that is spread across the whole body. (This view is quite compatible with the seemingly contrary evidence of feelings being deadened over time due to overexposure to a stimulus.) Hearing a haunting melody can analogously cause a pervasive tragic optimism. That is, the warmth and pleasantness (or their opposites) of sensations have their parallels in the psychic disposition of the entire organism. And most prominently, if enough cells are pained in the central nervous system, the animal or human being as a whole feels pain, unless, once again, anesthesia, paralysis, or meditative discipline intervene. These cells have their own individuality and minute independence, as well as a rapport among themselves. Further, they have a rapport (either by way of aversion or adversion) with the microindividuals in the thing causing the pain (PP, 17, 201–3, 244–47).

I do not want to overstate the case for Hartshorne's panexperientialism. The sense in which the red-seeing optic nerve and the brain become red in our experience is somewhat problematic on *any* view, whether materialist, dualist, or panexperientialist. What is clear in Hartshorne's panexperientialism, however, is that red as it is in the nerves and red as we see it is a relation between individual units of feeling and the overall quality of a complex of such units. At the very least, belief in nerve cells as individually sentient helps us to understand better than through materialism or dualism the mysterious relationship (Whitehead's "transmutation") between local pleasure/pain and overall experience of pleasure/pain. That is, in panexperientialism there is experience or feeling "all the way down," whereas in reductionistic materialism there is the notorious problem, pointed out by Thomas Nagel and other contemporary philosophers, of explaining the mysterious appearance of experience and consciousness at the level of whole animal individuals. Living cells are important because they occupy a halfway position between the higher animals and human beings, which are undeniably sentient, on the one hand, and the simplest physical entities (or better, pulsations), like electrons or photons, at which points the analogy to animal sentiency is pushed to its limits, on the other.

If Hartshorne's analogy holds, however, then physics would turn out to be the most primitive branch of comparative psychology. Those who think that the analogy will not hold will no doubt accuse Hartshorne of anthropomorphism, but it should be noticed that it is not so much mind or rationality that is traced to the simplest physical pulsations, but feeling; hence if a negative term is to be attached to panexperientialism it should be "zoomorphic" or "biomorphic" rather than "anthropomorphic." That is, the panexperientialist abstracts away from the specifically human in order to isolate the lowest (animal-like or lifelike) forms of feeling (PP, 248, 250, 265, 270).

The implications of Hartshorne's panexperientialism for aesthetics should now be clear. Aesthetic experience is not a mere subjective reaction, rather it implies a self-motion or a decision (literally, a cutting off of some possibilities and a movement toward others) or a value in the object analogous to that in the experience itself. Pleasure is felt *in* the sound of a merry voice or *in* the delightful song of an oriole. And the agony of a dog penetrates our sensation when we hear him whine. How could one, Hartshorne wonders, separate the pleasantness of our experience of the smell of a rose from the rose itself (or more exactly, from the living cells in the rose)? We *experience* the smell as coming from out there in the rose. Aesthetic experience can be seen as starting with a living outer wall in sensation that is permeated with the value it receives; the value is not experienced as being dumped after the fact on the sensation.

At the very least, Hartshorne does not grant the materialist's or the dualist's *assumption* that aesthetic pleasure and the objective elements in experience are ontologically separate; such a separation, if there is such, must be demonstrated. For the valued aspects of experience to be *there* at all they must strike us as magnificents or uglies or beautifuls that attract or repel us. The panexperientialism Hartshorne defends is not compatible with the claim that the rain mourns, in that raindrops are insentient aggregates of protosentient parts; however it does insist that we cannot easily, if at all, pass beyond, or deny the existence of, the value of active singulars in the world (OD, 233, 236, 239–40, 253–55).

In a process worldview, the locus of value is experience; hence the importance of the effort to consider the range of experience in nature: without at least nascent subjective experience there would be no locus for aesthetic satisfaction. S1, we have seen, goes all the way down the scale of becoming in nature. Where S2 starts is a more difficult matter. Perhaps at least the beginnings of sentiency per se (S2) are to be found in mollusks or crustaceans. Clams, for existence, have three pairs of interconnected ganglia, but no central brain. Because of ubiquitous S1, however, there are good grounds for claiming there is an unbroken continuum of aesthetic satisfaction in nature. This continuum is nonetheless compatible with the discontinuity in nature described by quantum theory. Quanta may be discontinuous, but qualia (such as S1) can still be continuous. Further, qualia are crucial in an aesthetic appreciation of nature, as in the aforementioned primacy of tertiary qualities.

It is obvious that Hartshorne's panexperientialism is out of the philosophical mainstream at present, but once again Thomas Nagel is a major analytic philosopher who takes panpsychism seriously. He defines "panpsychism" as the view that the basic physical constituents of the universe have mental properties, which include sensations, feelings, or desires of some sort. The plausibility of panpsychism lies, Nagel thinks, in the fact that such mental properties cannot emerge out of nonmental properties, but must be composed of them. That is, emergence is an epistemological condition rather than an ontological one: "The supposition that a diamond or an organism should have truly (not just epistemologically) emergent properties is that those properties appear at certain complex levels of organization but are not explainable in terms of any more fundamental properties."[15] To explain the mental (which, once again, includes sensation and feeling, according to Nagel) one must explain the subjective features of a thing, the phenomenological qualities of experiences, which neither reductionistic materialism nor dualism can do adequately. Although Nagel shies away from any comparison to Whitehead or Hartshorne, and although Nagel is confused regarding the connection between the mental states of whole animals and the "proto-mental properties of dead matter" (S1?), he is nonetheless unknowingly supportive of Hartshorne's view.

Nagel's support should not be surprising when we realize that cells, at least, are living organisms; thus they are analogous to us in this important respect: they have a qualitative or inner aspect. It is precisely this qualitative or inner aspect that reductionistic materialism cannot explain; dualism might explain it, but only inadequately in terms of a soul that is in some puzzling way connected to a physical body. The weak way to put the case for panexperientialism is to say that there is no conceptual or *a priori* criterion that limits feelings to higher organisms with S2. Having a brain is no more necessary to feeling in general than having lungs or a stomach is necessary to oxygenating and digesting in one-celled organisms (MB, 81).[16]

More typical than Nagel's reaction among analytic philosophers is the response of L. Bryant Keeling, who notices that for Hartshorne feeling is a metaphysical principle in that it is not explained by anything more general: all concrete singulars feel both in the actual world and in any conceivable world. To put the point in Plato's terms, to be is to have the dynamic power either to have an effect on others or to be affected by others, in however slight a way (see *Sophist* 247E). Keeling admits that Hartshorne knows more about analytic philosophy than analytic philosophers typically know about neoclassical metaphysics, but he still wishes to criticize Hartshorne's panexperientialism, as well as the view of Stephen Toulmin that any arguments that justify biochemists speaking of genes as molecules of extreme complexity also justify speaking of atoms and molecules as "organisms of extreme simplicity."[17] Keeling's basic criticism is based on the assumptions typically made by ordinary language philosophers like the later Wittgenstein, Austin, Strawson, Ryle, and Searle. In its everyday use, Keeling thinks, "feeling" refers to the experiences of human beings or other animals having central nervous systems. As such it is not completely general in reference, and hence it is not a metaphysical category. If the meaning of an expression is to be elucidated in terms of its use, then Keeling thinks that Hartshorne's use of "feeling" deviates substantively from its ordinary use.[18]

Most people would be uneasy with the idea that an earthworm feels remorse over what it has done, Keeling thinks, or with an amoeba feeling pain. There is no possible behavior by an electron (or by the universe as a whole, to be treated in a later chapter) that is sufficiently analogous to human behavior to make it possible to apply the word "feel" in its ordinary sense. The problem is not merely that we do not have scientific evidence for such feeling, Keeling thinks, but rather that we do not know what it *means* to use the word "feel" here. The source of Hartshorne's difficulty, in Keeling's view, is that his use of introspection to connect the word "feel" to an internal reality yields a private language, with all of its notorious difficulties pointed out by Wittgenstein: "When we abandon circumstances and behavior as criteria for feeling, we are in an 'Alice in Wonderland' kind of world."[19] Although it is meaningful to say that a cat can do arithmetic, even if such a claim is false, to say that an atom can do arithmetic leaves us at a loss as to what is being claimed. The same problem arises, Keeling thinks, regarding the claim that an atom can feel.

Hartshorne's response to Keeling's thoughtful criticism involves at least three points. First, Hartshorne does not hold, as Keeling alleges, that human beings have direct access only to human feelings. Rather, in human sensation we have feelings of subhuman bodily constituents. Hence from the start, our feelings and the language we use to describe them push us far beyond a private language. Second, regarding application of "feeling" or "sentience" (i.e., S1) to nonhuman feelings other than those of our own bodily constituents, behavioral criteria are all we have. Hartshorne's critique of behaviorism is not meant to make behavioral criteria unnecessary, as Keeling implies, but to supplement the merely behavioral with a more direct, aesthetically appreciated criterion. And third, whereas in sensation the datum of experience that is aesthetically appreciated is the just-previous subhuman feelings of our bodily constituents, in introspection, which is really retrospection; the direct datum that is aesthetically appreciated is the previous human feeling itself (CK, 67; LP, 151, 154).

The behaviors exhibited by subhuman reality outside of one's own body, Hartshorne thinks, include those that show evidence of receiving influence from the immediate past and the surrounding environment that elicits self-initiated activity, including motions, that indicate something expressive of anticipation, desire, purpose, or satisfaction, to however slight a degree, regarding the future. The evidence of these behavioral criteria being met by atoms, even by electrons, along with the inability of contemporary physicists to deny the self-activity of these dynamic realities (as in the irreducibly statistical half-life of the transformation of radium atoms into lead) confirms the banishment of merely inert units from science. Concerning larger dynamic realities like amoebas, it seems that they do not look far ahead or vividly recall the distant past, but their behavior seems to indicate *some* memory of the past and *some* anticipation of the future. As Hartshorne's ZF argues in detail, the gap between some finite amount of a quality, however small, and none of it whatsoever is quite large from a metaphysical point of view. That is, from a metaphysical point of view it is crucial to explore carefully both the lower limits of comparative psychology as well as the cosmic feelings of the all-inclusive, divine being-in-becoming. (We will see that in addition to the givenness of the feelings of our own bodily microconstituents, Hartshorne thinks that human feelings of God are also given.) One of the purposes of philosophy in general and of aesthetics in particular, Hartshorne thinks, is to help future scientists to transcend mere common sense (CK, 68–72).

It is fruitless for Keeling to wonder whether earthworms can feel remorse, but it is not at all fruitless to wonder what sort of feelings the earthworm (or its parts) has in general. Hartshorne wonders why ordinary language is sacred to some philosophers, who would be worried about uses of "feeling" that deviated from ordinary use, when ordinary language is refined or abandoned in nearly all academic disciplines. Baseball announcers notoriously misuse "velocity," as that term is defined in physics, for example. Ordinary language works wonderfully at the job for which it is intended, but this job is not the one philosophers (including metaphysicians and aestheticians) intend to do. In ordinary language we use "inanimate" things without considering what they are apart from our use, whether their parts have aesthetic experiences, or what they might be like as experienced by God. The use of "feeling" in Hartshorne's metaphysical aesthetics is not so much meant to *violate* ordinary language, however, as to *extend* it for the purposes of philosophy. There is no criterion for the absence of feeling that is not also a criterion for the absence of concrete reality itself. The problem is logical as well as phenomenological/empirical. All of these reasons support Hartshorne's contention, arrived at early in his life, that reality is "an ocean of feelings" (CS, 71, 142; WP, 148, 179).

Aldrich asks what he seems to take to be rhetorical questions, but these are questions that nonetheless point out the important link between the claim that sensation is a type of feeling and a defense of panexperientialism:

> Well, how can you experience the sadness of your neighbor's face? Or in his voice? Similar perplexities arise even here if you have a sneaking suspicion—as some philosophers have—that, strictly speaking, your perception presents you with nothing but a physical object in motion. The rest, the animation, has to be conjured up, according to them, by subjective associations and analogies. Well, *is* it?[20]

Clearly not, from Hartshorne's point of view. On an experiential basis alone we should be open to the possibility that Hartshorne's "ocean of feelings" is a plausible hypothesis. Works of art enhance this plausibility: even paintings by Kandinsky that are largely devoid of representational content nonetheless convey, like pure music, pervasive moods. We have seen that the experience of beauty is not a purely passive affair, but an active re-creation of objective beauty that is, from a religious point of view, expressive of a cosmic purpose. As the psalmist proclaimed, the heavens declare the glory of God. An aesthetic experience of a sunset as dynamic beauty, if not explained in terms of the annex theory that Hartshorne rejects, seems to point toward *something* in the natural world that is vibrant and with which we can resonate.[21]

It may seem that Hartshorne's panexperientialism is at odds with Whitehead's view if Ivor Leclerc's interpretation of the latter is considered. Leclerc resists the claim that Whitehead was a panpsychist or panexperientialist, but the debate between Leclerc and other interpreters of Whitehead seems to be a verbal one merely, such that Hartshorne's panexperientialism is quite compatible with Whitehead's view. Leclerc's legitimate point is that as a result of seventeenth-century philosophy we have a tendency to strictly bifurcate rationalism and empiricism, subjects and objects. By way of contrast, Aristotelian hylomorphist views popular before the seventeenth century saw anima included in the physical as a principle of life and feeling. The extrication of soul from the physical is what Whitehead wants to avoid, in Leclerc's interpretation, by claiming that actual occasions are dipolar: they are *both* physical (receptive) and mental (appetitive). Leclerc rightly criticizes panpsychism, and he rightly notes that Whitehead was not a panpsychist, *if* by "panpsychism" we mean the extrication of soul from the physical or the denial of the physical. But this is not what Hartshorne defends. Once again, Griffin's term "panexperientialism" (rather than "panpsychism" or Hartshorne's "psychicalism") may help to make this a bit clearer than it would be otherwise. One consequence of Whitehead's and Hartshorne's (updated Aristotelian) view is that genuine aesthetic appreciation of, and knowledge of, nature requires not reason alone, with its criteria of internal consistency, etc., but also sensation and a fair depiction of the phenomenologically given; hence there need be no strict bifurcation of rationalism and empiricism in Hartshorne.[22]

We have seen in a consideration of the aesthetic attitude that very often those who are the most interested in experiences as such are artists, which is why both Whitehead and Hartshorne profess a particular fascination with the poetry of Wordsworth. Husserl, by contrast, came to experience largely through logic and mathematics without any detailed consideration of poetry. Heidegger certainly considered poetry carefully, but he often gives the impression of being remote from logic and mathematics and science. An Anglo-American phenomenology like Hartshorne's is preferable because experiences as such are considered from the perspectives of logic, mathematics, psychology, physics, poetry, and, as we will see, religion (AP, 59–71).

One of the reasons panexperientialism is difficult for some to accept is that it involves the (supposedly counterintuitive) belief that psychology is the most fundamental subject in that it studies both ways of knowing: from within and from without, or directly in addition to indirectly, respectively. Once again, Hartshorne is not claiming that nature is known only through direct awareness of our own experiences; he is not an epistemological idealist. Rather, in addition to direct (albeit retrospective) awareness of our own experiences, we have direct, aesthetic awareness of the organisms in our bodies. Localized pain is really remembered feeling that happened a fraction of a second before; hence remembered localized pain is really re-remembered feeling. It is true that on the evidence of this feeling we ought no more to attribute sweetness, as a quality, to sugar than we ought to attribute pain to the thorn that pricks us. However, this admission is nonetheless compatible with the view that "nature is composed exhaustively of sentient individuals" (PU, 83). For example, the "I" is composed of ten billion interacting cells, each of which is composed of a huge number of interacting molecules. Because these cells have lives that are different from those they would live outside of an animal individual, they must also, however inadequately, aesthetically feel our feelings. It is in this fashion that psychosomatic illness, which is virtually inexplicable on reductionistic materialist grounds, is to be explained (PU, 81–85).[23]

The *harmony* of the central nervous system is truly remarkable when it is considered that there is such intense unity to *my* life in the midst of monumentally complex diversity of constituents. Amoebas, however, also establish unity in the midst of subamoebic feelings. The clear danger in analogizing human and subhuman aesthetic feeling is outweighed by the far greater danger of failing to do so. By refusing to use such an analogy we are left with an inert, lifeless world that is both amenable to exploitation and the source of monotony. On the basis of this analogy, physics becomes the psychology of the most primitive and the most widely distributed types of aesthetic experience. Chemistry and microbiology are not far behind. Even philosophical theology is an attempt on the part of animals such as us to conceive the thoughts of, and to feel the aesthetic mode of awareness of, a truly cosmic agent or superanimal: philosophical theology is an attempted psychology of deity wherein, as Peirce noted, one escapes the reductionistic materialist view that leaves the world as unintelligible as it finds it (PU, 86–90).

Hartshorne thinks that if God is truly the greatest conceivable being, then God can aesthetically feel a human being's entire feeling, not of course as God's entire feeling, but rather as a human being's entire feeling. The greatest conceivable being would have the capacity to assimilate in an unlimited way the variety and richness of the aesthetic feelings of others. To claim that no being can really feel another's feelings does violence not only to religious belief but also to our own sensations, which rely on our being able to feel the feelings of others (the microorganisms in our own bodies). If I have a stomachache and a headache at the same time, I can compare the qualities of the two because there are two sets of suffering members. That is, neither self-identity nor otherness is an absolute.

All feeling is participatory in some way. Even introspection (actually retrospection), as we have seen, is the participation of one's present moment of experience in the just-previous one. In one sense, the alleged truism that no subject can ever feel the feelings of another subject is the opposite of what Hartshorne sees as the correct view that *every* subject feels the feelings of some other subjects. In another sense, however, it must be admitted that human beings have (telepathy aside)[24] a hard time participating in the feelings of other human beings. To take an interesting example from Hartshorne, it would be hard for us to make a symphony out of bits of Beethoven, bits of Bartók, etc., because each human being has an individual mode of aesthetically appreciating the world that is quite different. We desire, and to some extent require, mutual externalities. Such an ability to take the styles of distinct and aesthetically sophisticated individuals and then turn them into a "su-perstyle" is, in a word, divine (ST, 87–93).

CHAPTER SEVEN

Beauty Merely in the Eye
of the Beholder?

BEFORE MOVING EXPLICITLY TO THE AESTHETIC elements in religious experience and to divine beauty as Hartshorne sees them, it will be worthwhile to consider aesthetic relativism. This is a popular view, even among those who are not ethical relativists. Beauty is *merely* in the eye of the beholder, it will be alleged. (In any defensible view, beauty is in the eye of the beholder in *some* sense.) In one sense aesthetic relativism makes sense when the vagaries of taste are considered, as we will see. At a deeper level, however, aesthetic relativism is a problematic view that deserves criticism, Hartshorne thinks. I will concentrate first on color and then on music in my treatment of his view.

We should note at the outset that aesthetic objectivism has been the norm throughout most of Western history. We have seen that Francis Kovach does an excellent job of detailing the compatibility between *some* sort of aesthetic subjectivism and aesthetic objectivism in medieval philosophy. The basic idea was that the beautiful, which was seen as a transcendental property of every being regardless of its limiting mode, gives disinterested aesthetic delight. Medieval thinkers like Saints Bonaventure and Thomas Aquinas admitted that not all beings are perceived as beautiful. This could be due to a lack of accidental integrity or proportion on the part of the object or due to a deficiency on the part of the subject. In any event, there is much compatibility between this sort of aesthetic objectivism and Hartshorne's aesthetic objectivism, despite the fact that in other areas Bonaventure's and Thomas' classical theism is at odds with Hartshorne's neoclassical view.[1]

For those who have been positively influenced by the aesthetic objectivism of classical theists, opposition to aesthetic relativism might seem to be a rather pedestrian stance. But we will see that Hartshorne's reasons for being opposed to aesthetic relativism or to an overly aggressive aesthetic subjectivism are anything but pedestrian. That is, his opposition to the idea that beauty is merely in the eye of the beholder involves several "bold" claims in the Popperian sense of the term, wherein one stops just short of overstatement in order to focus attention on the claims in question.

Consider initially a sensation of the color red. This sensation is felt or appreciated as warm, insistent, or advancing. By way of contrast, blue is experienced as cool, gentle, and receding, while yellow is felt as lighthearted or cheerful. Finally, violet is appreciated as quiet and wistful. Of course the objection will be raised against Hartshorne's view that these aesthetic feelings are associated with individual history or social convention and hence will vary at the very least from age to age and from culture to culture, if not from individual to individual. In fact, in many circles this objection is nothing short of axiomatic (PP, 165).

But is it correct? In the case of colors, at least, there is no clear evidence, as we will see, of such cultural or historical differences. It is clear that *the use of* colors is different from culture to culture, but it is crucial to notice that this is not necessarily due to the same colors expressing different feelings to different people. Rather, different peoples have different feelings to express. A famous example is provided by the use of white (along with other colors) in Chinese funerals. According to Hartshorne, this example in no way proves, as many cultural relativists assume, that the Chinese feeling for white is different from the Western one. People the world over see a certain purity in white, a certain detachment from the passions. The Chinese, however, do not share the historical conviction in the West that a funeral should solely, or largely, convey darkness, which underlies the traditional use of black in Western funerals (PP, 171).

Black and white convey the same feelings in China, North America, and even in Africa (or among African Americans, for whom black is quite legitimately seen as an aesthetic value involving moral seriousness), even if different peoples have different conceptions of death.

In any tradition of ancestor worship, a funeral is, in part, a matter of placating departed spirits or a pleading for the deceased person's purity. And the origin of black clothes at funerals in the West seems to be associated with a warning to others to beware of the dangers involving a corpse, according to Hartshorne. Culture rather than our emotional responses to colors influences which colors are appropriate at a funeral or wedding or rite of passage (PP, 170–71).

The empirical evidence on which Hartshorne's view of color (in PP and IS and elsewhere) is based is considerable. Early in the twentieth century Havelock Ellis studied the psychology of red and yellow in particular.[2] Since that time there have been several biological studies of the pleasure of color sensations[3] and several related psychological studies of color sensations[4] that have confirmed Hartshorne's views. It must be admitted, however, that the evidence for affectivity in color sensation might be challenged by those who claim to have visual sensation without affect. Hartshorne's response to this challenge is, once again, in terms of the claim that dull color sensations may *appear* to be devoid of affect, but the missing affect can easily be discovered if the appropriate means of observation are established. A neutral or dull patch of color that seems worthless nonetheless affects us enough for us to make such a judgment. Further, those who criticize Hartshorne's view may confuse affective response to color and color preference. As Wayne Viney points out in his careful treatment of Hartshorne's view of color, both the Romans and the early Christians saw yellow as a color that elicited a festive response, joy, and delight.[5] Yet the early Christians largely spurned yellow, a color that was often worn by the prostitutes in Rome, because they saw it as inimical to their faith. Gauguin's "Yellow Christ" did little to endear him to the Church. But the ancient Romans and Christians of all ages presumably have the same affective response to yellow.

Neurobiologists still tend to be reductionistic materialists and defenders of what Hartshorne calls the annex theory of value, where emotional affect is added to sensation after the fact. But on the basis of their own discoveries, there is good reason to call these views into question. For example, there is a well-documented syndrome called Kluver-Bucy, wherein damage to the amygdalar region in the brain leads to an absence of emotional "reaction" to sensory stimuli. The effects of this syndrome are devastating: a monkey, say, who developed this syndrome would not long survive because it would be indiscriminately fearless, placid, or unresponsive in its "psychic blindness" or "visual agnosia." That is, Kluver-Bucy syndrome illustrates *(per impossible)* what life would be like with sensation but without emotional affect.[6]

Aesthetic "associations" or connections common to the human species, as opposed to those that are idiosyncratic or merely cultural, are often shared with animals, as Langer also notes, indicating a biological basis for aesthetic feeling too often ignored in our present age, in which social constructivism is in many ways the norm. Consider the fact that for most day-living animals (excluding, of course, those that are color-blind) there is something beneficent about the orange or yellow of sunlight. Hence textbooks for those who work in the visual arts will typically refer to certain colors as warm or joyous.[7] Such patterns of "association" or connection are more than idiosyncratic or cultural (hence the need for scare quotes) in that they are rooted in our biological pasts, in Hartshorne's view.

The warm insistency of the color red, indeed its aggressiveness in some tones, can be ascribed to the fact that it is the color of blood, the only crucial and pervasively present red object in nature, once again as also noted by Langer.[8] Blood is also of highest concern to us. The greater physiological arousal to red than to other colors, amplified by conditioning to stop signs and the flashing red lights of emergency vehicles, is a potent mixture. Similar correlations with other colors are too tight to be lightly dismissed as fanciful, according to Hartshorne. Visual artists *depend on* these correlations in their works in various subtle ways that confirm rather than contradict the universality of the biologized color correlations or connections or "associations" (the scare quotes, once again, are needed to distinguish these from idiosyncratic or cultural associations per se). The making of a work of visual art would be merely a roll of the dice, Hartshorne thinks, if the artist had to rely solely on the trivial idiosyncrasies of personal history. Further, the perception of a work of art by people in other cultures would be a roll of the dice if the artist had to rely solely on the idiosyncrasies of her own culture regarding color. Artists reasonably assume, however, that they can elicit feeling in the viewers of their work *in spite of* personal or even cultural barriers (PP, 172–73).

Consider the possibilities. First, it is possible that the pervasive correlations between colors and feelings are not inherited but are developed *ab initio* in each individual. If this hypothesis were true, however, one would have an extremely hard time explaining the uniformity of result, Hartshorne thinks. A second hypothesis is that the uniformity of result is due to the fact that most cultures face roughly analogous environmental factors (the blueness of sky, the greenness of foliage, the redness of blood), and the reactions people have to these factors get sedimented into cultural tradition, which in turn is extended by artistic usage.

This second hypothesis gets us closer to the truth than the first. The problem with the second hypothesis, Hartshorne thinks, is that it fails to explain why city dwellers and those who live in rural areas do not have drastically different responses to color or why those who live in polar regions do not have drastically different responses to color than those who have never seen snow. Perhaps in the latter case the people who have never seen snow have seen many clouds.[9] In any event, the key point is that visual artists tend not to fear that their viewers will have drastically different responses to color from themselves, and they tend to believe that such variations that do occur are not to be feared, even such variations that are cultural rather than personal.

The third hypothesis to be considered, the one that Hartshorne adopts, is that color correlation is in some way innate or due to biology. This hypothesis, if true, would dovetail with the treatment of sensation as a type of feeling found above in Chapter 5. That is, in this view one does not first sense a color and then later add feelings or associations (whether individual or cultural) to the sensation. Rather, the sensation of color itself involves feeling tones and emotional affect, as Langer also shows.[10] Feelings inhere in, or are fused with, color sensations rather than tag along after the fact (PP, 173–75).

It must be admitted that in one work of art (say a Raphael painting) red may seem rich and dignified, whereas in another it may seem rude and annoying. This difference is most likely due to the relief provided by other colors and the balance (or lack thereof) among the parts of the work of art. When masses of color are simultaneously perceived, certain dynamic forces are put into play that do not contradict what has been said thus far in this chapter about Hartshorne's view. The subordination of a single element to the total pattern still depends on the former having its effect as an aesthetic feeling (PP, 183).

For example, although yellow is a gleeful color, if it is introduced into a painting that is mostly somber it may affront us as out of place; it may even strike us as violent rather than cheery. Thus in certain circumstances yellow may even have an effect on us that is characteristic of black, Hartshorne notes. But this is perfectly compatible with Hartshorne's thesis that what we notice in such a painting is that the lightheartedness of yellow seems out of place in the prevailing melancholy of the painting, or that it is placed in the painting intentionally by the artist to achieve an aesthetic effect, with the artist assuming the lightheartedness of yellow in itself.

Visual artists do not assume any strong relativity of color, but rather they know how to juxtapose colors so as to depict or elicit the totality of emotional possibilities, as Shakespeare analogously did with words. Yellow itself has no varying emotional character, even if at times we prefer it and at other times we do not. In conjunction with other colors and other factors yellow can elicit something other than cheeriness, just as the playfulness of children can lead an adult in a morose mood into an ever more intense negativity. The children are still merry, Hartshorne notes (PP, 184–85).

Variations of taste can be preserved in the nonrelativistic theory Hartshorne is defending. Some of these variations may be explained in terms of biological defects, as in partial color-blindness. But even with perfectly functioning sense organs one's distribution of attention leads to certain variations, as when some people concentrate on one part of a visual field, some on another part, as Gestalt psychologists have emphasized.[11] But if sensations were *not at all* valued in themselves they would not even be sensed. At the other extreme, if color sensations were valued *entirely* for themselves, our practical affairs would come to a grinding halt in that we would fixate on the red of the stop sign without putting a foot on the brakes, as is practically required of us. Aesthetic value in general is both expressive of feeling *and* convenient.

That is, there is variation in the explicitness of the intrinsic or instrumental values that we bring to our attention (PP, 186–87).

The emotional variability of visual works of art, therefore, is only partly due to individual inconstancy of association; some people, for example, seem to become less and less capable of attending to intrinsic aesthetic values as they move through the practical concerns of adulthood. Hartshorne puts the matter as follows: "The art of aesthetic appreciation is to 'associate' with the object solely the images and reactions whose affective content will permit the sensory content to remain in the focal center rather than such as will replace it" (PP, 188–89).

As before, the nonrelativity of color is connected to the nondualism of sensation and feeling, in Hartshorne's view. When one closes one's eyes and thinks of warm "out there," one's conception quite naturally involves a reddish or orange glow, as when we feel warmth when we sense red or orange with our eyes open. The same is true regarding other colors. The dependability of these feelings is no doubt due in large part to the strikingly simple distribution of colors in the natural environment: green is the color of vegetable life and is very often in the foreground; blue is the color of distant masses (the sky, the sea, distant hills); red, as we have seen, is the color of blood, danger, combat; yellow is the color of sunlight; white the color of light and snow; black the color of night or of deep shadows. If we except the arctic regions, from which human beings did not originate and in which few of them have settled, vegetation would have been the dominant foreground throughout most of the world, as Hartshorne notes. And throughout the world red carries with it emotions regarding the crises of life; hence it makes sense that we experience it as the most stirring and dramatic of colors. More than any other color, we must take it seriously (PP, 204, 221, 232–34, 253–56).

To admit that one's view of color is psychological as well as biological is not to make it easier to defend aesthetic relativism. For example, it may well be the case that Eskimos have a more refined appreciation of white than non-Eskimos, but these northern peoples have traditionally spent part of each year amid vegetation, as have desert dwellers. Further, human appreciation of color was settled hundreds of thousands or millions of years ago, before people settled in either the tundra or desert.[12] No doubt some of our feelings *about* sensations have changed over the years and across cultural boundaries, but it is doubtful that there has been much change regarding those feelings that *are* the sensations themselves. The association of cowardice with yellow is an example of the former, which is individually and culturally conditioned rather than built by the more distant evolutionary past. This cultural association is not adaptive like the sweetness of fruits or the serenity of green or blue (PC, 603–4).

Hospers is once again helpful in the effort to sort out the key features of the Hartshornian view. He is correct to notice that in the effort to flee relativistic associationism, both individual and cultural, Hartshorne lands in a different sort of associationism: universal "associationism," wherein people all over the world, because of the comparative similarity of the earth's separate ecosystems (all peoples have come into contact with green vegetation, a blue sky, water, etc.), have connected green with quiet cheerfulness.[13] These universal "associations" (with the scare quotes needed to distinguish this view from what is normally meant by associations, both individual and cultural) are common to humanity in general and perhaps to the higher animals as well.[14]

It must be admitted that if we had been able to live with different bodies on Mars or in another galaxy (as in some science fiction), perhaps we would have been in a position to refer to this view not as culturally variable but as environmentally variable or as planet variable. Clearly red is warm and not cold, however, in *any* human, earthly culture. For the sake of clarity I will continue to refer to Hartshorne's aesthetic view as nonrelativistic.

The nonrelativity of color-feeling applies as well to sound and other aesthetic feeling. It is customary to say that responses to music are inescapably subjective and relative to each individual. But it is of paramount importance to note that the affective quality of a musical work may remain constant even when people differ as to whether they like it or not. Some people may like a joyous tune, some dislike it, and yet they can all agree that it is joyous. Indeed the tune may depress the person who is grieving *precisely because* it is joyous. That is, to say that the affective quality of a work of art is *contextual* is more accurate than to say that it is *relative to* the individual or culture.[15]

As in visual art, the point can be better made if we consider smaller units (without subscribing to an aesthetic atomism—all perception, including aesthetic perception, is inescapably contextual). It is one thing to get agreement regarding the affective quality of a short musical passage, but this is quite different from getting agreement regarding the prevailing mood of a complicated symphony, where the affective qualities of sound are constantly shifting. The difference of opinion is often due to one listener being reminded of one passage and another listener being reminded of a different one, as in various colors displayed on an iridescent gown, to use Hospers' helpful example. Or regarding a single passage there may be disagreements that are merely verbal, as when one listener describes it as "majestic" and another describes it as "triumphant." Our affective vocabulary is still rather inexact.[16] Whitehead is especially helpful regarding the poverty of language for subjective states.[17]

Some musical passages from Richard Strauss strike some listeners as dissonant if they are not familiar with the other works that Strauss presupposed. And those who are only familiar with Haydn and Mozart will find the latter the apotheosis of passion; becoming familiar with Beethoven changes this estimation quite a bit, however. A final example: it may well be the case that some future composer will come on the scene who will alter our reception of Mahler's violently agonized passages. The overall point here is that for "individual relativism" or "cultural relativism" we should substitute "contextualism."[18]

To cite some simple examples of constancy, consider the fact that everyone would agree that the sound of a trumpet is more aggressive than the sound of a flute and that the sound of a French horn is more melancholy than that of a piccolo. The interval of a major third (C-E) is felt as positive and uplifting, whereas the interval of a minor third (C-E-flat) is felt as sad or melancholy, Hartshorne notes. *Compositions* in a minor key (involving appropriate melodic and tonal devices) need not be sad, but a minor chord is. No one calls music calm or restful if it is dominated by staccato passages, wide jumps in pitch, and rapid accelerandos and crescendos. These features of music obviously resemble restless people or animals who just cannot keep still. So also, slow, subdued music captures the emotions of sad people; no one calls such music excited (PP, 172),[19] as Langer also notes.[20]

All of the higher animals know that harsh sounds express harsh attitudes and hence spell danger; the same is analogously true regarding taste and olfactory qualities that indicate that some stuff can be safely eaten and some stuff should be avoided, Hartshorne emphasizes. A similar case can be made for musical sound as a universal language because it is not only intercultural (when in Vietnam and China and India and Egypt I was profoundly moved by music that I did not at all understand intellectually; and the Chinese and others appreciate jazz despite their conventions), but also interspecific. No animal has to learn through repetition what a snarl or a growl means. And human infants do not have to be taught to cry when they hear these sounds. As with color, the basis of music lies deep in our evolutionary pasts (ZF, 208–9; PC, 603; PP, 171).[21]

Some commentators might point to the dissonance of twentieth-century music as evidence for the thesis that beauty is merely in the ear of the listener, in that listeners in previous ages would not appreciate dissonance. But there is another way to look at the matter. The popularity of a certain combination of sounds that was previously condemned does not necessarily mean that the feeling tones themselves are appreciated in a new way but that in a more saccharine age people were not able to appreciate the dissonant combinations of feeling tones. We appreciate dissonant music (if we do) *precisely because* of its painfulness or dissonance.[22] And behind all cultures there is the biological aversion to harsh grindings and groanings, in which inhere feeling tones that are only with difficulty turned into music, although the task is not impossible. Krzysztof Penderecki's "Threnody for the Victims of Hiroshima" is a great accomplishment in music *precisely because* of the obstacles posed by such grindings and groanings and eerie high-pitched sounds (PP, 171, 174).

A harsh discord in one melodic context can be quite satisfying in another, especially due to the emotional qualities of several instruments in the orchestra, several keys, pitches, etc. Just as one's gaze can wander about a painting, one's attention at a symphony concert has endless possibilities. The conclusion to be drawn here, however, is not the relativistic one but rather that from the fact that sensing is a type of feeling we should not too quickly jump to the view that sensing/feeling is sufficient for aesthetic satisfaction. This satisfaction requires various background factors, both idiosyncratic and cultural and integral to the artistic medium in question. That is, the idea that sensations are feelings is necessary for an account of aesthetic satisfaction, but it is not sufficient. A composer can weave any number of delicate shades of feeling that we can all identify into her work, but there is no guarantee that the listener will be habituated to assimilate them in a satisfying way (PP, 183, 185–87).

Finally, the phenomenon of synesthesia is complex, but its very existence supports Hartshorne's aesthetic objectivism. No one will say that a Beethoven symphony is painted all in gray; everyone understands the analogy between the taste of sugar and a sweet melody; it is easy to describe the low tones of stringed instruments as warm and the higher notes of the trumpet as scarlet, etc. (PP, 204, 232–34).

Here regarding synesthesia and elsewhere, Hartshorne's views are often related to those of G. T. Fechner, whom Hartshorne frequently cites. It should be emphasized that Hartshorne was first exposed to panexperientialism through his Harvard teacher, Leonard Troland, who was, in turn, influenced by Fechner. The topics concerning which Hartshorne is influenced by Fechner, whether positively or negatively, include the following, topics that tend to unify his aesthetics: (1) sensed qualities are essentially aesthetic, not in the sense that they are strictly contemplative and are thus irrelevant to behavior, but rather in the sense that they balance our "incipient impulses to act"; (2) this view is at odds with the influential view of sensation defended by Helmholtz; (3) from the evidence of the body as a vast society of cells, both Hartshorne and Fechner conclude to panexperientialism; (4) there is an intersensory continuum. Based on the foregoing points, Hartshorne and Fechner are opposed to any strong version of aesthetic subjectivism (PP, 28, 30, 112, 176, 181–82, 206; PS, 243–46; 10, 248–49).[23]

We have obviously only scratched the surface of the topic of aesthetic relativism in that color is only one part of visual art and music theory is an enormously complex field that involves more than feeling tones, etc. But it is my hope that we are now, as a result of this chapter, better prepared to tackle the issues that are Hartshorne's primary concerns: the religious dimensions of aesthetic experience and divine beauty. Hartshorne's theses examined thus far—beauty as a dual mean, the difference between the aesthetic attitude and the instrumental one, the existence of nonanthropocentric aesthetic value, the convergence of sensation and feeling, panexperientialism, and the nonrelativity of aesthetic value—will come to bear on the remaining three chapters dealing with religious experience and God. To assume at the outset that aesthetic value is relative is to trivialize any effort to explore the religious dimensions of aesthetic experience.

Hartshorne's aesthetics is obviously connected to his affective theory of sensation. That is, aesthetic subjectivism is built on the assumption that it is entirely *our* perception that accounts for the beauty of an object. As Donald Viney characterizes this view: "beauty is something that we put in the world, not something we discover there."[24] It is precisely this assumption that Hartshorne rejected as early as his dissertation in the early 1920s (OD, 233). While it is true that aesthetic value is in the subject, this value can become an object for other subjects; thus value is an objective quality. It is, of course, possible that we can try to ignore our feelings toward things, but this in itself does not provide good evidence for aesthetic subjectivism. This alteration of feeling itself presupposes an element of stubborn fact, as Viney points out: "There is a kind of heroism in overcoming a fear of thunder, and an element of pathetic tragedy in becoming blinded to the gaiety of sunshine."[25]

Further, disagreement on aesthetic matters is often taken to support an argument in favor of aesthetic subjectivism. But Hartshorne insightfully emphasizes that such disagreements are usually outweighed by uniformities of opinion regarding the value of flaming sunsets, the smell of roses, etc. (OD, 234). The same approach can be taken regarding cultural relativism as an aesthetic stance. The fact that members of one culture can understand or perhaps even influence the aesthetic sensibilities of members of another culture only makes sense if there is aesthetic common ground. As an American I love Mahler; grunge rock from Seattle was the rage in the youth culture of the early 1990s in France, Poland, and Laos; classical music from India can be appreciated by classical music lovers from the West; etc. Disagreements among individuals and among cultures are quite compatible with aesthetic objectivism. The incredible amount of shared aesthetic opinion is much more of an embarrassment to aesthetic subjectivism, Hartshorne correctly argues, than is disagreement to aesthetic objectivism.

Sherburne, in his analysis of Whitehead's aesthetics, notes that aesthetic subjectivism was enhanced in the mid-twentieth century by the existentialists' attempt to shift attention from what they called the *Sein* (of entities of thought) to "the here-now-Da-ness of this Sein in concrete human experiences." This effort to catch concrete experience on the wing is to be applauded, at least as long as it does not also involve what Sherburne sees as a "linguistically confused and romantically irresponsible" aesthetic subjectivism. Even pure music, he thinks, which does not specify in detail the expressive nature of the psychical movement conveyed, nonetheless conveys a dynamic element that in broad outline is identifiable. Even without Beethoven's dedication(s) of the third symphony, we would know that the music is heroic, and even without the title *Sonata quasi una fantasia* ("Moonlight Sonata") all attentive listeners would know something of the expressive nature of this piece on the evidence in the music itself.[26]

Of course one person may like heroic music whereas another may detest it, just as some people like red automobiles while others hate them. But liking or disliking a quality of experience is not an unambiguous test of its feeling tone. Further, the fact that sensations are intelligible, rather than ineffable simples, counts against aesthetic subjectivism. For example, Hartshorne conceives of a circle of saturated colors bisected by two lines (intersecting at neutral gray) anchored on

Dimensions of Color
(PP, 222)

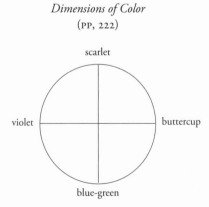

the four "psychologically primary colors," to use Hartshorne's designation: scarlet red at the northern end of one axis with blue-green, its opposite (or better, its complementary), at the other end of the same axis; buttercup yellow at the eastern end of the bisecting axis with violet, its opposite (or better, its complementary), at the other end of the same axis. This model helps us to understand why orange is experienced by most people as both reddish and yellowish: it is, at the very least, like other secondary colors, a compound of the psychologically primary colors. It is also possible on the basis of this model to explore three important contrasts regarding color: warmth/coldness (e.g., red is warmer than green), activity/passivity (e.g., red is more active than green), and brightness/dullness (e.g., yellow is brighter than violet). This model also improves on the related model from Troland, a square model where the corners mark the psychologically primary colors, thereby suggesting that these colors would be farther from the center than the others and hence would have greater saturation than the others, which is not the case.[27] The circle model that Hartshorne prefers has as its radius the dimension of saturated color (PP, 47, 165, 211, 222, etc.; IS, 174, 177–83). The circle model also enables us to amplify the thesis that beauty is a mean:

> In aesthetics it has long been recognized that complementaries [e.g., scarlet red/bluish-green], although not necessarily the most harmonious, are definitely far from the least harmonious of color combinations. In other words, the unity-in-variety which is axiomatic for aesthetic value, is by no means contradicted by complementary opposition. This is exactly in conformity with the geometry of the situation. (IS, 180; also see PP, 165)

It should be emphasized that this circle model of color, which Hartshorne calls an "unscientific hypothesis" in that he is not trying to do optics, is meant to help us understand the four *psychologically* primary colors, not the three primary colors of physics (i.e., red, yellow, and blue). Although the connection between the psychologically primary colors and the primary colors of physics is unclear in Hartshorne (e.g., the presence of violet as a psychologically primary color seems to be due to both impurities in the eye as well as to a mixture of longer wavelengths of light [PP, 215]), the existence of both of them, singly or combined, counteracts any strong version of aesthetic subjectivism. Aesthetic subjectivism is defective for the obvious reason, not to be examined in the present book, that it is at odds with our scientific knowledge of color. For example, it is known that color is a physical phenomenon of light (in causal relation to visual perception) that is associated with various wavelengths that are quite definite when detected by a technique known as colorimetry.[28]

It is simply erroneous, Hartshorne thinks, to assume that feelings of aesthetic value refer primarily to oneself or to one's likes and dislikes. Aesthetic values are objective in the sense that, although they can elicit reactive feelings in us, the aesthetic values themselves are intuited as residing or as arising outside the body and separated from us with a type of psychic distance. The crucial error lies in thinking that because one may or may not like purple, for example, it follows that beauty is *merely* in the eye of the beholder. But however much one likes or dislikes purple, one simply cannot *see* in it the gaiety of yellow. To reiterate a common theme: the thesis that beauty is merely in the eye of the beholder is problematic on several grounds, not least of which are phenomenological (SQ, 169–70).

CHAPTER EIGHT
The Religious Dimensions of Aesthetic Experience

Now that Hartshorne's general view of aesthetic experience is on the table for criticism, including his view of subhuman aesthetic experience, we are in a position to consider in particular the religious dimensions of aesthetic experience so as to prepare the way for the next chapter, where cosmic or divine beauty is considered.

Hartshorne characterizes aesthetic value in general as intrinsic, immediately felt value, and he characterizes economic and ethical value as much more extrinsic and eventual. Intrinsic values are only found in *experiences* of some sort, whether human, subhuman, or suprahuman; they exist everywhere for a *pan*experientialist. It is an unfortunate feature of the contemporary world that we tend to have too little appreciation of intrinsic value, Hartshorne thinks; hence we tend to depend on extrinsic, instrumental values (see ER). This seems odd when we consider that what makes life worthwhile is the variety and depth of harmonious (intrinsically valuable) experiences we or others can have (RE, 9–12).

Extrinsic or instrumental value is good only because it eventuates in intrinsic value, which, as we have seen, can be appreciated even by animals and is longed for by them when it is missing, as when they experience monotony or boredom, as Dale Jamieson argues in his careful studies of animals in zoos.[1] But because the experience of intrinsic value is immediate, it tends to be momentary or at least impermanent, a problem that quite explicitly leads to religious questions. For example, in some Buddhist views this universal impermanence is seen as the key feature of reality,[2] whereas some Christian views respond to the problem of impermanence of intrinsic value in terms of faith in—or in Kant's case the postulation of—an immortal soul.

In aesthetic terms, however, one wonders whether immortality of the soul or subjective immortality would be an aesthetic good. Just as a poem needs a first and last line or a symphony needs a first and last note, so also a personal career needs birth and death, as we will see in detail in the last chapter in the book on death and contributionism. In this view it is appropriate to notice that extremely old animals, including humans, tend to be bored with or tired of life. The problem of the preservation of enjoyed harmonies of experience can be responded to in several different ways, even within the context of the Abrahamic religions (Judaism, Christianity, and Islam). For example, rather than subjective immortality there is also the possibility of "objective immortality," Hartshorne thinks, where all of our enjoyed harmonies are given permanence not by us but by a imperishable deity who remembers them and who is the one life worthy of infinite variations through time. It would be one thing to live forever, quite another to do so like God without loss of zest (RE, 13–14).

It is precisely such zest that is lost in belief in an omnipotent God who timelessly imposes order on the world, unless, of course, one sees "zest" in a single act of creation, as did Saints Augustine and Thomas Aquinas. Part of the beauty of divine and creaturely life, in Hartshorne's contrasting view, lies in spontaneity that is unprogrammed. As before, beauty is a mixture of (divinely persuaded) order and (divine and creaturely) variations. The traditional argument from design only imperfectly captured the point urged by Hartshorne here. This argument was asserted to be empirical, such that the nature of things was seen as so orderly and beautiful that only God could account for it. In this view, however, it would seem that a less beautiful world would call into question the existence of God.

There are many reasons to be suspicious of the claim that God is omnipotent (see 00). A belief in God as *omni*potent often leads to belief in creation ex nihilo, construed as the belief that God creates the world out of absolute nothingness. Such a belief is unintelligible at the very least because any effort to articulate what absolute nothingness *is* proves to be futile, as Plato and Bergson, among others, have argued.

Perhaps it will be objected that by creation ex nihilo we should not mean creation of the world out of absolute nothingness but rather that God is the source and exemplification of being itself: it is the universe without God that is contingent or a possible nothing. Hartshorne would agree that it is not possible to understand the aesthetic unity-in-variety of the world without God, but he would wonder whether it is possible to understand God's eminent knowledge and love without the necessary existence of a world to be known and loved. Without *some* world to love (although not necessarily the one that exists at present), divine love would have to be self-love. It is by no means clear that *this* sort of love, if it is such, is the greatest conceivable. The biblical tradition, for example, gives us a (Hartshornian) view of love as care for *others.*[3]

Belief in God as omnipotent also leads to the most vicious form of the theodicy problem (e.g., a mother might ask, why did God send me a deformed child?) and to an attenuated appreciation of the beauty of the world. At its best, however, the argument from design is an attempt to respond to the question: What can it be that imposes judicious limits on the creativity of creatures? To respond that such limits are the result of pure chance is to offer an explanation that theists, in general, find gratuitous and unconvincing. Indeed, many theists find the claim that the intricate order and beauty of the world are gratuitous or the result of sheer chance to be as miraculous as any claim made by theists, including that regarding virgin birth.[4]

There is no need to jump to the conclusion that the best way to avoid such an unconvincing response is to defend belief in divine omnipotence. What is required instead is an orderer who optimizes the opportunities for creativity and minimizes *to the extent possible* the risks of such creativity. The evils in the world are due to these risks, which cannot be eliminated entirely if creaturely freedom itself—even on a microcosmic level—is to be preserved. *Any* world, even one with a great number of evils in it, is possible only if divinely ordered (or better, persuaded). That is, the argument from design can be articulated in an *a priori* fashion such that it can supplement the ontological argument: *if* God is possible, then God is necessary, for to try to conceive of the greatest being-in-becoming existing only contingently is to contradict oneself. And if God is not possible, it is hard to see how anything could be possible given the orderliness of the world (see AD and LP).

The ontological argument by itself is insufficient because it does not show that God is possible. However, what the ontological argument brings to Hartshorne's global argument for the existence of God that is not clearly supplied by other components is the concept that God exists necessarily or not at all: God's existence cannot be contingent. The argument from design strengthens the case for the possibility of God: without divine design, why is the world so beautiful?[5]

To say that God is an orderer who optimizes the opportunities for creativity and minimizes to the extent possible the risks of such creativity leaves partially open the questions as to how much power God has, what sort of power God has (persuasive power only or also coercive power?), and whether our resistance to evil must be nonviolent in order to be imitative of divine power. I personally (along with Brightman) respond to this last question in the affirmative, whereas Hartshorne sees pacifism as morally flabby (DR, 147–55; BH, 26–27; MV, 166–73; HB, 35–40).[6]

In Hartshorne's view, the many enjoyments of beauty in the world are contributions to the divine enjoyment of beauty. Of course it is one thing to know *that* God exists, another to know *how* God exists in God's own concrete mode of enjoying the world (see EA). But we should not assume that the mode of divine existence is analogous to a judge sentencing prisoners or to a computer programmer dictating the features of a software package. Perhaps God *enjoys* the world on the analogy of our enjoying the playing of kittens, or better, on the analogy of our enjoying the healthiness of cells in our body.[7] We should seriously consider the possibility that aesthetics rather than legal bookkeeping is the key to responding to religious problems.

We should serve God, in Hartshorne's aesthetic view, not because it is in our self-interest to do so, but rather because such service contributes to cosmic beauty. And it may very well be that the best service we can give is an enlightened interest, rather than self-interest, in beauty.[8] The fact that creaturely opportunities are inseparable from risks should not be taken to imply a fatal limitation in the power of the divine artist. If being *is* power to affect or to be affected by others, as Plato argues in the *Sophist* (247E), then all power over others, even God's power over creatures, is influencing or persuading others who have *some* power of their own, rather than sheer coercion or making of the others out of absolutely nothing, whatever that might *be*. In effect, the creative process as experienced by artists is an apt model for cosmic reality. Artists create order in diversity out of the recalcitrant material before them.[9]

Throughout this book we have seen Hartshorne argue that in art as well as in nature, beauty should be, and generally is, seen as organic unity-in-variety. Variety is the spice of life, it is said, but a steady diet of it is not very healthy. Aesthetic value involves both contrast and likeness. The universe as a whole contains more contrasts than anything else that exists, in that *all* contrasts fall within it, but it also exhibits sublime unity. Beautiful contrasts in the broadest sense are *dramatic* constituents of the whole, hence we need not be surprised to find Hartshorne holding that drama is the essential art and that all other arts tend to serve drama, including poetry and the visual arts. (This holds true even for an artist like T. S. Elliot, who was one of the greatest poets but was not terribly successful as a dramatist in the specific sense of "dramatist" rather than in the more expansive use of the term intended here.) If there were no drama in the world—that is, if there were no dramatic contrasts—there would be no beauty at all. The interplay of human personalities is especially dramatic and hence especially a potential source of creaturely beauty (MV, 212–15; CD, 246).

Aldrich like many aestheticians sees something histrionic and unnecessary in arranging the arts in a hierarchy, as was often done in the nineteenth century. But even he sees literature as potentially the greatest among the arts. Hartshorne sees drama as the highest art, in a sense, however, because it includes literature, sometimes even great literature, as in the cases of Shakespeare, Shaw, or O'Neill. But Hartshorne wavers between two uses of "drama": one in the ordinary sense of a theatrical performance and the other in a wider sense that refers to any device of representation in which there is both unity and dramatic contrast among various forces and actors. In this latter sense Hartshorne offers us, along with Balthasar, a "theo-dramatics" or a performance in which we all play a part, although Balthasar's version of theo-dramatics is a classical theistic one, concerning which Hartshorne is skeptical. He is skeptical as to whether either we or God could really play meaningful roles in a classical theistic scheme.[10]

Throughout nature we are confronted with the drama of personality: we are fascinated by animals because of their approximation to human personalities, by electrons because of their nascent personalities, by divinity because of God's mysterious super-personality. Both above and below human personality we struggle to find language adequate to describe the dramatic beauty found there, in Hartshorne's view. A materialist view of the world perhaps gives us a more parsimonious description of the world, but it deprives us of many of the main contrasts (and hence beauty) of life. The most dramatic contrast is that between God and creatures, between the greatest conceivable knower and appreciator of beauty and the creaturely knowers/appreciators.

Atheistic materialism loses out not only regarding contrast, however, but also regarding unity in that in this view the world does not follow a single persuasive plan, but is rather a mere concatenation of parts. Higher beings integrate more of the variety of the world than lower beings, and only the highest being-in-becoming could integrate the cosmos as a whole. If the world really were a jumble of parts with no intelligibility, it would be tremendously ugly, like cacophonous piano notes played at random. We do not experience the world as clueless, however. Our pragmatic purposes, at the very least, presuppose an orderliness and a general (if not absolute) predictability to reality (MV, 215–17).

The issue is complex. On the one hand, atheistic materialism is aesthetically problematic because if the world is a jumble of parts, it lacks unity and hence is the source of cacophony and confusion. On the other hand, atheistic materialists have very often been determinists who stress *too much* unity. In aesthetic terms, they have made the world more monotonous than it really is (CS, 306). The task, therefore, is to explain the *unity-in-diversity* (i.e., the beauty) of the world.

The key contribution of process theism to the topic of divine beauty lies in a sort of moderation between cosmic monotony (entailed by classical theism, despite the protests of some classical theists, as well as by atheistic materialism if it is deterministic) and the world seen as a vast jumble of parts (entailed, once again, by atheistic materialism): "Since the beautiful must contain contrast, it is as necessary that there be variety, multiplicity, in God as that there be unity" (MV, 217). That is, the unqualified simplicity in God urged by some would lead to unmitigated monotony. In fact, divinity requires not only contrast but *maximal* contrast in order to embody both the perfection associated with divine permanence and that associated with divine change. God also incorporates the contrast between the abstract and the concrete (MV, 218).

To deny God change is to deny God contrast with divine everlastingness; hence it is to deny God beauty, Hartshorne thinks. In the traditional view God becomes ugly by way of defect of variety, whereas in atheism the natural world has a tendency to become ugly by defect of unity. Through divine omnibenevolence and omnipresence God embraces the world; God cares even for the fall of a sparrow, as in the biblical trope. Hence monotony and discord, the Scylla and Charybdis of aesthetic failure, are preeminently avoided by the greatest conceivable being-in-becoming as understood in process or neoclassical theism. Aesthetics and metaphysics are alike in their need to avoid extremes; the difference between the two lies in the fact that the conditions of value in the former are found in their most concrete form (feeling), whereas in the latter they are found in an extremely abstract form requiring logical coherence (MV, 219–20).

If God were *pure* actuality, as many traditional theists hold, then all contrast would vanish because to compose a pattern that actualizes all possible contrasts is, in effect, to compose no pattern at all. Such a composition would exhibit the sheer continuity of the strictly possible and not be actual at all. We get definiteness by restricting the possible, and this restriction can be put in context only by other restrictions. In this regard we should note that both the Incarnation and the Trinity are doctrines that involve such restrictions: Jesus was born here rather than there, etc. Despite the protests of some classical theists, both doctrines seem to be at odds with the concepts of divine pure actuality and impassibility.[11] To take another example, to combine all hues of green with all hues of yellow is to accomplish nothing aesthetically even if one *says* that one has actualized them all. However, to combine a particular shade of green with a particular shade of yellow is perhaps to produce a harmonious contrast (MV, 221–22).

Some alternative possibilities are incompatible (such as writing a poem in iambic pentameter and simultaneously writing it in free verse), and some things that were once possible are so no longer (such as the possibility that Mahler could have written an opera). Not even God could write such a poem or now have Mahler compose such an opera. To actualize a potential is not aesthetically superfluous but is at the heart of aesthetic creativity itself; hence one denigrates God by referring to divinity as an unmoved mover who is already fully actualized. Luckily, neither the atheistic ugliness (of unordered diversity or gratuitously ordered diversity) nor the ugliness of traditional theism (of a monotonous actualization of all possibilities) exhausts the alternatives (MV, 222–23).

A God who knows the world but has no feeling tones of it, a superintellection devoid of intuition of aesthetic contrast, is not a divinity worthy of worship in that such a divinity would be hideously cold. An aesthetically empty "God" could hardly be omnibenevolent. Aesthetics is that part of philosophy that leads us to take concrete feelings seriously as excellences. These excellences, in turn, have implications for ethics and for philosophy of religion. In fact, in Hartshorne's view not only is it a mistake to refuse to attribute aesthetic feeling to God, but the exact opposite is the view that is most appropriate regarding the greatest being-in-becoming: a life with feeling tones more comprehensive and richer than those found in any other life, a matchless power to hold *harmonious* contrasts together. Indeed, the greatest conceivable being-in-becoming by definition holds all contrasts together that are noninvidious. An example of an invidious contrast would be the contrast between good and evil, as we saw in the introduction. The greatest conceivable being-in-becoming could not *do* any evil in any way, even if such a divinity would have to *feel* the evil done to others. God's omniscience and omnibenevolence require this (MV, 224).

If God were *pure* actuality, then there would not be much hope for a world that contained partly unactualized potencies because such a "maxed out" God would have nothing left to offer such creatures. Speaking of God, Hartshorne says the following:

He is the . . . never ending poem of which all actual poems are phrases, all cosmic epochs yet elapsed are verses, and whose "to be continued" is the promise of infinite poetic creation to come. He is the poet as enjoying this poem, the poem as the life of the poet down to the given present. But the phrases of the cosmic poem are themselves poets enjoying their poems. In this respect many aesthetic analogies are false. (MV, 222)

One difficulty with the poet-poem analogy itself is that God must deal with lesser artists; hence a chorus director or a stage manager in this respect is a more helpful example: a stage manager or a director still depends on the skills of the actors themselves (CD, 246). Hence, he alerts us to the fact that

God's art is superior to man's not because he "controls" his materials more absolutely, but almost the contrary, because he knows how to set the limits within which the living units of his work are to control themselves, to do as they happen to please, not precisely as even he would foresee. Of course this means that the resulting art work cannot exhibit "perfect" harmony (whatever that would be), and certainly discord, evil, hatred, suffering exist in God's world if anything exists there. The play of the world is a tragic as well as comic play, for players and for playwright. The social nature of existences makes tragedy in principle, though not in particular, inevitable. (MV, 227)

That is, God, as the greatest being-in-becoming, cannot *do* evil. However, as the greatest being-in-becoming, God must care for the *victims* of evil and include them, by virtue of divine omnibenevolence, in the divine life as feelings of suffering.

The only timeless absolute that applies to divine beauty is the abstract principle of unity-in-contrast itself, not any particular unity-in-contrast or any particular sum of such unities. "Let there be as much unity in contrast as possible" (MV, 229): this aesthetic imperative is as much the voice of God, Hartshorne thinks, as any other command. Serving God can, in fact, be seen in terms of behavior that conforms to rules, but it can also be seen in terms of a creative contribution, especially difficult in light of an understandable reverence for old values, of beautiful parts to a grand whole.

By criticizing divine omnipotence, one is in a position to understand the claim that it is divine beauty rather than divine power that moves the world. As Whitehead put the point, it was a mistake to give God the properties that belonged to Caesar.[12] God's power is not coercive but consists in the aesthetic appeal of divine love; the power of divine beauty is evidenced in the worship such a God inspires.[13] However imperfectly we respond to such divine beauty, we can nonetheless better understand on a neoclassical basis than on a traditional basis the claim that God *is* love (OO, 14; CA, 112).

It was a significant mistake when traditional theists moved too quickly from the necessary existence of God to the idea that God is noncontingent in every respect. In aesthetic terms this means that God would be devoid of definite contrast, and hence of beauty. God's concrete actuality, as opposed to God's bare existence, is contingent in the sense that creaturely events make a difference in the divine life. Human experiences properly called religious point toward an all-embracing Interest rather than toward an unmoved mover or a pure actuality outside of time (LP, 78; OD, 37).[14] It is especially odd that Christian thinkers subscribed to classical theism, along with its concept of divine impassibility, given the fact that they also wished to defend belief in the Incarnation. How *could* the divine and the human ever interact on classical theistic grounds?

The greatest beauty obtains where the parts both have maximum individuality and are integrated into a single reality. This is why drama (in the specific sense of the term) is a greater art than interior design: the parts in the former are human characters, whereas the parts in the latter are shapes and colors. Of course it might be objected at this point that interior design is like drama in consisting in the organization of human space in light of our forms of existence, psychology, perception, and historical consciousness.[15] Seen in this light, there is indeed something "dramatic" about interior design, and hence something profound.

Plato and Plotinus, for all of their genius, did not quite get it right when they identified *simpliciter* beauty with oneness, and hence with soul rather than with divisible body. It is true that without unity nothing could exist, but it is worthwhile asking, without multiplicity what could things amount to? Unity is always unity of something that is not unity. When Plato and Plotinus speak positively of variety, however, they do so in a whisper, whereas they shout when praising unity (PS, 4, 212, 220).

There is nonetheless a legitimate insight in the view that God is unified and self-contained in the sense that nothing could threaten the continued *existence* of God (this is the whole point to the onto-logical argument). But God's relations with creatures entail that the tragic beauty of creatures, especially their sufferings, enter into the divine life in some way. That is, God's *actuality* (i.e., *how* God exists) is very much affected by the creatures. This distinction between divine existence and actuality can plausibly be claimed to be Hartshorne's most significant contribution to philosophy of religion (see EA). We participate in the divine life when we love relatively unselfishly, when we sympathize somewhat graciously, and when we glimpse through a glass darkly the peace that transcends sorrow (PS, 414). The past is the sublime record of creaturely efforts to participate vicariously in these ways in the actual divine life (PS, 414; RS, 151).[16]

Hartshorne argues that there is aesthetic value in both order, rep-etition, and predictability, on the one hand, and disorder, freedom, novelty, and surprise, on the other (MV, 302). These aesthetic values are applicable to creatures—especially animals, human or otherwise—as well as to God. The latter fosters the beauty of creatures, that is, the harmonies and intensities of their experiences. These harmonies and intensities are valuable both in themselves and in the contributions they make to the divine life. One of our chief aesthetic weaknesses is our inability eventually to enjoy the harmonies and intensities of experience that we contribute to the everlasting whole of things, and one of our chief moral weaknesses is our overestimation of our own importance.

"God alone inherits all the harvests for which he, or anyone, sows the seed" (CS, 309), Hartshorne says. However, traditional theism in effect forbids God to enjoy the harvest. To the objection that if we make God's enjoyment of our harmonies and intensities of experi-ence the standard of their value, we are making God selfish, the fol-lowing reply should be made: selfishness comes into play only when someone overestimates her importance, but the greatest conceivable being-in-becoming, by definition, could not do this because selfishness is incompatible with the logic of perfection. The greatest conceivable being-in-becoming, by definition, could not be apathetic or jealous with respect to creatures; hence in this regard the jealous God of the Hebrew scriptures is an inaccurate guide to divine perfection. God is unique in at least this sense: because of God's all-inclusive love, only in God are self-interest and altruism coincident. For God to will divine benefit is to will creaturely benefit. God can be endlessly enriched aesthetically by particular harmonies and intensities, but the rightness of the divine aesthetic aim itself is always perfect just as it is (cs, 310).

God's *existence* is necessary, but God's *actuality* (i.e., the mode of God's existence) is better than any absolute, nonchanging thing could be. The traditional view of God, as we have seen, is simpler than Hartshorne's neoclassical view, but simplicity simply as such is not an unqualified aesthetic good. Whitehead's dictum was, in fact, to seek simplicity, but he also thought that we should then distrust it.[17] Especially problematic is the monopolarity of traditional theism, wherein it is too easy to model God on human police or soldier functions because, on this overly simple view, God acts but does not receive. Once again, such a God is not compatible with the doctrine of the Incarnation. (It should be noted, however, that Hartshorne himself shies away from explicitly theological topics like Incarnation and Trinity.) Without some power or freedom in the creatures, however slight, there would be nothing at all, especially if the Platonic view is correct that being *is* power (*dynamis*—once again, see *Sophist* 247E) to affect or be affected by others. Both complete order without freedom and complete freedom without order are inconceivable states of affairs (zf, 212–14).

There is no need to worry about whether the harmonies and intensities of our experiences will become purely instrumental if they find their measure in their contribution to God. For example, even our everyday sensations have some value in themselves; if they did not, they would not even be sensed as the smell of *this* rose or the color of *that* chair. But it would not be a good thing if they were valued totally in terms of their intrinsic value both because practical life would come to a grinding halt and because the contributions of present beauty to the divine life would dry up. The effort to appreciate the present in its presentness is hampered by the fact that we are always thrown into new experiences. Valuing things in themselves and valuing them instrumentally are both limit concepts. That is, we inhabit a world where aesthetic and ethical/economic value interpenetrate, even if the two can, in fact, be intellectually distinguished (PP, 187).

The religious elements in aesthetic experience (in contrast to the aesthetic elements in religious experience) come to the fore when present intensities and harmonies are experienced as parts of a mighty, cosmic yet personal, whole. Just as a young child or a musically uncultivated person will probably not enjoy a symphony, so also those who are not attentive to the religious elements in aesthetic experience will not hear what the ancients and medievals referred to as the harmony of the spheres; they will not experience themselves as parts of a mighty, cosmic yet personal, whole. The issue is, in part, empirical. In any event, an experientially adequate aesthetics will at the very least reserve a place for the beauty of piety as well as for the beauty associated with both immense tragic events and quotidian sensations (PP, 187–88; PC, 605).

Jane Austen, Willa Cather, and other great novelists have mastered the art of simultaneously expressing the beauty of everyday reality and that of metaphysical truths. Everyday aesthetic values that point to the pretty are nonetheless different from those that point to the sublime in at least two respects. The former are both *simpler* and *less intense* than the complexities exhibited in sublime events. Certainly what we have seen throughout this book about Hartshorne's concept of beauty as a dual mean, and in this chapter about the sublime character of the religious dimensions of aesthetic experience, is subject to doubt. But so are aesthetic theories (like Aldrich's, to cite one example)[18] that exhibit despair regarding the very effort to define beauty, or that have given up on the very idea of core aesthetic values, or that play a game of musical chairs wherein there is never a place for the religious dimensions of aesthetic experience to find a seat.

It is to be hoped that intellectual progress can be made when all of these doubts are on the table and all of the relevant considerations are openly discussed. It is the purpose of the present book to make a small contribution to aesthetics as a whole in this regard (PC, 605–6).

One crucial element in this intellectual progress, from Hartshorne's point of view, is the awareness that just as we aesthetically experience the experiences of our cells, so also God aesthetically experiences our experiences and beliefs as part of the divine life without necessarily accepting those beliefs as true. Brightman, it should be noted, rejected Hartshorne's claim that selves participate in each other's lives; rather, Brightman thought, other selves and their experiences are inferred or constructed. By contrast, Hartshorne thinks that what it means to have a religious element in aesthetic experience, indeed what it means to have a religious experience itself, is to add complexity to our normal experiences, a complexity that comes about in a quite real participation in the experiences of others (or of The Other, in the case of religious experience) on the analogy of our participation in the flourishings or sufferings of our own cells (HB, 60, 105, 126).

The fear that some aestheticians will no doubt have is that by bringing such heavy metaphysical baggage to aesthetics, and by searching for the religious elements in aesthetic experience, we would ignore what is integral to the aesthetic attitude itself as that attitude was described in an earlier chapter. But Hartshorne's aesthetics is perfectly compatible with both the aesthetic attitude and the distinction between the content of a work of art and its subject matter. The latter is external to a work of art, whereas the content of a work of art is the subject matter *as formulated in* a certain medium. That is, a Hartshornian can easily distinguish between religious subject matter and the way that subject matter is depicted as the content of some particular work of art. It is with respect to this content that we can adopt the aesthetic attitude. The issue has been hotly debated among aestheticians themselves, quite apart from Hartshorne's views on the matter. For example, J. W. N. Sullivan, in a fascinating book on the spiritual development of Beethoven, argues against purely formal music, which he calls "isolated" because it is seemingly devoid of subject matter altogether (assuming for the moment that this is possible), as well as against the opposite extreme of pure program music, which reduces music to literature or philosophy. The intermediate sort of music, concerning which Sullivan thinks that Beethoven was a genius, Sullivan refers to as "spiritual." Hartshorne would agree with Sullivan, as far as I can tell, that "pure" music and "pure" listening are probably not completely pure in the sense of being isolated from spiritual or religious concerns.[19]

It would make sense for Hartshorne to agree with John Richmond that there is a symbiosis between aesthetic and religious experience, with the latter construed as perceiving or feeling divine influence.[20] Viladesau defends a similar symbiosis, relying on Whitehead. The basic idea here is that a language or a work of art is not a universal mode of expressing all ideas; rather, language and art are limited modes that have been used for specific purposes. Encounters with God, with the divine relativity, are sources of excess that enable us to say or paint or sculpt more than we have said historically. These breakthroughs, a prime example of which is Bernini's "Ecstasy of St. Teresa," enable existing languages or art forms to be expanded, reinterpreted, and transformed. Another example is the way that the traditional religious music of Bach and Mozart has been reinterpreted and transformed by new religious composers like Gorecki, Tavener, and Part.

To claim that aesthetic and religious experiences are symbiotic is to imply that aesthetic experience contributes something to religion as well. Such experience both concretizes what might otherwise be a formless mist and offers a text or an image for a religious believer to analyze further. In addition, art works have what can be termed a sacramental power to dissuade us from reductionistic materialism. In the final analysis, there is not much success to be hoped for when trying to demarcate rigidly between the religious dimensions of aesthetic experience and the aesthetic dimensions of religious experience, although both Viladesau and Whitehead are correct to point out the possibility of "degeneration" or a "merely aesthetic" view wherein art can be used to support the case for atheism or agnosticism (as in the novels of Hardy).[21]

This symbiosis view is nonetheless problematic. Throughout religious history there have been iconoclasts (especially in Islam, but also Plato) who feared that by "materializing" God we are left with a misleading version of divinity. The fear is that the artistic image will be taken "for real." An attenuated version of this view is found in St. John of the Cross, who permits religious images but only as long as they are simple and take no longer than a day to make. In this way our anthropomorphisms will not get out of hand, he thinks.[22] (Quite ironically, John's own simple drawing in Ubeda of Christ on the cross as seen from above—i.e., from the perspective of God the Father—inspired the elaborate masterpiece by Dali with the same subject matter.)

To understand the religious dimensions of aesthetic experience adequately, it will be useful to be precise regarding three different uses of language in Hartshorne, all of which have been employed by either neoclassical or classical theists in the effort to describe God. What is crucial from a Hartshornian point of view is that two extremes be avoided: that we can capture deity in some verbal, visual, or other formula devoid of any doubt or obscurity on the one hand, and that we are totally in the dark in the effort to describe or imagine God on the other. The latter extreme leads to atheism, or at least to agnosticism or fideism, whereas the former extreme leads either to intolerance or idolatry (EA, 39).

"Literal" terms applied to God, as Hartshorne uses the word, are not matters of degree, but must be matters of all or none. That is, literal terms express a purely *formal* status by classifying propositions as of a certain logical type. For example, the categorical terms "absolute" and "relative" have a literal meaning when applied to God as an individual: either God is independent of (i.e., absolute with respect to) creatures for divine existence or not, and either God is related to creatures in the divine actuality or not. (However, when considering the *concrete* way in which God is independent of or related to others, we can say that God is *supremely* absolute and *supremely* relative, hence indicating a matter of degree.)

"Analogical" terms applied to God, as Hartshorne uses the word, by way of contrast admit of matters of degree as they apply to different entities *within* the same logical type. For example, concrete individuals feel aesthetically in different degrees of intensity and with different levels of adequacy, with God being the supreme example of feeling.

And "symbolic" terms applied to God, as Hartshorne uses the word, are used to apply locally and not cosmically to a particular kind of individual in a particular culture, and so on, with an even greater degree of specificity than analogical terms, as when God is referred to as a shepherd or a king.

There is an obvious distinction at work in Hartshorne between formal and material predication. To compare God with a rock, a king, a shepherd, or a parent is a material description that cannot be literal. Formal or nonmaterial predication is illustrated when one refers to God as noncorporeal or nonrelative *or* (and this point is often missed) when one refers to God as corporeal or relative. That is, when the abstractions "concreteness" or "corporeality" are applied to God, one is not identifying God with any particular concrete or corporeal thing but contrasting the abstraction "materiality" with the abstraction "immateriality." Hartshorne emphasizes that the formal (literal) predicates of deity are not exclusively negative. If God's very existence cannot be contingent, the question arises: Is God's necessary existence to be conceived as having the ability to be related to creatures or simply as the absence of relativity? These are two categorically or formally opposite ways of interpreting the necessary truth of the proposition "God exists." In either interpretation, something literal is being said of God. In between the formal, literal terms (absolute-relative, being-becoming, etc.) and the most material, particular, symbolic ones (shepherd, monarch, etc.) there are analogical terms (love, personality, feeling, etc.). To the extent that analogical terms involve qualitative distinctions of degree, they are removed from the all-or-nothing character of literal terms. Who can say literally how divine love differs *qualitatively* from ours (LP, 134–41)?

Neither abstractness nor concreteness have been properly understood by classical theists, overly influenced as they are by the tradition of negative theology. It is easy enough to say that one is being modest in claiming that human language cannot properly apply to God; hence we cannot speak literally about God. But according to Hartshorne, the negative theology of classical theists itself may be a sort of presumption:

So it is held to be quite safe to say, without qualification, that he is *not* finite, *not* relative, *not* passible or open to influence. I think, however, that the modesty is only apparent. We dare to forbid God to sustain relations, to accept the definiteness that comes through limits, to respond to the creatures and thus be influenced by them. He may, we conclude, do these things "symbolically," whatever that may mean, but we tell him in no uncertain terms that he must not literally do them! Is this modesty—or is it monstrous presumption? Have we this veto power upon divinity? (CS, 151)

It makes sense to say that God is not literally but only symbolically a shepherd or monarch, because shepherds and monarchs are quite specific sorts of things. To "forbid" God to be a shepherd literally does not really restrict God:

> It is, however, a very different affair when we treat utterly abstract terms like "finite" or "relative" in this same manner. There are not an infinity of miscellaneous possible positive forms of reality alternative to being relative; there is only being non-relative or absolute. If God is not literally finite and relative, then he is literally and exclusively infinite and absolute. For there is no third possibility; here the law of excluded middle must, I submit, apply. (CS, 152)

It may well be the case that if God is not a shepherd God could be a super-shepherd, whatever that means, but "super-relative" can only be thought of as an eminent form of relativity if "relative" implies in some way or other being constituted by contingent relations: "either one might, or one might not, have been otherwise. *Tertium non datur*" (CS, 153).

The modesty of negative theology is suspect because it puts a human veto on the wealth of the divine life:

> Traditional theological theory had a headlong tendency, almost wholly ungovernable, and even today in many circles largely uncontrolled, to "plump" for one side—the negative side—of the ultimate polar contraries, in application to God. But this indeed "limits" God—for instance, if we deny him all definiteness, or all responsiveness to the contingent creatures. . . . And we think to honor God by offering him this vacuity as his sole portion! (CS, 153)

All abstractions, even the abstraction "concreteness," are impassible. But this does not mean that God is entirely impassible if God is both abstract in one sense and concrete in another, contra traditional negative theology.

Hartshorne's view is that regarding abstractions we can speak literally about God, and regarding the most specific, concrete predicates we can speak (indeed we must only speak) symbolically. But in between there are psychical terms like "knowledge," "will," "aesthetic feeling," and "love." These denote states or functions like the human ones, but as is well known, there is a central philosophical issue regarding how far psychical or experiential terms can be broadened beyond the human application. Hartshorne's response to this problem, we have seen, is to suggest the broadest possible meaning of psyche terms, a meaning that is applicable to all concrete singulars, from atoms to God. This meaning is so broad that psychic or experiential terms are almost categorical, like absoluteness or relativity. "There is, however, a difference," Hartshorne notes. "For only individuals, not abstractions, can feel or think or remember, whereas both individuals and abstractions (other than those of uttermost generality) can have aspects of relativity, can depend in some way and degree upon contingent relations" (CS, 154). In some abstract way God's knowledge is like human knowledge in that merely absolute, wholly nonrelative "knowledge" is an impossibility for anyone. In fact, Hartshorne goes so far as to claim that "the veto upon literal relatedness (a veto which must itself be literal or else merely misleading) is in my view unwitting blasphemy" (CS, 155).

But to say that, because God knows, God is literally relative is not to deny that we should be sensitive regarding the *levels* of knowledge and relativity that different beings possess. That is, in one *abstract* aspect of the divine nature, God is relative, and this can be stated literally, but regarding what it is like to be *concretely* related to the entire world through aesthetic awareness or knowledge, as God is, can only be talked about in outline, or analogically, with the full details of concrete occurrences left out of the picture (OO, 11). We cannot speak literally about what it is like to *be* God. At times Hartshorne confuses matters by saying that the concrete complexity of divine awareness and knowledge can only be talked about symbolically rather than analogically (EA, 41), but his overall point remains that we can only speak of God in literal terms if we do so abstractly; we can only talk about what it is like to *be* God concretely in, at best, analogical terms. But if there is no sense whatsoever in which univocal meaning or literal terms (roughly equivalent in Hartshorne) can be used regarding the concept of God, then talk about the concept of God is not of much use. Maximal conceptual flexibility is perhaps needed regarding analogical and especially symbolic terms, but there is a real impediment to progress in philosophy of religion and aesthetics when vague or flabby analogies or symbols are used regarding philosophical abstractions (MV, 194, 221).

Before leaving the issue of literal terms or univocal meaning connected with the concept of God, it is necessary that we treat a second sense of the term "literal," in addition to the sense in which Hartshorne usually uses the term—that is, to refer to those abstract terms that can be used to describe God as exhibiting a certain logical type or not. Confusing as it sounds, the second sense of the term (hereafter: literal-2) refers to a certain distinction within the use of analogical terms. It is a commonplace in philosophy of religion that we start with human aesthetic experience or human psyche and then analogize regarding God. In learning the meaning of words, we necessarily follow the us-to-God path, but once we reach some understanding of the concept of God, the reverse path is also crucial. As Hartshorne puts the issue:

> I have . . . sometimes argued that, unless we have in our own natures instantiation of concepts (say that of decision-making) which we use to conceive God, we could not have these concepts. But I have also sometimes argued that we can conceive our own form of knowing, say, by introducing qualifications into what we know of divine cognition. God knows—period; we—partially, uncertainly, vaguely; and much of what we can hardly avoid taking as knowledge is erroneous belief. The appearance of contradiction here has sometimes occurred to me. (EA, 38)

As Feuerbach and others have (over)emphasized, God has always somewhat resembled human beings, but theists have also always been convinced that there is something deimorphic about human beings.

There is a sense in which analogical terms apply literally-2 to God and only analogically to us. We are said to be aesthetically aware of or know certain things, but we are always liable to make mistakes. Our having "knowledge" means that we have evidence, which falls short of indubitable proof, that certain beliefs are true. The indefiniteness of our "knowing" is in contrast to the divine case. God, as infallible, has conclusive evidence regarding all truths: "God simply knows—period" (LP, 141). God literally-2 knows. In effect, what Hartshorne is doing is issuing a call not so much for the old negative theology as for a new negative anthropology. And he has the same view of feeling and love as he does of knowledge, in that human love is intermittent and mixed with apathy, vanity, and fear. Human love enables us to analogize so as to talk about divine love, but once one has experienced divine love, one realizes that "God appreciates the qualities of all things—period" (LP, 142), whereas we love in a bastardized way. If we allocate to ourselves properties like loving or knowing in a literal way, there is little left to characterize deity. This is precisely the monumental error made by negative theologians, including many classical theists overly influenced by negative theology. Consider the issue of memory. We remember only tiny scraps of the past and these indistinctly. By way of contrast, God remembers literally-2. God remembers—period.

It is true both that we form the idea of divine aesthetic feeling, love, and knowledge, and so on, by analogical extension of our own aesthetic feeling, love, and knowledge *and* that we know what aesthetic feeling, love, and knowledge are partly by feeling, loving, and knowing God: "To 'know' *ought* to mean, having conclusive evidence, such as God has; but to apply this idea to man we must tone it down drastically indeed" (CS, 155). It is precisely the amphibious nature of analogical terms that makes them so problematic. Analogical terms are problematic for Hartshorne, however, for a different reason from that which makes them problematic for classical theists. Hartshorne denies that human knowledge is a mere symbol for an otherwise inaccessible divine reality (the classical theistic view) at the very least because human "knowledge" is, in a sense, derivative. What Hartshorne has accomplished through his treatment of literal-2 terms (he refers to them simply as literal terms, thereby creating confusion for some interpreters)[23] is a way of understanding the importance of mysticism in the religious life. Those who have, to use Alston's term,[24] "perceived" God's feeling, love, and knowledge (or, to use Hartshorne's word, "intuited" these) make it possible for us to use literal-2 terms regarding God, terms that push our analogical terms closer to literal-1 terms than to symbolic ones, as Hartshorne emphasizes:

> The real trouble is less in the exaggeration of literalness than in the idolatry of infinity, being, cause, and absoluteness, accepted as substitutes for the divine unity of the contraries, finite-infinite, being-creativity, cause-effect, absolute-relational. . . . [M]any theological terms are more or less symbolic; others may be now symbolic (here better termed analogical), now literal, depending upon the availability of religious intuition; but the most completely abstract general terms applicable to deity are quite literal. (cs, 157)

God is the literal-2 instance of analogical terms because God is the preeminent instance of them. It is by self-flattery that we think of ourselves as loving beings when we notice the limitations of our social awareness. This is in contrast to God, as the Soul of the World, who is socially aware—period. The heavy influence of the *via negativa* on classical theism has created the illusion of safety in what is not said regarding description of God. But negative theologians have typically atoned for their paucity of discourse by an orgy of metaphors. Hartshorne is not opposed to metaphor; in fact, he thinks religious metaphor has a crucial role to play in moving the emotions toward God. But description must be based on *some* literal terms (whether literal-1—those of the metaphysicians—or literal-2—those of the mystics) "or it is a scandal" (DR, 37). Analogy itself, as a comparison between things that are somewhat similar and somewhat different, ultimately rests on there being *some* univocity of discourse so as to secure the similarities. It is true, however, that the contingent or the concrete (as opposed to the abstraction "contingency" or the abstraction "concreteness") transcend reason in the sense that these realities must ultimately be felt as sheer facts. Regarding God as contingent or as concrete we can talk analogically or symbolically, but when God is symbolized as judge or monarch there is always the danger of distorting what the best available arguments indicate is the case metaphysically:

> It is one thing to know an individual as distinguished from all others. It is another to know the same individual in its actual "state." . . . To know the actuality of deity, as relative to the present and past actual universe, would be to know that universe as God knows it. (DR, 40)

Hartshorne's aesthetics, informed as it is by his theistic metaphysics, has nothing to do with the belief in divine madness as the source of artistic creativity, as argued in several of Plato's dialogues, including the *Ion*. Creativity involves both of the following, to use Sherburne's terms: *vertical transmutation* (whereby macroscopic perception advances beyond the experiences of the microscopic occasions in one's body) and *horizontal transmutation* (whereby at the macroscopic level certain experiences, intuitions, or concepts are seen as *significant*). The significance involved in horizontal transmutation is what is meant by the religious dimensions of aesthetic experience. For process theists, God is seen as the source of novel dimensions that are incorporated into horizontal transmutation. That is, the artist discovers a lure for feeling or a potentiality made possible by God *and then* brings it into actuality in some artistic medium. Thus it is equally true to say both that the artist discovers the religious dimensions of aesthetic experience and that the artist creates them.[25]

CHAPTER NINE

Absolute Beauty?

The Anselmian (and Hartshornian) view of God as one who surpasses all others is implied in God's being the proper object of worship. But what does it mean to be the greatest being? If a loving being is superior to a nonloving one, then God must exhibit eminent love and other ethical qualities in the best way possible, Hartshorne emphasizes. But what if the value in question is not ethical but aesthetic? We can verbally mouth the words "absolute beauty," but it is by no means clear to Hartshorne what these words mean. They cannot refer merely to the absence of ugliness or pain. If they did, a simple musical passage would meet the former criterion (absence of ugliness) and a snail would meet the latter (absence of pain) (CS, 261–62).

In order to do intellectual work for us, aesthetic criteria must be positive, as in intensity of experience or harmony among an integrated variety of contrasts. However, just as there can be no greatest possible number, there can be no greatest possible variety that is integrated; hence there can be no "absolute beauty." Likewise, there can be no such thing as absolute intensity if each new configuration of the cosmos at each moment brings about a new divine intensity and harmony of experience.

That is, aesthetic value is without upper limit even if it is true to say that God is unsurpassable by others. We should note, however, that there *can* be a greatest possible variety or greatest intensity for a particular creature. We have seen that the diagram for beauty found in Chapter 2 must vary to fit individuals, as when some melodies may be hopelessly complex for some birds. This leaves open the possibility that God could be surpassable by God, that God could always surpass previous instances of divine greatness. This does not mean that the previous moments in the divine life were defective, since they were at that time the greatest responses to creaturely variety. New moments bring with them new possibilities for eminent divine re-sponse.

In the traditional view of God as pure actuality, God could not respond to creatures' sufferings; hence this being was not really worthy of worship in that God could, at most, offer "inde-sponses" to the creatures. That is, to hyphenate the word re-sponse is to point out the Hartshornian belief that God's existence is an everlasting series of moments of experience; God is not eternal in the Boethian sense of being outside of time altogether.[1]

To be God is to appreciate the beauty of the entire cosmos, whereas to be us is to be able to appreciate only a fragment of this beauty, to get but a glimpse of it. However, our aesthetic sensibilities are sophisticated enough for us to experience fragments *as* fragments, indicating some sort of vicarious experience on our part of the cosmic whole. The romantic poets made much of this, as in Wordsworth's appreciation of the whole through the ruins of an old building in "Tintern Abbey."[2] It is true that God cannot exhibit the courage that a human being can exhibit when facing death, but through divine omniscience and omnibenevolence God can participate in the harmony and especially in the intensity of this experience (cs, 262).

That is, God can participate in a human being's experience of the process of dying without God being afraid of death, contra the claims of Brightman (see HB, 43, 46, 83) and, more recently, of Henry Simoni-Wastila. Simoni-Wastila thinks that Hartshorne's view is inconsistent because it entails that God has acquaintance with the feelings of every actuality, yet the radical particularity of creaturely experiences makes a full sympathetic divine grasp of them impossible. Donald Viney ably shows that what is problematic with this criticism is that it misrepresents Hartshornian prehension. In "feeling of feeling" the subject of the second feeling is admittedly not *identical* with the subject of the first feeling, nor is the subject of the second feeling a mere replica of the subject of the first feeling. The subjective form of the second feeling is its own and is not to be reduced to the first: this preserves the particularity, if not the radical particularity, of the subject of the first feeling. As a result, God can sympathize with the ignorant without having a moment of contingent ignorance that is identical to that of the ignorant human being. Viney even goes so far as to suggest that the differences between God and the creatures, which are fully appreciated by God, may even increase divine sympathy for creatures, on the analogy of our greater sympathy with the helpless than with those who are capable when we notice their differences from us.[3]

Hartshorne is famous (or infamous) for his position matrices that logically exhaust the possible options regarding a particular problem. Regarding the question of whether the cosmos as a whole has beauty, and whether there is anyone to enjoy it if it does, there seem to be four alternatives, as we have seen in detail in a previous chapter, relying on cs (287, 289–91). The first is that there is no beauty of the world as a de facto whole. If this were true, however, then the world would be either a chaos or mere jumble of parts (in which case science would be impossible and our experience of order illusory) or a monotony (in which case our experience of inquisitiveness and Aristotelian wonder would be quite out of place). If reality is essentially active and at least partially unpredictable, there are always new promptings that would militate against monotony. To be more exact, if the world really were complete chaos, nothing could be possible. However, the thinkers against whom Hartshorne is arguing (those who claim that *we* are the ones who impose order on the world) are not committed to the claim that science is impossible. Rather, they are committed to an instrumentalist view of science, which has problems of its own, as we will see below in an examination of Hartshorne's ss.

The second and third options are equally problematic. The second possibility is that there is a beauty of the world as a whole, but no one enjoys it. But it should be noticed that even when *we* think of "the world as a whole," we have a glimpse of its beauty in that such a thought is not totally without aesthetic content, as in our ability to appreciate not only the pretty but also the sublime. Thus one is led to consider the third option, that there is beauty in the world as a whole, but only nondivine beings enjoy it. The problem here is the disproportionality between our localized aesthetic sensibility, which only imperfectly appreciates the sublime beauty of the whole, and the cosmic scope of the beauty in question. In effect there is a very informal argument for the existence of God at work here that suggests that the state of affairs postulated by this third option would leave us with a basically flawed reality. That is, it would leave us with a reality that is ugly: there ought to be an Ideal Valuer for the aesthetic value that is cosmic in scope.

Obviously this "argument," if it is such, is weak on its own. But we have seen that it nonetheless supplements the other components in Hartshorne's global argument, as in Peircian strands in a cable that mutually reinforce each other. The ontological argument assures us, Hartshorne thinks, that *if* God is possible, then God's existence is necessary. This informal aesthetic argument supplements the design and other arguments in the effort to show that God is possible. If we notice that the beauty of the world is cosmic in scope and of a complexity that is largely beyond us, it is at least possible that there be a cosmic aesthetic appreciator for this beauty.[4]

An astronaut on the moon can view the earth as a whole in aesthetic terms, but we can at least imagine that there are aesthetic values associated with seeing the astronaut do this, a seeing that we know we cannot really have. If we put a viewer on Mars the same problem would replicate itself *ad infinitum.* Only on the fourth hypothesis, that there is a beauty of the world as a whole and God alone *adequately* enjoys it, is the world truly beautiful. This gesture toward an aesthetic argument for God's existence has as its primary strength a making explicit of what the denial of theism entails. One can believe theism because all of the alternatives are unbelievable, or at least they do an injustice to both our (admittedly limited) experience of sublime cosmic beauty and our sense that the world would be defective if there were not an Ideal Valuer for cosmic aesthetic value. At the very least this aesthetic "argument" for God makes us more aware than we would otherwise be of the alternatives open to us (cs, 287, 289–90).

If the world is beautiful it makes sense to wonder about the possibility of "absolute beauty." This expression is not bothersome, according to Hartshorne, if: (a) it refers to maximal unity in maximal variety, and (b) maximal variety is not interpreted to mean all *possible* variety ideally integrated in that any variety that is actual is capable of being surpassed (10, 29). Plato and Plotinus had a glimmering of the idea that it was the multiplicity of partially free creatures that made absolute order impossible, but they mistakenly appear to have thought that some definite order could be an absolute good forever (CS, 116–17).[5]

Just as there cannot be absolute beauty *in the sense of* the integration of all possible variety, so also at the other extreme there cannot be absolutely negative aesthetic value, sometimes personified as the Devil. Absolutely negative aesthetic value would mean something that completely lacked integrity or oneness, for these are positive values, yet an individual with no integrity whatsoever is a contradiction in terms, Hartshorne thinks. Traditional theism was correct to hold that to be at all is to be good (or beautiful) in *some* sense. That is, absolutely negative aesthetic value is to be equated not with an extremely ugly being, but with absolute nonentity, assuming for the moment that such is conceivable. The clarification of the extremes of absolute beauty and absolutely negative aesthetic value is crucial in the effort to highlight the contribution made by multiplicity, as when a symphony exhibits greater aesthetic value than a chord (CS, 248; NT, 15).

The realization that "all possible variety" is no definite variety at all (because not all possibles are compossible) should not lead us to despair regarding the aesthetic importance of variety. All beauty is unity-in-variety. We have seen that a chord and a symphony may be equally unified, but the former's lack of complexity makes it less likely, other things being equal, to achieve the aesthetic value of the symphony (AD, 28). Someone thrown into prison unjustly can be as morally virtuous as before, but this person's life is aesthetically diminished due to the lack of variety, indeed the monotony, of the surroundings and daily routine. God, the greatest being-in-becoming, could not remain unmoved if this virtuous person were removed from jail and was free to more easily appreciate the beauty of the world again. If the world first lacks, and then gains, new harmonies and intensities of experience, new forms of aesthetic richness are available to a being-in-becoming with the most refined and inclusive aesthetic sensibilities. Of course, some remarkable prisoners discern the beauty even in a prison (OO, 9).

It is to Plato's credit, and also to Peirce's and Whitehead's, that they viewed God as the divine artist or as the poet of the world. In these views even God is limited by the recalcitrant material that divine creativity has to shape. But limit here (the Greek *peras*) is a positive term in contrast to a formless surd *(apeiron)*. Likewise, a symphony by Brahms is limited in the sense that it cannot embody the values associated with one by Dvorák. "Any actual being is less than there could be" (oo, 10). But this is a good thing, Hartshorne thinks, in that it leaves open the possibility for additional values, for a better, more beautiful, world.[6]

It is nonetheless a mistake to assume, along with the Plato of the *Republic* (Books 4–6), that a perfect being would not change, for, it is alleged, if the being in question were really perfect there would be no need to change. Plato comes closer to the truth in his later dialogues *(Phaedrus, Timaeus, Laws,* etc.) when he identifies God as the soul for the body of the world and when he identifies soul with motion, specifically with self-motion. This latter motion provides the metaphysical basis for a caring God who can make the responses to creaturely suffering appropriate to the greatest possessor of aesthetic feeling (zf, 2).

The divine being-in-becoming may aesthetically enjoy all that exists and yet want what does not exist, as in the amelioration of the sufferings of sentient creatures. Of course the traditional theistic belief in divine omnipotence would lead to the further belief that all that exists is due to divine decision or at least to divine permission. The more refined neoclassical or process theistic belief, however, is that God's enjoyment of the world is truly social in that it depends on the partial self-determinations of the creatures. Once again, if being *is* the power to affect or to be affected by others, then no being, however insignificant, can be utterly coerced by another power, not even by maximal power. For example, the weaker being at the very least recoils from its persecutor or leans toward its liberator. God, in this view, is not beyond all multitude, whatever that might mean, but is the measurer and appreciator of the multitude (mv, 36–37).[7]

Some values must be renounced not because of human or divine limitations but rather because values are, in principle, subject to incompatibilities, Hartshorne thinks. A short story excludes the merits of a philosophical essay and vice versa. This is why absolute beauty or absolute happiness cannot be equated with mere contentment, as found, say, in a scallop that is not being agitated. The higher animals are higher precisely because they can be discontented in many ways. The reason for this is their rich, complex, more inclusive lives when compared to those of scallops. Absolute happiness, like absolute beauty, cannot possibly mean the aesthetic satisfaction of all possible desires (an advertiser's dream!) but, if it means anything at all, refers to the aesthetic satisfaction of all logically possible desires in their most harmonious and intense combination. Absolute happiness, on the same lines of absolute beauty, could only mean the best unification and appreciation of all of the concrete (rather than possible) variety of the world (PS, 10).

Hartshorne sums up his view in the following terms:

> We can verbally speak of "absolute beauty" or absolute happiness; but as soon as we seek criteria for the maximal degree of beauty or happiness we find difficulty. To be free from ugliness or suffering is not enough. A musical chord is one, a contented oyster may be the other. Aesthetic criteria must be positive, something like intensity, variety or scope of contrasts, completeness of integration or harmony. . . . But just as no number is the greatest possible, so no actual variety can be the greatest possible. And what can be meant by unsurpassable or absolute intensity? We thus have good reason to take aesthetic value to be without upper limit. It follows that in aesthetic enjoyment even God must be surpassable. However, it is another question whether he could in this respect be surpassed by another than himself. If the beauty of the entire cosmos is bound to be fully appreciated by deity, while anyone not divine can enjoy but a fragment or partial glimpse of this beauty, then, though the cosmos may grow in beauty and God's enjoyment with it, no one else can ever be his rival in this respect. Thus God may be the "greatest possible" by those criteria which make this conceivable, and the greatest actual, yet without possible rival, by other criteria. Either way, as beyond rivalry, he is worthy of worship. (CS, 262)

For the purposes of this book it should be emphasized that from the evidence of there being no upper limit to aesthetic value, Hartshorne does *not* infer the iconoclast or apophatic conclusion, as we saw in the previous chapter.

In fact, Hartshorne agrees with Bergson that each of us is an artist who, at least in part, creates his/her experiences in the art of living. But Hartshorne is different from Bergson in the way he balances the abstract and the empirical. Unfortunately, Hartshorne thinks, Bergson confirmed in William James the latter's greatest weakness: underestimation of the philosophical utility of formal logic. Hartshorne's and Whitehead's dogged pursuit of the data of intuition requires an appropriate use of logic (largely absent in Bergson and James) in seeking the right questions to address to intuition or immediate concrete experience. Hartshorne accuses Bergson of relying exclusively on immediate concrete experience without the guidance provided by abstract logical thought (BA, 369–70).

Perhaps this is why Bergson denies the intersensory continuum, wherein high-pitched sounds are similar to bright colors. It is not enough that one pay attention to experience; one must also have some idea where to pay attention and what to look for when one does so (BA, 369–71).[8] Further, if one relies *exclusively* on empirical data, one runs up against the same problem faced by Hume in the first section of the *Treatise:* even though one has never seen a particular shade of blue, one can, given other shades of blue on either side of it on a spectrum of color, *conceptually* supply the missing shade. This is not a trivial exception to the attempt to rely exclusively on empirical data—that is, to the exclusion of conceptual input.[9] At the other extreme, Hartshorne does not give as much importance to the conceptual as does Whitehead, whose list of eternal objects would presumably include an eternal object for the precise shade of missing blue. In Hartshorne's view, by way of contrast, all except the most abstract of universals (concerning the structure of creativity itself) are in process, including those for colors.

Bergson's radical empiricism nonetheless led him to appropriately understand the fact that the prime characteristic of space is symmetry, whereas that of time is asymmetry.[10] The past might be a necessary condition for the present (with the necessity discovered only retrospectively), but it is not sufficient. Hartshorne agrees with Bergson that duration (i.e., becoming with permanence in the sense that dynamic reality preserves its products) pervades reality, with God being the highest conceivable form of becoming or duration. It is precisely this dynamic character of deity that makes "absolute beauty" impossible. Retrospective unity in durational process does not entail prospective unity. This is why we can do nothing more than make probability estimates regarding what will happen in the future: if the future were here already to be known in detail, it would not be the future. Not even the present is fully actual in that, in its presentness, it is *becoming* actual (BA, 372–77).

Hartshorne also agrees with Bergson that spontaneity is a variable with innumerable degrees, the preeminent example of which is divine spontaneity. On the basis of religious experience (without the aid of the arguments for the existence of God, including the ontological argument), Bergson realized that the idea of deity as an eternal, Boethian constant was a big mistake. God's bare existence, without consideration of *how* God actually exists, *is* constant, but this is to consider God as a mere abstraction. God's spontaneity or freedom is, like God's power, limited only by the spontaneity or *dynamis* of others. As we have seen, however, in Hartshorne's view God is nonetheless powerful enough to persuade the world toward such order as will reliably limit mutual frustration and chaos (BA, 378–79).

Despite Bergson's help in showing the inadequacies of the concept of absolute beauty, there are dualistic tendencies in his thought due to his denigration of logic and his overemphasis of experiential examination of one's intuitions; such procedures make one's own mind, at least, and perhaps that of others, seem radically different from the rest of the world. Hartshorne finds the same defect in a temporalistic American theist whose views are, in others respects, compatible with his own: H. N. Wieman (see PS, 395–408). Throughout Hartshorne's aesthetics there is a constant effort to find a proper mix of abstract thought and empirical detail. For example, using the model of beauty as a dual mean, he carefully records the songs of birds to see if they corroborate the model and, if they do not, to modify the model accordingly. Or again, regarding the affective quality of sensation and the intersensory continuum, he tries to get clear regarding the theoretical options so as to see which of these options most closely fits the empirical data of sensation; that is, he does not assume that the ordering of primary, secondary, and tertiary qualities inherited from modern philosophy is the last word on the matter. And regarding the concept of God, Hartshorne is famous for his explication and defense of the very abstract ontological argument and other components of his overall global argument for the existence of God *as well as* his careful attention to the data of religious experience, both his own and that of others.

The same sort of interplay can be found in Hartshorne's treatment of some theological mistakes and their effects on modern literature. Poets and novelists deal with concrete topics in a more intimate way than philosophers, but they often express, or at least imply, philosophical beliefs in their writings. For example, various philosophers (e.g., the Stoics, Spinoza), theologians (e.g., Jonathan Edwards), and literary writers have moved from the animal feeling that we are subject to momentum coming from the past to a full-fledged determinism. This move is not due to an animal faith, however, but to a philosophical/ theological mistake, Hartshorne thinks. Thomas Hardy is an obvious example of a literary writer who makes this move, but Hartshorne thinks that several others have done the same: Robinson Jeffers, Robert Frost (whom Hartshorne nonetheless sees as the greatest American poet of the twentieth century), and Mark Twain. There is a way to avoid this mistake, however:

> Statistical laws of gases first, then quantum theory, have shown that the religious alternative to absolute order need not be absolute chaos, but may be freedom, individual creativity, sufficiently influenced by a divine vision of cosmic order to make what happens partially predictable, but not wholly so even for God. (ML, 60; see also 55–59)

Unfortunately, neoclassical theism has not yet received a great poet who does justice to this position, Hartshorne thinks, the way Dante did for classical theism. (However, Darren Middleton and I have tried to make the case for Nikos Kazantzakis' mythopoesis of process thought.) Much is at stake here, as Hartshorne sees things, because it is the combination of theological determinism (and its concept of supposed absolute beauty) and the obvious evils that exist in the world that leads many reflective people, including many poets and novelists, to religious skepticism (ML, 64–65).

Even in mathematics there is an interplay of abstract thought (obviously) and empirical observation (e.g., in the inspection of diagrams). Both in mathematics and in science there are two basic reasons motivating participation in these disciplines: (1) these disciplines, through their applications, are useful, and (2) these disciplines enable us to get at truth, at that sort of truth that is beautiful, as opposed to trivial truths that are cute, at best. Scientific beauty consists in "a reasonably complex system of contrasts, an adequately diversified unity or adequately integrated diversity" (SS, 89). Even Darwin ended his first great book with a prose poem to the beauty of the web of life.[11] But this beauty is not due to an absolute source of beauty, if such is defined in a way that the first noun in the formula "unity-in-variety" is seen as more important than the second. As we saw in the introduction to the present book, to view God as dipolar is to see that the logic of perfection leads us to believe in *dual* transcendence: God is both more unified than any other unity, in that God brings together the whole cosmos, and more diverse than any other collection of diverse elements, in that God aesthetically feels, loves, and knows *all* of the diverse elements of this cosmos (SS, 85–90, 102).

Some scientists, however, like some literary writers, import sheer determinism from philosophy and theology and then impose it on their data, even on the data that do not fit the deterministic thesis. But by excluding chance, spontaneity, and freedom they fail to do justice to the data of experience themselves; hence determinism is to be rejected, in part, because it leads to bad empiricism:

> The real world keeps turning out to be more thrillingly beautiful, in a vastly greater variety and intricacy of ways, than our previous dreams. How dull and unaesthetic the Newtonian picture seems now; how messy the notion of special creation in biology, or of the movements of heavenly bodies in Ptolemaic astronomy. (SS, 95)

In this light, science can be defined as a sort of sympathy for or love of reality as open to observational inquiry. Rather than searching for surface beauties (or better, prettinesses), scientists are, or ought to be, lovers of nature in its depth, in its dynamically sublime beauty. But this is still not "absolute" beauty (ss, 91–96).

From the above it would be correct to conclude that Hartshorne rejects any rigid distinction between the natural and human sciences (*Naturwissenschaften* and *Geisteswissenschaften,* respectively). There are, he thinks, three abstract, philosophical possibilities for the long-term development of science: (1) physicalistic monism, (2) psychophysical dualism, and (3) psychicalist (or panexperientialist) monism. A theory of emergence does not count as a fourth option but rather consists in a transition from (1) to (2). Hartshorne is quite clear regarding what is problematic with this and other dualisms:

> A mere dualism is unscientific, since it is a denial of the unity upon which all beauty depends. And science is the sense of the discoverable beauty of things. But shall the unity be in physical or in psychical terms? In *method* science must be physicalistic and behavioristic, since only behavior is intersubjectively observable. But "method," "intersubjective," "observable," are psychical terms; and so behaviorism taken as a materialistic monism is inconsistent with its own argument. . . . Its [psychicalism's] view is that matter, including behavior, is how mind on certain levels is given or appears to other mind. . . . Psychical terms are indispensable. (ss, 97)

The unity mentioned in this quotation is not absolute but dynamic, just as the diversity of the natural world is exhibited in various kinds of experiences, whose lower levels constitute what we call "matter" in everyday discourse. These lower levels of psyche must indeed be dealt with behavioristically, with "behavior" here referring to the way in which lower level experiences are observable by minds at our level, unless, of course, these lower levels of experience are constituents of our own bodies, in which case we literally feel their feelings (ss, 98).

Reductionistic materialism, the belief in vacuous actuality, *should* lead us to conclude that there is no feeling or thought anywhere in the universe, but there *is* feeling and thought, hence the implausibility of this position. Hartshorne thinks that the natural world is much more interesting and aesthetically richer than any world that could be consistently described in materialist terms:

[S]cience . . . is search for the hidden but indirectly observable intellectual beauty of the world. A strictly deterministic cosmos, with all
conclusions foregone . . . is not really beautiful. . . . And it is plain
for all to see that the zest and beauty of the life of inquiry itself is
partly due to the unexpectedness of its results. Physicists in general
now seem happy with their statistical laws. Certain philosophers and
a few colleagues may tell them they should not be happy, but they
feel that it is a superlatively beautiful world of order-in-disorder
which they have discovered. Einstein's inability to sense this beauty
rendered his last period, so far as a layman can make out, singularly
unfruitful. (ss, 99)

The unpredictability and freedom in the natural world is exhibited
even at a supreme or divine level, "by which all lesser freedoms are
coordinated sufficiently to keep conflict within bounds. This idea too
is grand and beautiful" (ss, 100).

Metaphysics, in Hartshorne's view, is like mathematics in consisting in a search for abstract beauty. In fact, metaphysical ideas are at
such a level of generality that all other ideas presuppose them or their
equivalents, nor can they fail to be instantiated in existence of some
kind or other. These metaphysical ideas include at least the following
three. First, there is the idea of event or happening. To suppose that
there could be no events is to speak without any clear idea in mind, in
that *any* idea, including the idea of God, presupposes the idea of event
or happening. Second, there is the idea of value, not in the sense of a
particular value, but value as such or mattering of some sort. Even in
seemingly insignificant events there is *some* value or mattering, either
in terms of aversion or adversion to the inherited past and an appeti-
tion, however slight, toward some future or other. And third, there
is the idea of God, as argued in the ontological argument and other
components of Hartshorne's global argument for the existence of God.
To claim that God's existence is a metaphysical concept is to say that
it is not a factual matter but a logical one, as philosophers as diver-
gent as Norman Malcolm, Alvin Plantinga, and J. N. Findlay argue
in agreement with Hartshorne.[12] Unfortunately, these three authors,
despite their debt to Hartshorne's heroic defense of the ontological ar-

gument in the middle decades of the twentieth century, largely ignore Hartshorne's equally important neoclassical concept of God; hence all three are vulnerable to succumbing to the claim that God's beauty is "absolute" (ss, 101–5).

Although whether God exists is a logical question, God's existence can also be felt, at least by those who are receptive enough, or attentive enough, to divine influence. An adequate philosophical theology, in both its conceptual and empirical dimensions, Hartshorne thinks, is both compatible with and helps us to explicate a defensible scientific alternative to reductionistic materialism (i.e., panexperientialism or psychical monism). Hartshorne himself relies on Ilya Prigogine and Henry Stapp in this regard.[13] This alternative to reductionistic materialism helps us to understand the limits within which we can aesthetically enjoy the various kinds of balance and imbalance in the natural world. Further, this alternative to reductionistic materialism enables us to understand the claim (which Hartshorne attributes to J. S. Haldane) that if biology is ever reduced to physics, it will be because physics has become more like biology, not because biology has become more like physics (ss, 107–19).

As a psychologist (see PP) and ornithologist (see BS), Hartshorne exhibits a great deal of experience as an empirical researcher, and as a defender of the ontological argument (see AD and LP) and of position matrices, he shows a familiarity with a quite different kind of knowledge. Hartshorne's hope is that these two sorts of knowledge can be brought together within the same philosophical methodology. Metaphysicians are notorious unifiers, even if they are doing psychological or ornithological research. As a result of his conceptual and empirical efforts regarding birdsong, for example, Hartshorne concludes that music really is a universal human language, such that we can make *something* of music that is initially foreign to us, even if it comes from a source not merely from another culture, but from another species.

To believe in God as the source of absolute, changeless beauty not only runs into conceptual difficulties, it also encourages a state of mind biased toward the fixed and the immutable that distorts our ability to record, or even to notice, the most concrete events in nature (ss,

120–27). Hartshorne summarizes the history of the transition from classical theism, with its fixation on God as absolute beauty, to neo-classical theism in the following way:

> What I call classical theism was formulated in two words by Aristotle as the "unmoved mover"; it's the immutable cause of all becoming and all change. It influences everything, but nothing influences it. So if you pray to that God, you can't possibly have any influence on it. By definition you can't have any influence, yet there were lots of prayers addressed to it. The result is rather paradoxical. And worse than that, that God was supposed to know the world. Now Aristotle knew better. He knew that that kind of God couldn't know the world because to know something is to be influenced by it. So Aristotle denied that God knows the contingent details of the world. But in the Middle Ages they felt religious obligations to a certain God who knows all about us. So they had Aristotle without Aristotle's limited consistency. Spinoza saw that problem, and therefore he denied the contingency of the world so God could know everything without being contingent in any respect. So that's a long dialectic covering many centuries. But soon after Spinoza the Socinians decided that they'd solve the problem in a different way. They asserted the contingency of the world and asserted that God knows the world; they said therefore there's something contingent in God, namely the world as he knows it. And since we are free, we have power to determine, to some extent, what God is going to know about the world. We influence God. So the Socinians were the first process theologians. And Fechner in Germany had a similar idea. (ss, 128–29)

Hartshorne's assumption that getting at the truth, both conceptually and empirically, will get us closer to beauty will no doubt be called into question by some interpreters. They will wonder whether we need to judge Hamlet's "To be, or not to be" soliloquy as true or false in order to find beauty in it. We should return at this point to Whitehead's belief, congenial to Hartshorne with modifications, that a work of art exhibits the primary propositional character of being a lure for feeling. In fact, for Hartshorne reality is a surging mass of microscopic feelings. But these are transmuted vertically into macroscopic emotional tones and horizontally into significant, intellectual propositions that are lures not only for feeling, but also for thought and action. As was argued earlier in the book, there is something worthwhile in the art-for-art's-sake position when trying to focus attention away from everyday affairs and toward the aesthetic attitude wherein we can better appreciate intrinsic value. In the final analysis, however, art is not for art's sake but rather for life's sake, for the sake of richer, more beautiful, aesthetic contrasts that yield a better, truer understanding of our creaturely place in the world. Thus, Hartshorne's aesthetics is ultimately in accord with Keats' famous dictum regarding the coalescence of truth and beauty.[14]

Hartshorne even talks of an aesthetic imperative as "the voice of God": let there be as much unity-in-contrast as possible! This imperative is obeyed consciously by some human beings, but also unconsciously by birds. There is tremendous variation among bird singers, as in the riotously happy song of the bobolink, the sadness of the mourning dove, and the Handel-like leisurely tempo of the American wood thrush (MV, 229; DL, 88). Obedience to this imperative is diametrically opposed to belief in absolute beauty:

> The ideal by which the artist is inspired is not any notion of "absolute beauty" as either a supreme sample or a fixed total of possible beauty. The artist wishes, taking the past of culture as given, to add something new which is both intrinsically valuable or enjoyable, and is appropriate to, enjoyable together with, that past, though by no means deducible from it. He wishes in a small way to simulate the cosmic adventure, to create a note in the next phase of that adventure as visible from his corner of the world. . . . The only static "beauty as such" or timeless absolute which the artist ever contemplates, even subconsciously, is purely abstract, such as the principle of unity in contrast; not any definite unity in contrast or any absolute sum of such unities. . . . Let there be as much unity in contrast as possible. . . . This is the aesthetic imperative which the artist feels laid upon him by the scheme of things, and it is the voice of God as truly as any other imperative. As Berdyaev says, the service of God consists, not in rule-conforming correctness of behavior, but in that creativeness of new values together with respect for old ones by which man can most truly imitate the everlasting creator. (MV, 228–29)

At least a few poets (e.g., the Persian Omar Khayyam, the Englishman Edward Fitzgerald, and the American Sidney Lanier) are instructive in this regard. They direct us to a belief in both creaturely freedom and a God (not the classical theistic one) who is thoroughly compatible with this freedom (TP, 261–75).

CHAPTER TEN

Death and Contributionism

We have seen that two extremes are to be avoided in our language about God, in Hartshorne's view. One is that we could "capture" deity in a verbal formula that would eliminate doubt, and the other is that we cannot say anything coherent about God. The former extreme leads to dogmatism or idolatry, whereas the latter leads to agnosticism or atheism (EA, 39). In between these two extremes lies a judicious mean, he thinks, wherein three levels of discourse about God can be distinguished: literal, analogical, and symbolic (or metaphorical). Literal concepts and terms deal with the formal and most abstract matters in philosophy of religion. These concepts and terms are not matters of degree but are absolute. For example, either God is absolute or *necessary in existence* or not. Or God is either relative or *contingent in actuality* (i.e., in the mode of divine existence in relation to creatures from moment to moment) or not. Literal terms when applied to God classify propositions of a certain logical type (LP, 140). Only God is in one aspect (existence) strictly and maximally absolute and in another aspect (actuality or mode of existence) strictly and maximally related to others (DR, 32).

We have also seen that at the opposite end of the spectrum of intelligible discourse about God is that which relies on material (i.e., on symbolic or metaphorical) concepts. An example of such material predication is found when we describe God as monarch or shepherd or soul for the body of the world. This last symbol is crucial in the present chapter. Here we are clearly dealing with a matter of degree rather than with all-or-nothing possession of the property in question (EA, 21, 28, 38, 41).[1]

In between the most formal and the most material levels of religious discourse is analogical discourse about God, concerning which Hartshorne exhibits a significant, albeit largely unacknowledged, debt to St. Thomas Aquinas. As in St. Thomas, there is the interesting question as to whether analogical discourse ultimately depends on literal discourse: if an analogy points toward some similarities and some differences between the things compared, *some* literal terms are required to secure the similarities. For example, analogical language about God depends on the literal distinction between God's necessary existence (as demonstrated, say, in the ontological and other arguments) and our merely contingent existences.

For my purposes in this chapter it is crucial to notice that the key analogical terms applied by Hartshorne to God are feeling or sentience (rather than higher order thinking), terms that have been at work throughout Hartshorne's aesthetics regarding the capacity for aesthetic sensitivity. There are some notable differences, however, in the way God feels in contrast to the way we feel. For example, God eminently feels all creaturely suffering, whereas we feel it in a fragmentary way that is mixed with our own self-interested desires. But to claim that we are *completely* ignorant of God's aesthetic mode of appreciating the world would be to concede the agnostic's or atheist's case. Feeling terms (including love) are the truly inclusive ones, as we saw above in the chapter on Hartshorne's panexperientialism. In this view God has inclusive aesthetic experience of all the subordinate feelers; God is the universal subject of experience. Feeling may be ubiquitous, but not feeling of *all* other feeling (EA, 26, 31, 41). (There is a peculiar sense, however, in which for Whitehead, at least, everything is everywhere at all times, but only by way of negative prehensions where occasions exclude all of the data in the universe except those that are relevant at the moment.)[2]

Before further explicating both the *symbol* of God as the soul for the body of the world and the *analogy* of God as the universal subject of aesthetic feeling (there being no rigid distinction between symbols and analogies—the former approximate the latter), one other sort of religious language in Hartshorne should be mentioned again. It is a type of literal language that I have labeled "literal-2" so as to distinguish it from the formal, literal-1 language discussed above. It is our normal religious practice to start with human concepts and terms, which we often take to be literal, and then apply them analogically to God. But strictly speaking, when dealing with a feeling such as love it is God who literally-2 loves, whereas the creatures do so only analogically or symbolically. We do not love in exactly the same way that God does, but our love nonetheless counts for something when we imitate God's love rather than the other way around, Hartshorne thinks. To put the issue differently, it is not so much that where there is religious experience or experience of beauty on our part there is awareness of God, as it is that our experience of God or of divine beauty enables us to experience love or beauty in other creatures. God knows in the best way possible, in a literal-2 way, whereas we know vaguely and selectively. It is not so much that God is anthropomorphic as that we are deimorphic, in Hartshorne's view (EA, 25, 30, 33, 38).

One of the reasons for all of these distinctions is to contribute to a conception of God and to language about God that will enable us to avoid Pascal's conclusion that the God of the philosophers is not the God of religious experience.[3] Pascal's conclusion is justified regarding traditional theism, however. The effort to develop a conception of God that helps to clarify, rather than to render unintelligible, religious experience has been hampered by the Kantian assumption that whereas science is empirical in a straightforward sense, this is not the case regarding religious experience. For example, many contemporary philosophers would point to the pervasiveness of nonbelievers as strong evidence against universal human experience of God and as at least prima facie evidence against *any* trustworthy evidence for God.[4]

The premodern world, however, did not feel as acutely as we do today this sharp distinction, in that premodern believers (along with American pragmatists like James and Peirce) did not automatically dismiss the empirical claims made by religious believers regarding divine influence in their lives. The Hartshornian response to the Kantian distinction mentioned above is to urge the following: There are two levels of human experience. On one level we vaguely experience "the inclusive something," and on a higher level we experience "the inclusive something" *as* "the inclusive something." The former may be ubiquitous in humanity even if the latter is not. It is only when someone consciously experiences the inclusive something as such and realizes that it is the model for all experience that one comes close to approximating one's *telos* as a human being. Agnostics and atheists do not seem as far removed from theists as they sometimes think, however, when one considers that they also have contact with the first level of experience when they move about in a world that is not felt as alien to them and which, at least in aspiration and to some degree in practice, makes sense. An experience of the mighty whole at this level, it should be noted, often occurs in atheists or agnostics along with a denial of the corresponding experience at the second level (EA, 20, 31–32).

The aim of life for those theists who affirm the inclusive something *as* the inclusive something is to enrich life and to contribute beauty to the all-inclusive life that is alone capable of enjoying the total beauty of all creation, according to Hartshorne. As Mohammed Valady puts the point, in this view the Hartshornian categorical imperative is to facilitate those aesthetic and ethical values that one would like to see as part of the inclusive value—God.[5] Our contributions to the divine life are easy to miss if we, like other animals, tend to see ourselves, or at least our group, at the center. We have a tendency to be egocentric or ethnocentric rather than theocentric. Some human beings also have the unfortunate tendency to view their lives as (divinely or scientifically) determined. For example, Hardy wrote great literature, but his deterministic, distorted view of life (which contains a satirical view of a God who mismanages the world) is hardly a livable philosophy that is conducive to a defensible aesthetic, as Hartshorne sees things. That is, determinism leads to a grim theology at odds with the partially open future involved in process contributionism (ZF, 52, 54).

The contributionist view not only involves a symbolic description of the world in terms of God as the soul for the body of the world and an analogical description of God as preeminent aesthetic feeling; it also involves a view of the afterlife. Two main options can be considered once the reductionistic materialist view that death ends all is dismissed. First, the afterlife may involve the continuation of a person's career into the indefinite future in some supernatural form (without a body, with a resurrected body, with a different body, etc.). The second option, however, is to believe in God as the end of our lives rather than as a means toward the continuation of our own careers. In this second view, God everlastingly possesses whatever beauty we or others have experienced. God makes possible the (Whiteheadian) immortality of the past in that God's actuality, rather than God's bare existence, is the ultimate heir of our aesthetic achievements. This will no doubt fail to satisfy those who prefer the first option and who assume the first option's orthodoxy. It should nonetheless be noted that the effect of the first option is to make us rivals to God in our infinite careers. That is, otherworldly belief in personal immortality not only distracts us from our real problems, but it tempts us into thinking that we, rather than God, exist necessarily (ZF, 57).

However, two different questions should be separated: Do we use God as a means to our ends? and Do we have a personal career after death? Kant, for example, separates these two when he famously claims that we should strive not to gain the rewards of heaven but to be worthy of heaven's rewards. At times Hartshorne seems to conflate these two questions, perhaps because: (a) many or most believers in personal immortality do so themselves and (b) personal survival may seem to signal a return to the idea that there is no genuine tragedy. However, Hartshorne thinks that it is obvious that there *is* genuine tragedy. To be fair to those who believe in personal immortality, however, we should be clear that such a belief does not in itself have to be connected to a self-interested theory of motivation.

Some great novelists, Austen among them, have treated what it takes to find real happiness on earth without the idea of personal immortality and without threats of everlasting punishment or everlasting bliss for *us*. But no great artist has artistically concretized the abstract philosophical and theological ideas of process theism the way Dante or Milton and the (Italian and northern) Renaissance painters did for traditional theism. It is quite amazing how Dante and other writers and visual artists squeezed artistic value from the "theological catastrophe" of traditional theism, Hartshorne urges (ZF, 59, 61). If this language sounds hyperbolic, it should be remembered that for centuries traditional theists have saddled religious believers with literally gut-wrenching questions regarding why an omnibenevolent God would send a plague, a deformed child, or the death of a young mother to a family.

The answer to these questions is partly philosophical/theological, in that divine omnipotence is not theoretically defensible once it is realized that being *is* power, and partly aesthetic, in that a divine tyrant who has, or could have if *He* wanted it, a monopoly of power is an aesthetic monstrosity.

The proposition that there is a being who enjoys complete control over all other beings is a commonplace in traditional theological theories. According to Hartshorne, this implies that no other beings could have freedom at all if what "freedom" means is the ability to decide things for oneself without complete determination from the outside. Of course some (e.g., Nelson Pike)[6] will object to Hartshorne's view here by claiming that there is a distinction between God *having* all power to completely determine the creatures and *using* that power. That is, some will claim that although God chooses to allow creatures to make their own choices, God could completely determine them. Hartshorne would respond to this argument in at least two ways. First, if being *is* the power to make some decisions (once again, literally the cutting off of some possibilities), then it is by no means clear that we can make conceptual sense of the view that creatures are *or could be* completely determined. And second, if God could prevent innocent suffering, but chooses not to do so, as some of Hartshorne's critics allege, then these critics would at this point be saddled with the nastiest version of the theodicy problem that neoclassical theism is meant to solve.

Absolute freedom in one being and zero freedom in all others, however, makes no sense metaphysically or experientially, as James showed in his famous essay "The Dilemma of Determinism."[7] One wonders how to make sense of determinism when we are in the process of making a *choice*. Metaphysically there is the quandary of how to make sense of an agent that deals only with puppets of itself rather than with (Platonic) self-movers. A complete absence of self-determination would seem to portend absence of a positive, coherent presence in the world. Freedom is, if anything, social and involves a plurality of influential agents. Not even atoms or radioactive waves are completely inert in that they are, in a sense, active singulars. A zero of free activity would seem to be equivalent to a zero of actuality.

In Hartshorne's view, in each free act we and other creatures add something to the definiteness of the divine actuality. The qualified indeterminism of the world is partly due to chance (the absence of fully determining omnipotence) and partly due to creaturely creativity itself. Some of the difficulty with the traditional theistic view is in the overuse of interpersonal symbols (e.g., God as father or ruler) rather than organic ones (e.g., God as mind or soul or nervous system for the body of the world). The latter symbol is not immune from criticism, as when it is combined with causal determinism in the Stoics or Spinoza. "Free beings" is, in a way, a redundancy, whereas a "wholly unfree being," as found in the Stoics or Spinoza, is a contradiction in terms, once again on the Platonic assumption that being *is* the power to affect, or at least to be affected by, others (zf, 62–63, 66).

Only by rejecting belief in personal immortality and accepting belief in at least limited human freedom are we in a position to embrace, or even to understand, Hartshorne's view implied in the lines of the Wallace Stevens poem "Sunday Morning": "Death is the mother of beauty."[8] Not only human freedom but human life itself is definitely bounded by birth and death. The definiteness provided by death can be seen, in the effort to appreciate the beauty of life, as the "gift of finitude," to use Hartshorne's phrase (zf, 66). To vaguely suppose that we can personally survive death is to rob life of its vividness, its intensity, he thinks. Stevens aptly calls these vague suppositions the "chimeras of the grave." Rather than hold out for personal immortality we should instead concentrate our aesthetic attention on the definitely beautiful career we have here (zf, 66).

To say that death is partially constitutive of the beauty of life is not to deny but to support, Hartshorne thinks, the belief that God cherishes the uniqueness we contribute to the divine life. Biologists in particular help us to appreciate the place of death in the overall scheme of things. If religious they may very well be especially cognizant of the intrinsic value of the natural process *even in* its instrumental contribution to God. Whereas nonreligious scientists nonetheless imply at the very least a vague feeling of the wondrous, beautiful whole to which every species makes its contribution, as in the aforementioned hymn in praise of the beauty of the web of life found at the end of Darwin's

The Origin of Species.[9] Both scientists and nature lovers, in general, have a tendency to need convincing when there is proposed a radical diminution of natural beauty, say through industrial or suburban "development." As before, each one of us is of more value than many sparrows, but how many more is open to question, especially when we exhibit a tendency to overconsume. Perhaps as individuals we are not more valuable than a whole sparrow species (WM, 94, 120, 126).

The final definiteness of a career that takes place at death lends support to the view that the fundamental values are not ethical but aesthetic, as Hartshorne details in an essay in WM titled "The Aesthetic Meaning of Death." This definiteness illuminates the fact that cognitive values are not universal in that we value experience not merely as a means to knowledge. That is, aesthetic experience is wider than and includes cognitive experience, such that getting clear on what makes aesthetic experience definite helps us to appreciate living experience as such. It is quite easy, however, to miss the definiteness of aesthetic experience by assuming, for example, that partial disorder is the opposite of beauty rather than partially constitutive of it. We have seen that orderliness unrelieved by surprise or irregularity (death being the prime example of these) does not yield perfect beauty but aesthetic disvalue in the form of monotony. Admittedly death or any other chaos is in itself not an aesthetic value but is nonetheless partially constitutive of the aesthetic value of life as a whole. Even a life lived in intermittent anticipation of death is aesthetically richer, Hartshorne thinks, than one of unremitting monotony (WM, 51–52).

We have also seen that in Hartshorne's view intensity is an aesthetic criterion that can be discussed in abstraction from other aesthetic criteria like unified diversity or differentiated unity. But in concrete reality it is hard to maintain a Zorba-like zest for life without sufficient variety and contrast of experience. A monotonous life tends to be lived in a correspondingly tepid way. The richer the contrasts integrated, and the richer the integration itself, the more likely we will be to lead our lives with *élan*. In fact, when these rich contrasts partially transcend our ability to integrate them, our lives take on a sublime character especially conducive to the flourishing of religious emotions (WM, 52–53).

This flourishing of religious emotions is not necessarily due to a monopolar view of God as a formless being who is infinite in every way. "Infinite" is not a synonym for "divine," in Hartshorne's view, in that God's *existence* may be infinite but not God's concrete *actuality* in relation to finite creatures. The greatest works of art, for example, are also finite: great novels, symphonies, and poems always have a last sentence, note, or word. In *this* regard we are finite like these works of art, whereas God, who is infinite in existence, is not (WM, 52–53).

With each moment of experience we add variation to our lives, which require both this variation and a certain degree of repetition, the latter of which is embodied in our "personality traits." The balance in this aesthetic theme of expectedness and variation, found in animals as well as in human beings, Hartshorne thinks, changes somewhat as we age and especially as we approach the end of a natural lifespan. The variations are added on to a wider and deeper base and are assimilated accordingly. At any age, however, death could rise up to surprise us, a fact that is easily understandable if the world is not determined by absolute power. That is, in order to respond adequately to the theodicy problem it is crucial to realize that divine purpose is not primarily illustrated in the time and manner of our deaths. In this sense all life is fragile and tragic, as wise people have always known, Hartshorne claims. (Hartshorne himself almost died at the age of twenty [RM, 289].) This fragility and tragedy are, via divine feeling and knowledge, transferred to the divine life itself. Once again, because God is, in a way, made finite by our tragedies, the best way to put the contrast between us and God is perhaps not in terms of our finitude versus God's infinity, but rather in terms of our fragmentariness versus God's all-inclusiveness (WM, 53–54).

Further, God's ability to re-spond to creatures implies real finite relations with finite creatures. If God were "wholly infinite" God would have to actualize all possibilities with all creatures, assuming for the moment that this is a possibility (which it is not, in Hartshorne's view). All concrete actualization is finite, definite: "To identify deity with the sheerly infinite is to identify deity with pure possibility" (WM, 55). The most poignant of God's finite, indeed individual, relations with creatures, so far as we know (angels?), are those with human beings, some of whom, unlike animals, experience their tragedy at a highly self-conscious level. It is precisely this self-consciousness that leads many human beings into self-pity and anthropocentrism and away from contributionism and theocentrism, the beliefs that the ultimate value of our lives consists in the degree to which we contribute something positive to the everlasting divine reality and that God is the central reality of the cosmos, respectively. Our medical powers to extend human life are wonderful examples of progress *only if* they do not seduce us into anthropocentric illusions about ourselves. These powers are genuinely progressive, however, when they enable us to contribute more beautiful moments, and beauty of a greater intensity, to God (WM, 56–58).

Just as we creatively advance through each new drop of experience, so also at each moment we experience the death of the previous one. Against the background of this Whiteheadian "perpetual perishing,"[10] death is nothing other than the final phase of this continual loss. (However, Hartshorne's belief that God preserves the subjective immediacy of our experiences leads him to dislike the language of perpetual perishing.) Death should confirm for us what we could know on the basis of everyday experience of loss: the meaning of life transcends the ego and instead consists in our contributions to the everlasting whole of things, the personification and concretization of which is God. The divine good is more permanent than the good of the individual or even of the species, assuming, of course, that Hartshorne is correct regarding the ontological argument and other components of his global argument for the existence of God. What is the value, say, of the ancient Celts, whom *we* now know only through a few of their artifacts? If they lived well or ill, what does it matter to us? Hartshorne has cogent responses to these questions not easily improved upon by the nontheist. The theistic contributionist thinks that although death is the termination of our careers, it is not the destruction of them.

Analogously, reading the last sentence of a book does not destroy that book: "God will read the books of our lives forever after" (WM, 61). That is, God will give our fleeting experiences abiding significance by accurately remembering them. Further, if we assume that God is omnibenevolent, then each "book" that God reads would be ideally valued and not contribute less in proportion to the whole as God reads more "books." Indeed, the gospel writer assures us that, according to Jesus, God cares even for the fall of a sparrow (Matthew 10:28), a claim that was not lost on Shakespeare, as evidenced in the last act of *Hamlet*. This is not to be interpreted as being absorbed into an impersonal absolute, but rather as participation in the abiding, personal, life of God, to whom we are to offer our entire hearts and minds, Hartshorne thinks, as the biblical tradition also attests (WM, 62). In fact, God (as the greatest knower and carer) not only remembers what we remember, but even remembers experiences of which we were never even conscious, and so has our experiences to a maximum of intensity in a way we never did.

The beauty of the world as a whole is, in a way, hidden from the nontheist, although the quite public discoveries of science indicate to us all how grand the cosmos really is. One of the prime tasks for the theist is to reconcile this grandeur with the obvious evil that exists in the world. Such a reconciliation is a much more likely prospect in process or neoclassical theism than in traditional theism. In fact, Hartshorne's process metaphysics elaborates the intelligible beauty of the world, abstractly conceived, whereas religious experience (or mysticism) conveys such beauty to us concretely. Both of these testify to the accompanying, divine melody of all existence (LP, 127, 287–88, 292, 297).

It was only with great difficulty that traditional theists like Jonathan Edwards could assimilate into their systems the idea in aesthetics that the greater the variety in equal uniformity, the greater the beauty. He, like most traditional theists, borrowed selectively yet unwittingly from the Greeks: beauty is unity, order, and avoidance of diversity or randomness. In nonhuman reality, as well as in the aesthetic practices of artists and critics themselves, however, beauty is just as much the avoidance of too much unity and order. The defense of aesthetic moderation, however, should not be confused with a lack of daring. Hartshorne himself agrees (albeit at an abstract level rather than at the concrete, contingent level) with the bold aesthetic thesis of Keats that beauty is truth, and truth beauty, as we saw in the previous chapter.[11] Necessary truths, in particular, including those in mathematics, cannot yield aesthetic disvalue; this is because contemplation of them is satisfying. Even contingent truths, however, have some aesthetic value, *some* immediate appeal or beauty above a mere zero level, Hartshorne thinks. Nonetheless, to say that beauty itself is good does not, obviously enough, provide us with a guide to action that can replace the very complicated decision-making procedures that are needed in ethics (CA, 24, 55–56). Likewise, agreeing with the above dictum from Keats does not mean that we are willing to do away with the very complicated procedures used in science that are needed to get at the truth, or at least to avoid falsity, regarding the natural world.

Each experience is an act, and every act realizes (or at least strives to realize) a value. At times, the values realized are ethical, but far more prevalent, Hartshorne thinks, is the realization of aesthetic value, broadly construed, which involves intuitive or concrete awareness of some sort. It is out of such concrete awareness that we build an ethics or a metaphysics or even an aesthetic theory. This last would have to include at least the following: an account of aesthetic qualities (as found above in Chapters 5 and 6 on sensation and panpsychism) and an account of aesthetic structures, in which aesthetic qualities are combined (as found above in Chapter 2 on beauty as a mean between extremes). The most successful aesthetic combinations can be called harmonies, which are relations between things that are both felt to be different from each other and felt as if they are in some way properly connected to each other. Octaves in music provide a primitive or insipid example of harmonies of this kind (RS, 44–45).

The failure to achieve any sophisticated harmony due to too little contrast (insipidity) or too little similarity (chaos) can be avoided both through bold use of contrast, wherein strength and vitality are given to a work of art, and through subtlety or delicacy, wherein an effete approach attracts our attention, Hartshorne thinks. And we have seen that the importance of contrast is not confined to art. For example, life's harmony is threatened when everything is reduced to uniformity, as is the case in an overly aggressive egalitarianism. Of course, Hartshorne's intent here is not to defend the violent inequalities of present capitalist society. Indeed, he thinks that present capitalism is problematic in part because it is ugly; there seems to be little unity shared between the wealthy and the disenfranchised. A far more beautiful contribution to God would be a mixed economic (Rawlsian?) system wherein the talented would be rewarded *precisely because* their talents would be to everyone's advantage, especially the least advantaged.[12] Unity-in-diversity is once again the key (RS, 46–47).

To use some helpful examples from Brian Henning, a novice pianist who plays "Greensleeves" produces only pretty music because the chords lack sufficient complexity. Conversely, a symphony with ten thousand different parts played simultaneously would be so complex that it would be impossible for us to grasp. The human brain, at present, seems like such a symphony in that it involves a complexity that is still largely beyond our grasp. Henning prefers to say that the beauty we can experience is "larger" than that experienced by a bird, with God's experience of beauty "larger" still than ours. In addition, the beauty we can experience is more complex, more profound, and more intense than that experienced by a bird.

I would like to come at this important issue in Hartshorne from another angle. Despite the fact that red is the opposite of green, in some circumstances the two harmonize. So also competition is the opposite of cooperation, yet in the aforementioned mixed economic (again, Rawlsian?) scheme the two can be harmonized. In both art and economics, nature can and often should be our model for aesthetically rich contributions to deity. It is seldom insipid or monotonous; even a tundra landscape provides more diversity than may initially be evident. And whereas the old physics offered us a world that was highly predictable and monotonous, the new physics is much more satisfying aesthetically, Hartshorne thinks. It is also satisfying, and not surprising, to know that it is more accurate than the old physics. It would be odd if the less accurate theory were the more beautiful one (RS, 47–48).

Science and art thus have a structural kinship despite their obvious differences. That is, these two disciplines ideally are harmoniously related in their everlasting contributions. In both disciplines we experience both expectation and surprise. Skillful artists knowingly provide the aesthetic pleasure of surprise, whereas in science it is impossible in principle to predict in advance the future of the discipline. Scientists actually predict nature better (although not even here with absolute assurance) than they do the future of science itself, Hartshorne notes. Process philosophers are famous (or infamous) for actually claiming not only that events in nature are to some extent unpredictable, but also that the *laws* of nature change over long periods of time. This is analogous to the claim that the particular way in which we experience harmony in art changes, as in modern appreciation of the dissonant "harmonies" in Stravinsky that would have been difficult for earlier aestheticians to appreciate. But the principle of aesthetic value as a dual mean has thus far remained relatively constant. Real change occurs, however, the moment we become too familiar with a piece of music such that we tire of it when we too definitely anticipate its passages. Unmitigated conservatism in art or science seems doomed (RS, 48–51).

The partial unpredictability of reality in general is aesthetically pleasant, but it is also sometimes a source of suffering and tragedy in that partially free individuals in great numbers are bound to clash at some point. In addition, suffering and tragedy are also partially due to the inner conflict in human beings themselves between the desire to facilitate the common good and the desire to pursue one's own or one's group interests. The sublime symbol of these facts in Christianity is the cross (RS, 148–49). The aesthetic dicta to "Be not too predictable" and "Be not too unpredictable" enable us to go a long way toward avoiding suffering and tragedy, but unfortunately there is still much suffering and tragedy that is unavoidable, in Hartshorne's view. By treating each day, indeed each moment to the extent possible, as a new opportunity for richness of aesthetic experience, we might come as asymptotically close as possible to blessedness in that such richness is ultimately contributed to the divine life (DL, 207).

The cosmos is nonetheless beautiful despite the clear examples of suffering and tragedy. This beauty is constituted, according to Hartshorne, of the innumerable centers of aesthetic experience creatively bound together in a harmonious way, a harmony that is best explained not in terms of a *principle* of divine love, but rather in terms of eminent divine love itself (NT, 106). This reinforces the view that aesthetic value of *some* sort, in this case love, is the generic category that includes other value. To return to the Keats dictum, it is probably more accurate to say that truth is a form of beauty than it is to say the reverse. Cognitive value (e.g., truth) and ethical value (e.g., goodness) are alike in being instrumentally important to the extent that they foster the intrinsic value of present or future experiences. When these intrinsic values are present rather than future, we can accurately say that virtue is its own reward (cs, 308). Once again, however, the point here is neither to trivialize ethics nor to do away with debate regarding the complex decision-making procedures that are needed to do ethics well.

Death can be a great evil if it is premature or ugly or painful, but death simply as such is a good, it is valuable. This is because it facilitates our realization that life is, among other things, an aesthetic problem: how to enrich a finite number of moments of experience, how to savor them in their finitude. Only the death of God makes no sense, as the ontological argument shows, in that the nonexistence of the greatest conceivable being is a contradiction in terms. Human life is appreciated in the living of it. Its worth, however, is *measured* by something partially external to it in terms of its contribution to something more enduring than itself. This aesthetic theory of death not only facilitates, but, in a way, *forces* us to value the excitements and longings of childhood, the productive work of middle age, and, it is to be hoped, the serenity of old age. Any human personality, even one like Hartshorne's that lasted over a hundred years, is a theme with a finite number of variations. In a peculiar way we can even say, Hartshorne thinks, that death does not pose a problem for us so much as it *solves* the aesthetic problem of life (cs, 309–10, 321; zf, 206).

The apophatic theologians were certainly correct to emphasize that it would be presumptuous of us to claim to know in minute detail what God's purposes are. However, this point can be exaggerated, according to Hartshorne. If God is at least preeminent love, then it seems we can know God's purpose at least in outline: it is the beauty of the world or the harmonious happinesses of the creatures. For example, even the writings of the great apophatic mystics of the Byzantine tradition are grouped under the title *Philokalia:* love of beauty.[13] Each creature has glimpses of, or feelings for, this beauty, but presumably, only God enjoys it adequately and everlastingly (oo, 25).

Hartshorne admires the Jews—ancient and some recent—who accept death as the end of a human career. We are distinct in being the only animals, as far as we can tell, who foresee the inevitability of our eventually dying. In *this* sense Frost and Omar Khayyam and other poets are correct in believing in the inevitability of death. Only a theist, however, would be concerned that one of the problems with belief in subjective immortality is that it makes us rivals to God; it is a sort of hubris. Dickens, for example, in *The Old Curiosity Shop,* makes it quite clear that the promise of everlasting reward and the threat of everlasting punishment are not needed to bring out a refined version of Christianity in little Nell, who comes to believe, as did the ancient Jews, that people live on after their death in the memory of others (BA, 380; ML, 61–65).

There is no obvious consensus among process thinkers, however, regarding immortality. Marjorie Hewitt Suchocki tries to bring about a rapprochement between Hartshorne's objective immortality or contributionism, on the one hand, and belief in subjective immortality, on the other. In the standard view of Hartshorne's position, she thinks, "we are like carbon become diamonds by the very intensity of pressure brought about as the weight of such infinity bears down upon our mortality."[14] Despite the fact that Hartshorne uses the terminology of objective immortality, he nonetheless lays the groundwork for subjective immortality, she thinks. If it is the case, as Hartshorne holds, that only God is able to prehend another occasion completely and vividly, without eliminations of any kind, then God prehends our subjective occasions *as subjective.* By contrast, our fragmentary prehensions "murder to dissect," to use Wordsworth's language so dear to both Whitehead and Hartshorne.[15] The question from Hartshorne at this point would probably be: Is the subjective immediacy that is retained in God to be associated with *our* subjective immortality? In any event, even if Suchocki is a bit ambitious in associating God's prehensions of our subjective immediacy with subjective immortality (in that these prehensions are God's, not ours), she nonetheless provides a service to neoclassical theists by pointing out the "balm in Gilead" that is discernable in Hartshorne's view. Her achievement consists in pointing out that prehension might work both ways in a sort of mutual immanence: God coexperiences our suffering with us, and we might coexperience its transformation (or better, its transfiguration) in God (see TD).

Randall Auxier is like Suchocki in relying on Hartshorne's TD in the effort to defend subjective immortality. And like Suchocki he argues that Hartshorne's own doctrine is objective immortality or contributionism, but it *should* be subjective immortality. But Auxier's view is somewhat different from Suchocki's, as is indicated when he says:

> But [Suchocki] is wrong in assuming that upon death the locus of subjective experiencing either shifts or is transformed in such a way as to be relocated in God. This shows a basic confusion regarding *what* our relation to God has been in life. There were always two loci of our subjective immediacy in life—our physical actuality, and our existence in God. That is, there was never any complete sense in which I, in life, am the only (or even the main) locus of my own experience. God is having my experiences *as I have them,* but to a much greater degree. God's experience of my subjective immediacy is more subjective and more immediate than my own experience of it in life. Let me suggest that after physical death, the only important difference in me is that a certain limitation upon my experience of my own subjective immediacy is lifted, and I come to experience even myself only as a self-in-God.[16]

Auxier's version of subjective immortality, in contrast to Suchocki's, involves the idea that the "I" that dies does not become less, but rather more, as a result of death.

In death we do not lose ourselves, but gain ourselves, he thinks, such that our present existence is merely larval. That is, at death our *actual* limitations are altered, but our *existential* ones are not. In Auxier's use of Hartshorne's distinction between existence and actuality, our existence is personal in the sense that we receive personhood only through an act of God, and such a reception is not negated by death. Indeed, Auxier thinks that subjectivity is enhanced at death. Because of this enhanced subjectivity, Auxier thinks that we need not get aesthetically bored with everlasting existence, as Hartshorne fears, nor need we give up, as Hartshorne does, on the idea that there might be some sort of final judgment, at least in the sense that God's just treatment of me in my subjective immortality will involve a sense of justice that is similar to a human one.[17]

One can imagine at least four different responses that Hartshorne could make to Suchocki's and Auxier's careful attempts to expand on Hartshorne's own principles regarding objective immortality so as to have them consistent with subjective immortality. First, there is indeed something of a systole-diastole sequence between subjective experience in human beings and divine prehension and transformation (or transfiguration) of that experience: first a human being has a vivid experience, God prehends and transforms (or transfigures) it, then some human beings who have religious experiences are aware of God doing this; the process subsequently starts all over again. But the fact that God prehends the subjective experiences of human beings as subjective does not alter the fact that such prehensions are *in God.* For Hartshorne it is true that all of our experiences are preserved *in God;* hence he winces whenever interpreters try to describe his view in Whiteheadian terminology like "perpetual perishing." However, if *God* preserves our subjective experiences as subjective, this is a far cry, he thinks, from our doing so. Analogously, we can imagine live cells in our bodies that have had their cell walls damaged by high heat that causes intense pain *for us.* Even after these cells die, we can still remember the localized pain that occurred when we were burned (even if we cannot do so with complete accuracy and vividness in the divine way). But the cells are still dead.

Second, a related disagreement between Hartshorne, on the one hand, and Suchocki and especially Auxier, on the other, surrounds a defensible use of pronouns. In the long quotation from Auxier above, it can be seen that Auxier is willing to refer to personal identity without having a body (see especially the use of the word "I" in the last sentence of the quotation). This indicates a flirtation with the seventeenth-century dualism that Whitehead (starting in *Science and the Modern World*) and Hartshorne have consistently opposed. Hartshorne's pan-experientialism can also be termed a type of dynamic hylomorphism or dynamic hylozoism, wherein every concrete, physical singular has an experiential or lifelike or psychic capacity. However, according to Hartshorne not only is it incorrect to posit a concrete singular without an experiential dimension, it is *equally* misleading to posit a psyche without some sort of concrete embodiment. Whitehead's language concerning each occasion having *both* a mental pole and a physical pole is helpful here.[18] And for Hartshorne, even God is embodied: God is the World Soul for the body of the world, or the natural world as a whole is the divine body. The implication of this sort of thinking, as Hartshorne sees things, is that when a human body disintegrates, so does the soul/body (or mind/body) complex. That is, for Hartshorne, human beings are not souls (Auxier would say "persons") who can live without bodies the way angels are alleged to live, whereas Auxier compares our lives after bodily death to the lives of angels. Nor are human beings bodies without souls or minds. Rather, in Hartshorne's view human beings are dynamic, mortal "soulbodies" or "mindbodies," to coin some terms that help to describe his view. Finally, one of the main problems with believing in disembodied, angelic cogitos is that such a disengagement from the natural world is precisely the seventeenth-century move that left the natural world devoid of psyche and hence amenable to exploitation in that it was seen to be composed of vacuous actualities. All of these matters are commonplaces in Hartshorne's writings.

Third, Hartshorne is convinced that human life is tragic, whereas Suchocki's biblical "balm in Gilead" and Auxier's belief in rewards, if not punishments, for the "I" in the afterlife run the risk of trivializing this tragedy. (I do not say that Suchocki and Auxier necessarily trivialize the tragedy of life, only that on the grounds of their respective views they run the risk of doing so.) Further, for Hartshorne it is crucial to notice that if tragedy occurs (the death of a teen, for example), no being with memory of that tragedy can ever escape tragedy in its future. That is, both Suchocki and Auxier, despite their caution, have a much stronger sense than Hartshorne that justice will (or could be) served in the afterlife. Hartshorne, by contrast, agrees with Wordsworth that that "Which having been must ever be."[19]

And fourth, in addition to running the risk of being in tension with Hartshorne's aesthetic concept of tragedy, Suchocki and Auxier do the same regarding his aesthetic concept of monotony. Although our subjective experiences are preserved everlastingly, it is God who preserves them. Throughout his career, and especially in his comparison of our songs and those of birds, Hartshorne emphasizes the fact that we are biological animals. As such, we are likely to find life less vivid when we are old in that each new and potentially exciting experience is added to a larger and larger base. This tends, however, to bring about a serenity and repose that is itself an aesthetic reward that is rare in young people. But even if we do not find life less exhilarating when we are old than we did when we were young, eventually our bodies quite simply wind down and with death prevent us from experiencing at the macro level. The parts of our bodies, in the process of decomposing, nonetheless go on experiencing at the microscopic level. One pays an aesthetic price if one continues for very long in a debilitated state; to do so everlastingly would, in fact, lead to what Hartshorne calls mo- notony. Of course one can deny this whole way of looking at things if one ultimately denies (as Auxier does, at least by implication) that human persons are biological animals.

No trivial issue is at stake here. It is not the case that one can ac- cept Hartshorne's philosophical theology and his aesthetics, but tag on at the end a doctrine of subjective immortality, without radically altering the philosophical theology and aesthetics. The key point, from Hartshorne's point of view, is that death be *accepted,* in that without getting clear on the meaning of death we lose out on the meaning of life. And, from Hartshorne's point of view, belief in subjective immor- tality indicates a certain refusal to accept death.

Life is good while it lasts; it is, like virtue and aesthetic value, its own reward. Hence there is the problem of trying to make death ac- cept*able.* There are three ways to do this, Hartshorne thinks. The first is to believe, along with Suchocki and Auxier, in subjective or personal immortality. Hartshorne is quite clear about what he thinks about this option (see the above four Hartshornian criticisms): "I think that the appeal of this view is largely a consequence of misconceptions about the nature of life as such, no matter where or when" (AC, 84). Another option that makes death acceptable to some is the belief that death is like a deep sleep from which one never wakes. Hartshorne is not convinced, however, that this option really makes death acceptable. Suppose a middle-aged person in good health were told that tomorrow she would die, with the supposed consolation being that the death would be painless and would lead to a deep sleep. Would this *really* make her death acceptable? Hartshorne thinks not.

The third way to make death acceptable is to transcend self-interest as our final concern, to regard our lives as contributions to the good of those who survive us, whether human or nonhuman. Once self-interest is transcended in this way, and only when this has occurred, can death be acceptable, he thinks. Hartshorne would have us consider the following case:

> Miserable people, even if they are useful, contribute less than happy people who are also useful. By giving posterity our misery to look back upon we do them no special favor. It is joys one wants to recall, more than sufferings. Even admitting the truth in the poet's phrase, "our sweetest songs are those that tell the saddest thought," still, in the composing and singing of these songs there is more than misery, there is satisfaction in the beauty of the expression of grief. (AC, 84)

The insight here is directly connected to Hartshorne's aesthetic theory as we have seen it unfold throughout the present book:

> [W]e are mere fragments of reality spatially and temporally. But then any work of art or beautiful thing is such a fragment, apart from the entire universe throughout time. Contentment with mortality is contentment with the finitude of our ultimate contribution to the whole of life. Should our careers have a last episode? Should a book have a last chapter? A poem, a last verse? Without beginning and end a work of art has no definite form or meaning. I personally regard a life as, with normal luck and good management, having something of the qualities of a work of art, and I see no reason why it should be endless; rather the contrary, it ought not to be endless. (AC, 85)

Life is interesting, in part, *because* it has a beginning, middle, and end. The drastic contrasts between infancy and youth, youth and adolescence, adolescence and early adulthood, early adulthood and advanced middle age, and advanced middle age and elderliness are, in a way, crucial in the creation of a beautiful life. It is common, for example, to fixate on one period and hence to miss out on the beauty of a whole life, as in the high school sports star whose remaining years are all downhill.

Perhaps it will be objected that we ordinarily think of books and poems as complete, the exceptions being those proportionately fewer novels and poems that are left half-written. But the massive amount of suffering that has existed historically (wars, plagues, famines, high infant mortality rates, etc.) has left the majority of human beings with incomplete lives. Thus, it will be claimed that the analogy between a life and a book or a poem is flawed.[20] A critic might even go so far as to say that Hartshorne's philosophy of death is elitist in that Hartshorne had the luxury of a long life such that only he and a few like him could bring some sort of closure to it.

One reply might be to say that *any* analogy consists in certain similarities *and* dissimilarities between the two analogues, and thus Hartshorne's critics here are doing nothing more than pointing out an important dissimilarity between a human life and a book or poem. Something more needs to be said, however: even if it is true that most human lives have historically been cut short, it is nonetheless crucial to notice that we see these lives as tragic only because of the assumption that all human beings have a natural lifespan of seventy years or so (i.e., a complete story that ideally ought to be written). Even in antiquity, or in primitive conditions where over half the children die of disease, such an assumption is made, as in Aristotle (*Nicomachean Ethics* 1100A), who thought that happiness requires a complete life.

Satisfaction with the present stage in one's life, indeed with the present moment to the extent that this is possible, does not require everlasting future rewards as found in belief in subjective immortality. In fact, belief in subjective immortality makes it even harder to achieve aesthetic satisfaction in the present. The meaning of life *can* survive its termination, but only if there is a divine form of life that can appreciate and preserve the goodness and beauty of such a life. Further, the contributionist acceptance of death has implications for the theodicy problem. Premature or aesthetically repulsive or painful modes of dying *are* evil, but death simply as such is not:

I am deeply convinced that it is a religious mistake to ask, in case of misfortune, why did God do this to me? God is not in the business of inflicting misfortunes upon anyone. It is other creatures, for example bacteria, or human thieves or mischief-makers, that inflict misfortunes. God makes it possible for there to be a cosmic order in which creatures can live and make their own decisions. . . . Only chance intersections of many actions by many agents can acceptably account for evils. The nontheological determinist is, in spite of himself, committed to chance, for the entire cosmic system, from which, according to him, every event is a necessary consequence, has itself no explanation and is as a whole like an immensely complex throw of the dice, with no intelligible account possible either of the dice or of the dice thrower. Chance must be admitted somewhere, but the place to admit it is everywhere, just as some aspects of order are everywhere. Quantum physics shows in principle how the two can be combined. Given certain limits to randomness (which limits I view as providential) and large numbers of similar happenings, there will then be statistical regularities, and yet each single agent can be making its own little decision. (AC, 86–87)

The aesthetic satisfaction of finding a meaning in life as we live it is obviously no small accomplishment. In this sense, heaven and hell are here now in our persistent blessedness or recurrent resentments, respectively, if such exist. In any event, there is an aesthetic need for finitude (AC, 87).

Hartshorne's opposition to subjective immortality dovetails with his critique of anthropocentrism, a critique that is informed both by his theocentrism and his defense of the rights of the subhuman world:

[A]n animal ought to be mortal. . . . [M]ortality is intrinsically appropriate to the status of being a fragment of reality such as each of us is. We are but parts of the spatial whole of things; we are also but parts of the temporal whole. The spatial fragmentariness and the temporal belong together. To be finite or limited in time is no more an injury or insult than to be finite in space. Immortality would be appropriate only for a being coextensive with the whole of things. If there is a truly cosmic being, there may well be an immortal being; otherwise not. (PD, 81; also see SH)

In this view death simply as such is not absurd, but the lack of death would be. Once again, however, in this view some deaths *are* absurd or ugly or immoral (e.g., as a result of murder) or tragic. Wisdom, Hartshorne thinks, consists in "making the best of what by chance comes our way" (PD, 82). Barry Whitney is likewise instructive in arguing that theodicies based on a God who has unilateral and coercive power are bound to fail because they lead people both to ask the wrong things of God and to expect more from life than is reasonable in a universe pervaded by self-movers.[21]

To ask why an animal's (even a human animal's) life has to end is like asking why Brahms' Fourth Symphony has to end; if it did not end, it would not be a symphony. Hartshorne is like the Greeks in thinking that aesthetic value has a definite form or limit *(peras)*, which is a good thing. If we lived forever, our lives would lack this form or limit and would be what the Greeks called *apeiron,* or limitless chaos. Only a being cosmic in scope could definitely handle limitless time, he thinks, but not even in this case would we find "absolute beauty," as we have seen. By contrast, each moment in *our* lives is a variation on the themes found in our distinct personalities. To think that a definite, fragmentary theme could have infinite variations is defective music theory, to say the least, because infinite variations on a finite or fragmentary theme would eventually produce monotony.

If it is true that life is aesthetically interesting, it is *because* of life-and-death, not in spite of them. The matter is, as Hartshorne sees things, "as simple as that" (PD, 83). Human beings have tried to conceal this fact or to refuse to accept death due to an understandable instinct for self-preservation. But if instinct is directed toward the *concrete* (this threat here and now), such instinct for self-preservation is compatible with the *abstract* acceptance of death simply as such, which is an object of thought. Animals (including human animals) could not survive without an instinct for self-preservation, but human animals are able to place this instinct within a larger, reticulative whole.

It is true that animals (including human animals) struggle to live out a natural lifespan, but this is quite different from trying to live forever. If biological desires have limited scope, then we have no instinct for subjective immortality, no invincible will to live forever.

However, if ethics is given hegemonic power over the aesthetic, then it must be admitted that belief in subjective immortality makes some sense in that there is no ethical reason for death, especially if the good die along with the bad, as they obviously do. But if ethics grows out of aesthetic considerations, as Hartshorne thinks, the matter can be seen in a different light:

> [A]ll life is a search for the golden mean between intolerably monotonous uniformity, on the one hand, and intolerably chaotic or discordant diversity on the other. . . . Monotony is an aesthetic, not an ethical category. . . . Life is diversification aimed at harmony. . . . Death is the ultimate barrier between us and hopeless monotony. (PD, 84)

Recent developments in genetics have led some to hope for a natural lifespan of 170 rather than 70 years. But if these developments come to fruition, they will not change the metaphysical situation: 170 years is not subjective immortality. Even a 170-year-old human being has to learn to appreciate life under certain limits (PD, 85).

As a result of a critique of divine omnipotence, personal experience of evil in the world, and a metaphysical analysis of being in terms of dynamic power, Hartshorne concludes that the details of the world are not arranged by divine fiat. Experiencing subjects must, to some extent at least, arrange themselves. This leads some to wonder whether we are faced with an aesthetic evil that is the opposite of monotony: confusion brought about by unbounded chaos. But there *are* bounds to creaturely freedom and chance, real enough as these are. Scientific probabilities, persistence of character traits, and legitimate expectations regarding the future based on past experience all attest to this. Hartshorne argues:

> If anyone asks for some profound reason why just his friend, or his child, or he himself, should die prematurely, I can only say, this is how the chances came out. Life simply is a gamble, and there is no remedy for that. Does it follow that the universe is meaningless? Not at all. (PD, 87)

Although we are not puppets in God's hands, in Hartshorne's view God nonetheless establishes the basic principles, statistical though they are, that govern both human and subhuman nature: "The cosmic drama is one in which the actors write the details of the dialogue and action. Only certain outlines are divine. Science searches for these outlines" (PD, 87). In this view even God is in some respects finite (e.g., in terms of concrete relations with creatures), but in no way fragmentary, a mere part of the whole of things.

Hartshorne, who died at the age of 103 while I was midway through writing this book, should have the last word:

> The variety, intensity, and harmony of the divine experiences require variety, intensity, and harmony in creaturely experiences. Since no two creatures are precisely alike, deity experiences ever-new contrasts in perceiving the world; moreover, the basic order of things (the divinely imposed limitations upon creaturely freedom) insures that there will always be unity in the variety of creaturely data for the divine participation. To be is to be divinely enjoyed. In this sense do we "live and move and have our being" . . . in [God]. (PD, 89)[22]

Notes

Introduction

1. Donald Sherburne, *A Whiteheadian Aesthetic* (New Haven: Yale University Press, 1961). Also see Sherburne's "Whitehead without God," *Christian Scholar* 40 (1967): 251–72.

2. Sherburne, *A Whiteheadian Aesthetic*, 184.

3. See, e.g., Richard Viladesau, *Theological Aesthetics: God in Imagination, Beauty, and Art* (Oxford: Oxford University Press, 1999), 6–7.

4. Susanne Langer, *Philosophy in a New Key: A Study in the Symbolism of Reason, Rite, and Art* (Cambridge: Harvard University Press, 1942), and *Feeling and Form: A Theory of Art* (New York: Scribner's, 1953).

5. On Hartshorne's treatment of the ontological argument in particular and of other arguments that combine to form one "global argument" (actually to form a metaphysical system), see Donald Viney's excellent book *Charles Hartshorne and the Existence of God* (Albany: State University of New York Press, 1985).

6. See Donald Viney, "Jules Lequyer and the Openness of God," *Faith and Philosophy* 14 (1997): 212–35. Also see Randall Auxier's and Mark Davies' commentary in *Hartshorne and Brightman on God, Process, and Persons: The Correspondence, 1922–1945* (Nashville: Vanderbilt University Press, 2001).

7. See Spinoza, *Ethics* (London: Dent, 1913), Book I, Propositions 29, 32.

8. See, e.g., Thomas McFarland, *Coleridge and the Pantheist Tradition* (Oxford: Clarendon Press, 1969).

9. Erazim Kohák, *The Embers and the Stars: A Philosophical Inquiry into the Moral Sense of Nature* (Chicago: University of Chicago Press, 1985), 124–25.

10. See the recent study by Mark Brimblecombe "Dipolarity and God" (Ph.D. diss., University of Auckland, 2000).

11. Sherburne, *A Whiteheadian Aesthetic*, 3–5, 108, 204–5.

Chapter One

1. See my forthcoming book *A Platonic Philosophy of Religion*. Also see Katharine Gilbert and Helmut Kuhn, *A History of Esthetics* (New York: Macmillan, 1939); and Bernard Bosanquet, *A History of Aesthetic* (1892; reprint, New York: Macmillan, 1904).

2. See, e.g., Francis Kovach, *Philosophy of Beauty* (Norman: University of Oklahoma Press, 1974). Also see Umberto Eco, *Art and Beauty in the Middle Ages,* trans. Hugh Bredin (New Haven: Yale University Press, 1986).

3. See Hans Urs von Balthasar, *The Glory of the Lord: A Theological Aesthetics, ed. Joseph Fessio and John Riches, 7 vols.* (San Francisco: Ignatius Press, 1983–1991); also Louis Roberts, *The Theological Aesthetics of Hans Urs von Balthasar* (Wash., D.C.: Catholic University of America Press, 1987); and Gerardus van der Leeuw, *Sacred and Profane Beauty: The Holy in Art,* trans. David E. Green (New York: Holt, Rinehart, and Winston, 1963).

4. See Jeremy Begbie, *Voicing Creation's Praise: Towards a Theology of the Arts* (Edinburgh: T. and T. Clark, 1991); Frank Burch Brown, *Religious Aesthetics: A Theological Study of Making and Meaning* (Princeton: Princeton University Press, 1989); J. Daniel Brown, *Masks of Mystery: Explorations in Christian Faith and the Arts* (Lanham, Md.: University Press of America, 1997); Garrett Green, *Imagining God: Theology and the Religious Imagination* (San Francisco: Harper and Row, 1989); Richard Harries, *Art and the Beauty of God* (London: Mobray, 1993); F. David Martin, *Art and the Religious Experience: The "Language" of the Sacred* (Lewisburg, Pa.: Bucknell University Press, 1972); John Navone, *Toward a Theology of Beauty* (Collegeville, Minn.: Liturgical Press, 1996); Aidan Nichols, *The Art of God Incarnate: Theology and Image in Christian Tradition* (New York: Paulist Press, 1980); Patrick Sherry, *Spirit and Beauty: An Introduction to Theological Aesthetics* (Oxford: Clarendon Press, 1992); Viladesau, *Theological Aesthetics;* and Nicholas Wolterstorff, *Art in Action: Toward a Christian Aesthetic* (Grand Rapids, Mich.: Eerdmans, 1980).

5. Alfred North Whitehead, *Religion in the Making* (New York: Macmillan, 1926).

6. Viladesau, *Theological Aesthetics,* 70, 242, 275. A thinker who is like Viladesau in mentioning, but who does not treat in detail, Whitehead (as well as Hartshorne, John Cobb, and Schubert Ogden) regarding the connection between aesthetics and thought about God is John Dillenberger; see *A Theology of Artistic Sensibilities* (New York: Crossroad, 1986), 218, 222.

7. See David Ray Griffin, *Reenchantment without Supernaturalism: A Process Philosophy of Religion* (Ithaca: Cornell University Press, 2001), 181–82, 239–40.

8. See, e.g., Alfred North Whitehead, *Process and Reality: An Essay in Cosmology,* corrected ed., ed. David Ray Griffin and Donald Sherburne (New York: Macmillan, 1978), 68. Whitehead cites James; see William James, *Some Problems of Philosophy* (New York: Greenwood, 1968), chap. 10.

9. See Alfred North Whitehead, *Modes of Thought* (New York: Macmillan, 1938), 120. Also see Sherburne, *A Whiteheadian Aesthetic,* 8, 10–22.

10. On the differences between Whitehead and Hartshorne, particularly regarding their views on eternal objects or universals, see especially Lewis Ford, ed., *Two Process Philosophers: Hartshorne's Encounter with Whitehead* (Tallahassee, Fla.: American Academy of Religion, 1973).

11. See Sherburne, *A Whiteheadian Aesthetic,* 24–26, 39, 43–44, 46–47, 49–51.

12. Ibid., 53–54, 56, 59, 73, 80–83.

13. René Wellek and Austin Warren, *Theory of Literature* (New York: Harcourt Brace, 1949), 151.

14. Whitehead, *Process and Reality,* 20. Also see Sherburne, *A Whiteheadian Aesthetic,* 98, 100–102.

15. See Whitehead, *Process and Reality,* 394–96. Also see Paul Kuntz, "Whitehead's Category of Harmony," *Process Studies* 29 (2000), 43–65.

16. See George Santayana, *The Sense of Beauty: Being the Outline of Aesthetic Theory* (1896; reprint, New York: Modern Library, 1955), 54.

17. Sherburne, *A Whiteheadian Aesthetic,* 105–7, 110, 112. Also see Benedetto Croce, *Aesthetic as Science of Expression and General Linguistic,* trans. Douglas Ainslie (London: Macmillan, 1922), and *Brevario di estetica* (Bari: Laterza, 1928).

18. Sherburne, *A Whiteheadian Aesthetic,* 113, 117.

19. Ibid., 118, 121–24. Also see Whitehead, *Process and Reality,* 256–65.

20. Sherburne, *A Whiteheadian Aesthetic,* 128–30.

21. Ibid., 130–32.

22. Ibid., 132–39. Also see John Cobb, "Toward Clarity in Aesthetics," *Philosophy and Phenomenological Research* 18 (1957), 169–89.

23. See Alfred North Whitehead, *Science and the Modern World* (New York: Macmillan, 1925). Also see Eliseo Vivas and Murray Kreiger, *The Problems of Aesthetics: A Book of Readings* (New York: Rinehart, 1953); and Curt Ducasse, *The Philosophy of Art* (New York: Dial, 1929).

24. Sherburne, *A Whiteheadian Aesthetic,* 140–42.

25. Ibid., 143.

26. Ibid., 143–45.

27. See Alfred North Whitehead, *Adventures of Ideas* (New York: Macmillan, 1933), 349.

28. Sherburne, *A Whiteheadian Aesthetic,* 166, 170–71, 178.

29. R.G. Collingwood, *The Principles of Art* (Oxford: Oxford University Press, 1958).

30. Sherburne, *A Whiteheadian Aesthetic,* 179–80, 190.

31. Judith Jones, *Intensity: An Essay in Whiteheadian Ontology* (Nashville: Vanderbilt University Press, 1998), 97, 145, 171, 186, 196.

32. Ibid., 44, 68–69, 178, 209.

33. See William Dean, "Whitehead's Other Aesthetic," *Process Studies* 13 (1983), 104–12.

Chapter Two

1. Hartshorne credits Max Dessoir and Kay Davis Leclerc for refinements to this diagram.

2. Whitehead, *Adventures of Ideas*, 252. Also see Jones, *Intensity.*

3. See John Hospers, "Hartshorne's Aesthetics," in *The Philosophy of Charles Hartshorne,* ed. Lewis Hahn (LaSalle, Ill.: Open Court, 1991), 124, 134, 600–606.

4. See Frederick Ferré, *Living and Value: Toward a Constructive Postmodern Ethics* (Albany: State University of New York Press, 2001).

5. Virgil Aldrich, *Philosophy of Art* (Englewood Cliffs, N.J.: Prentice-Hall, 1963), 90, 99–100, 103. Also see Jacques Maritain, "Beauty and Imitation," in *Art and Scholasticism, With Other Essays* (New York: Scribner's, 1930); and Nick Zangwill, *The Metaphysics of Beauty* (Ithaca: Cornell University Press, 2001). Arthur Danto's 2001 Carus Lectures, titled "The Revolt Against Beauty," have not yet been published.

6. Sherry, *Spirit and Beauty,* 63.

7. See Thomas Munro, *Toward Science in Aesthetics: Selected Essays* (New York: Liberal Arts, 1956), 140, 262. Also see Sherburne, *A Whiteheadian Aesthetic,* 5–6.

8. Whitehead, *Adventures of Ideas*, 257.

9. Sherburne, *A Whiteheadian Aesthetic,* 119, 124–26. Also see Jacob Bronowski, *The Ascent of Man* (Boston: Little, Brown, and Co., 1973), 360, on Hegel.

10. Sherburne, *A Whiteheadian Aesthetic,* 131, 137–38.

11. Ibid., 141, 155–57, 190, 197.

12. Donald Viney, *Charles Hartshorne and the Existence of God,* 119–20.

13. Ibid., 121–24.

14. Ibid., 125–26.

15. Ibid., 127–28.

16. Griffin, *Reenchantment without Supernaturalism,* 185–87.

17. Steven Weinberg, *Dreams of a Final Theory* (1992; reprint, New York: Vintage Books, 1994), 250. Hartshorne specifically mentions Weinberg's appreciation of the beauty of scientific theories in TI, 211–27. (Weinberg was Hartshorne's colleague at the University of Texas.)

18. Griffin, *Reenchantment without Supernaturalism,* 187.

19. Donald Viney, *Charles Hartshorne and the Existence of God,* 122. Regarding aesthetic theory, Hartshorne relies on the following sources, among others: Theodore Greene, *The Arts and the Art of Criticism* (Princeton: Princeton University Press, 1940), especially his theory of beauty as an Aristotelian mean (see RT); Irwin Edman, *Arts and the Man: A Short Introduction to Aesthetics* (New

York: W. W. Norton, 1939), which Hartshorne also uses (see RI); Charles Kay Ogden, I. A. Richards, and James Wood, *The Foundations of Aesthetics* (1922; reprint, New York: International Publishers, 1925); E. F. Carritt, *The Theory of Beauty* (London: Methuen, 1914), and *Philosophies of Beauty from Socrates to Robert Bridges* (Oxford: Oxford University Press, 1931); Louis Grudin, *A Primer of Aesthetics: Logical Approaches to a Philosophy of Art* (New York: Covici, Friede, 1930); Ernst Grosse, *The Beginnings of Art* (New York: Appleton, 1897); DeWitt Parker, *The Principles of Aesthetics* (New York: Silver, Burdett, and Co., 1920), and *The Analysis of Art* (New Haven: Yale University Press, 1926); Roger Fry, *Vision and Design* (New York: Brentano's, 1924); and Albert Chandler, *Beauty and Human Nature: Elements of Psychological Aesthetics* (New York: Appleton, 1934).

Chapter Three

1. See Hospers, "Hartshorne's Aesthetics," 125.
2. See my "Hartshorne and Heidegger," *Process Studies* 25 (1996), 19–33. For a clearer view than either Heidegger's or Husserl's regarding the claim that aesthetic experience is a dimension of experience more fundamental than ethics or knowledge, see William Dean, *Coming To: A Theology of Beauty* (Philadelphia: Westminster, 1972). Also see the instructive work by Timothy Menta, "The Origin and Development of Moral Sensibility" (Ph.D. diss., Boston University, 1996).
3. Henri Bergson, "Laughter," in *Comedy: An Essay on* Comedy *[by] George Meredith.* Laughter *[by] Henri* Bergson (New York: Doubleday, 1956), 90.
4. See my *St. John of the Cross: An Appreciation* (Albany: State University of New York Press, 1992).
5. Clare Palmer, *Environmental Ethics and Process Thinking* (Oxford: Clarendon Press, 1998). Palmer relies heavily on Aldo Leopold, *A Sand County Almanac* (New York: Oxford University Press, 1966).
6. Tom Regan, *The Case for Animal Rights* (Berkeley: University of California Press, 1983), 361.
7. See John Moskop, "Mill and Hartshorne," *Process Studies* 10 (1980), 18–33; and Thomas Nairn, "Hartshorne and Utilitarianism," *Process Studies* 17 (1988), 170–80. Also see, e.g., Hartshorne's SH. Finally, see my *Hartshorne and the Metaphysics of Animal Rights* (Albany: State University of New York Press, 1988).
8. Griffin, *Reenchantment without Supernaturalism,* 285, 287, 301–2, 305.
9. I. A. Richards, "Science and Poetry," in *A Modern Book of Aesthetics,* ed. Melvin Rader (New York: Holt, Rinehart, and Winston, 1960), 270–85.
10. See Edward Bulloch, "'Psychical Distance' as a Factor in Art and an Esthetic Principle," in *Problems in Aesthetics: An Introductory Book of Readings,* ed. Mor-

ris Weitz (New York: Macmillan, 1959), 646–56. Also see José Ortega y Gasset, "The Dehumanization of Art," in Rader, *A Modern Book of Aesthetics*, 411–19.

11. Vernon Lee, "Empathy," in Rader, *A Modern Book of Aesthetics*, 370–82.

12. John Dewey, *Art as Experience* (New York: Minton, Balch, and Co., 1934).

13. Aldrich, *Philosophy of Art*, 10, 12–15, 17–27.

14. See, e.g., James Johnson, "The Unknown Langer," *Journal of Aesthetic Education* 27 (1993), 63–73, who refers to Langer's philosophy as "organistic." Also see Donald Dryden, "Whitehead's Influence on Susanne Langer's Conception of Living Form" *Process Studies* 26 (1997): 62–85; Randall Auxier, "Susanne Langer on Symbols and Analogy: A Case of Misplaced Concreteness?" *Process Studies* 26 (1997): 86–106; and Rolf Lachmann, "From Metaphysics to Art and Back: The Relevance of Susanne K. Langer's Philosophy for Process Metaphysics," *Process Studies* 26 (1997): 107–25. Regarding Langer's own work see *Philosophy in a New Key* and *Feeling and Form*.

15. See Aldrich, *Philosophy of Art*, 70–71, 77. Also see Viladesau, *Theological Aesthetics*, 270–71.

16. See Aldrich, *Philosophy of Art*, 83–84, 91, 98. Also see Wilhelm von Bode, *Die Meister der Holländischen und vlämischen Malerschulen* (Leipzig: Verlag von E. A. Seemann, 1917); Robert Byron and David Rice, *The Birth of Western Painting: A History of Colour, Form, and Iconography, Illustrated from the Paintings of Mistra and Mount Athos, of Giotto and Duccio, and El Greco* (New York: Knopf, 1931); and W. J. Turner, *Orpheus; or, The Music of the Future* (New York: Dutton, 1926).

17. Alfred North Whitehead, *The Function of Reason* (Boston: Beacon Press, 1958).

18. Clive Bell, *Art* (New York: Capricorn, 1958).

19. Sherburne, *A Whiteheadian Aesthetic*, 95, 102, 108–9, 111–12, 116, 124, 146–47.

20. See Stephen Pepper, *Aesthetic Quality: A Contextualistic Theory of Beauty* (New York: Scribner's, 1937), 106–7.

21. Sherburne, *A Whiteheadian Aesthetic*, 148–51, 153–54, 192–96, 198–202.

Chapter Four

1. See Alexander Skutch, "Bird Song and Philosophy," in Hahn, *The Philosophy of Charles Hartshorne*, 65–76; also see 586–89.

2. See Lucio Chiaraviglio, "Hartshorne's Aesthetic Theory of Intelligence," in Hahn, *The Philosophy of Charles Hartshorne*, 77–90; also see 589–98.

3. See W. H. Thorpe, *Bird-Song: The Biology of Vocal Communication and Expression in Birds* (Cambridge: Cambridge University Press, 1961); also see Thorpe's "The Learning of Song Patterns by Birds," *Ibis* 100 (1958), 553–70.

4. See Peter Slater, "Birdsong Repertoires: Their Origins and Use," in *The Origins*

of Music, ed. Nils Wallin, Björn Merker, and Steven Brown (Cambridge: MIT Press, 2000), 49–64.

5. See Thomas Nagel, "What Is It like to Be a Bat?" in his *Mortal Questions* (Cambridge: Cambridge University Press, 1979), 175.

6. Carol Whaling, "What's behind a Song: The Natural Basis of Song Learning in Birds," in Wallin, Merker, and Brown, *The Origins of Music,* 65–76.

7. See Charles Birch, "Chance, Purpose, and Darwinism," in Hahn, *The Philosophy of Charles Hartshorne,* 51–63, 584–86. Also see John Haught, *God after Darwin: A Theology of Evolution* (Boulder, Colo.: Westview, 2000).

8. See Donald Viney, "Jules Lequyer and the Openness of God."

9. See Donald Viney, *The Life and Thought of Charles Hartshorne* (Pittsburg, Kans.: Logos-Sophia Press, 1997), 20, 37. Also see Donald Viney and Rebecca Viney, "For the Beauty of the Earth: A Hartshornian Ecological Aesthetic," *Proceedings of the Institute for Liberal Studies* 4 (1993): 38–44.

10. See my "Hartshorne and Plato," in Hahn, *The Philosophy of Charles Hartshorne,* 465–88, 703–4.

Chapter Five

1. See Hospers, "Hartshorne's Aesthetics," 113–25. Also see Hartshorne's reply on 601–3.

2. Ralph Ellis, *Questioning Consciousness: The Interplay of Imagery, Cognition, and Emotion in the Human Brain* (Philadelphia: John Benjamins, 1995).

3. See Ernst Cassirer, *The Philosophy of Symbolic Forms,* trans. Ralph Manheim (New Haven: Yale University Press, 1957), vol. 3, part 2, chap. 2.

4. See Langer, *Feeling and Form,* 10, 40, 46–47, 57, 71, 73, 76–77, 234, 249, 382, 388–90, and *Mind: An Essay on Human Feeling* (Baltimore: Johns Hopkins University Press, 1967), 1:107–52.

5. See, e.g., Langer, *Philosophy in a New Key,* 66, 68, 77, 82, 88–90, on discursive symbols, and 89–90, 123, 128, 164, 185, 197, 220, 237, on presentational symbols.

6. See Langer, *Mind: An Essay on Human Feeling,* 181.

7. See, e.g., Susanne Langer, *Philosophy in a New Key,* 180, 194. Through hypnosis one can be put into a state in which one is dissociated from one's pain, as when a woman hypnotized during labor later reports that the pains were not in her body but on the table on which she was reclining.

8. See Jean Piaget, *The Child's Conception of the World* (London: Routledge and Kegan Paul, 1929), chap. 7.

9. Natika Newton, *Foundations of Understanding* (Philadelphia: John Benjamins, 1996), 194.

10. See Paul M. Churchland, *Matter and Consciousness* (Cambridge: MIT Press, 1984).

11. Newton, *Foundations of Understanding,* 193–97.
12. See Ellis, *Questioning Consciousness,* especially 6–7, 9, 134, 153, 163. Also see Gerald Edelman, *The Remembered Present: A Biological Theory of Consciousness* (New York: Basic Books, 1989); and Jeffrey Gray, "Brain Systems that Mediate Both Emotion and Cognition," *Cognition and Emotion* 4 (1990): 269–88.
13. See Wayne Viney, "Charles Hartshorne's Philosophy and Psychology of Sensation," in Hahn, *The Philosophy of Charles Hartshorne,* 91–112. Regarding Helmholtz, see Richard Warren and Roslyn Warren, *Helmholtz on Perception, Its Physiology, and Development* (New York: John Wiley, 1968). Finally, see Leonard Troland, *The Principles of Psychophysiology,* 3 vols. (New York: Van Nostrand, 1929–32).
14. Wayne Viney, "Charles Hartshorne's Philosophy and Psychology of Sensation," 106–9.
15. Sherburne, *A Whiteheadian Aesthetic,* xxviii.
16. See Aldrich, *Philosophy of Art,* 7–9, 48–49, 51.
17. Edward Bullough, "The Perceptive Problem in the Aesthetic Appreciation of Single Colors," *British Journal of Psychology* 1 (1908): 443–48; and C. W. Valentine and C. Myers, "A Study of Individual Differences in Attitude toward Tones," *British Journal of Psychology* 7 (1914): 68–72.

Chapter Six

1. See the indices to Hartshorne's many books under "panpsychism" or "psychicalism," etc. On David Ray Griffin's use of "panexperientialism" rather than "panpsychism" or "psychicalism" see his *Reenchantment without Supernaturalism,* 94–128.
2. See, e.g., David Bohm and B. J. Hiley, *The Undivided Universe: An Ontological Interpretation of Quantum Theory* (London: Routledge, 1993).
3. See Cassirer, *The Philosophy of Symbolic Forms,* vol. 2.
4. See Karl Popper, "Of Clouds and Clocks," in *Objective Knowledge: An Evolutionary Approach* (1972; reprint, Oxford: Clarendon Press, 1979).
5. See, e.g., Jerome Frank, "Mind-Body Relationships in Illness and Healing," *Journal of International Academy of Preventive Medicine* 2 (1975): 46–59. Also see William Seager, "Consciousness, Information, and Panpsychism," *Journal of Consciousness Studies* 2 (1995): 272–88.
6. On this important distinction between the categories and the transcendentals in Duns Scotus, see Richard Cross, *Duns Scotus* (Oxford: Oxford University Press, 1999), 39, 167–68.
7. Cf. Robert Neville, *Creativity and God: A Challenge to Process Theology* (New York: Seabury, 1980).
8. Both the early debates between Einstein and Bohr and more recent experiments (both thought experiments and actual experiments) that make the case for the

irreducibly statistical character of quantum theory are summarized in *Quantum Theory and Measurement,* ed. J. A. Wheeler and W. H. Zurek (Princeton: Princeton University Press, 1983). Hartshorne explicitly shows admiration for some of Wheeler's views in ss (120).

9. See Ernst Cassirer, *Substance and Function and Einstein's Theory of Relativity,* trans. William Curtis Swabey and Marie Collins Swabey (Chicago: Dover, 1923), 351–456. Also see George Shields, "Physicalist Panexperientialism and the Mind-Body Problem," *American Journal of Theology and Philosophy* 22 (2001): 133–54; and Edgar Towne, "The New Physics and Hartshorne's Dipolar Theism," *American Journal of Theology and Philosophy* 22 (2001): 114–32.

10. See, e.g., Julius Adler and Wing-Wai Tsi, "Decision-Making in Bacteria," *Science* 184 (June 21, 1974), 1292–94.

11. In addition to the passages from Hartshorne cited above regarding this distinction, see Whitehead, *Adventures of Ideas,* 206. Also see, e.g., Alexander Cappon, *About Wordsworth and Whitehead: A Prelude to Philosophy* (New York: Philosophical Library, 1982). Finally, see Ananda Coomaraswamy, *Christian and Oriental Philosophy of Art* (New York: Dover, 1956).

12. See John Dewey, "Qualitative Thought," in *The Essential Dewey,* ed. Larry Hickman and Thomas Alexander, eds., (Bloomington: Indiana University Press, 1998), vol. 1, 195–205.

13. On Susanne Langer's nuanced view of the projection of feeling in art, see *Mind: An Essay on Human Feeling,* 73–106.

14. On empathy or intuition in aesthetics, see Cassirer, *The Philosophy of Symbolic Forms,* vol. 2, part 2, and vol. 3, part 2; Edith Stein, *On the Problem of Empathy,* trans. Waltraut Stein (The Hague: Martinus Nijhoff, 1964); and Max Scheler, *On Feeling, Knowing, and Valuing: Selected Writings,* ed. Harold J. Breshady (Chicago: University of Chicago Press, 1992).

15. Nagel, "Panpsychism," in *Mortal Questions,* 186, 194.

16. See Wayne Viney, "Charles Hartshorne's Philosophy and Psychology of Sensation," 104. Also see Donald Viney, *The Life and Thought of Charles Hartshorne,* 34.

17. See Stephen Toulmin, *Foresight and Understanding: An Enquiry into the Aims of Science* (New York: Harper, 1961), 78. Also see Stan Godlovitch, "Creativity in Nature," *Journal of Aesthetic Education* 33 (1999), 17–26.

18. L. Bryant Keeling, "Feeling as a Metaphysical Category: Hartshorne from an Analytic View," *Process Studies* 6 (1976), 51–66.

19. Ibid., 61.

20. Aldrich, *Philosophy of Art,* 46.

21. Sherburne, *A Whiteheadian Aesthetic,* 157–59.

22. Ivor Leclerc, "Whitehead and the Dichotomy of Rationalism and Empiricism," in *Whitehead's Metaphysics of Creativity,* ed. Friedrich Rapp and Reiner Wiehl (Albany: State University of New York Press, 1990), 1–20.

23. See the articles in *A Process Theory of Medicine: Interdisciplinary Essays, ed.* Marcus Ford (Lewiston, N.Y.: Edwin Mellen, 1987).

24. See David Ray Griffin, *Parapsychology, Philosophy, and Spirituality: A Postmodern Exploration* (Albany: State University of New York Press, 1997). Also see Leonard Eslick, "Bergson, Whitehead, and Psychical Research," in *Bergson and Modern Thought,* ed. Andrew Papanicolaou and Pete Gunter (London: Harwood Academic, 1987), 353–68.

Chapter Seven

1. See Kovach, *Philosophy of Beauty,* cha4–5. Also see Martin Vaske, *An Introduction to Metaphysics* (New York: McGraw-Hill, 1963), 203–5, 207.

2. Havelock Ellis, "The Psychology of Red," *Popular Science Monthly* 57 (1900): 365–75, and "The Psychology of Yellow," *Popular Science Monthly* 68 (1906), 456–63. Finally, see Myrtis Hodges, *Life Interpreted through Color* (Holyoke, Mass.: Towne, 1926).

3. See, e.g., Michel Cabanac, "Sensory Pleasure," *Quarterly Review of Biology* 54 (1979): 1–25. Also see Jay Shurley, "Profound Experimental Sensory Isolation," *American Journal of Psychiatry* 117 (1960): 539–45.

4. Hans Eysenck, "A Critical and Experimental Study of Colour Preferences," *American Journal of Psychology* 54 (1941): 385–94. Also see I. C. McManus et al., "The Aesthetics of Colour," *Perception* 10 (1981): 651–66; Isolde Martin, "Universal v. Learned Emotional Responses to Colors," *Arts in Psychotherapy* 9 (1982): 245–47; Robert Gerard, "Color and Emotional Arousal," *American Psychologist* 13 (1958): 340; and Faber Birren, *Color Psychology and Color Therapy: A Factual Study of the Influence of Color on Human Life* (1950; reprint, New Hyde Park, N.Y.: University Books, 1961).

5. Wayne Viney, "Charles Hartshorne's Philosophy and Psychology of Sensation," 101.

6. See John Nolte, *The Human Brain: An Introduction to Its Functional Anatomy* (St. Louis: Mosby, 1999), 556–60; and Eric Kandel, James Schwartz, and Thomas M. Jessell, eds., *Principles of Neural Science* (New York: McGraw-Hill, 2000), 988–93.

7. Langer, *Mind: An Essay on Human Feeling,* 3–4, 129, 141–46, 229, 343–44, 412, 418, 425, 439. Also see, e.g., Ralph Wickiser, *An Introduction to Art Education* (New York: World Book Co., 1957), 91–96; and Hazel Harrison, *How to Paint and Draw* (New York: Anness Publishing, 1994), 146–47.

8. See Langer, *Mind: An Essay on Human Feeling,* 181.

9. Regarding the biology and anthropology of color and other sensations, Hartshorne cites several sources: C. A. Strong, *The Origins of Consciousness* (London: Macmillan, 1918); G. H. Parker, *Smell, Taste, and Allied Senses in the Vertebrates* (Philadelphia: Lippincott, 1922); Durant Drake, *Mind and Its Place in Nature*

(New York: Macmillan, 1925); J. P. Nafe, "Psychology of Felt Experience," *American Journal of Psychology* 39 (1927): 367–89; Edward Bullough, "The Apparent Heaviness of Colors," *British Journal of Psychology* 2 (1909): 111 ff.; and C. D. Taylor, "Visual Perception versus Visual plus Kinaesthetic Perception in Judging Colored Weights," *Journal of General Psychology* 4 (1930): 229–46.

10. Langer, *Feeling and Form,* 79, 84–85.

11. Hartshorne himself (PP, 116) cites the Gestalt psychologist Wolfgang Köhler, *Gestalt Psychology* (New York: Liveright, 1929).

12. In addition to the studies cited above in n. 9, Hartshorne cites the following: Amédée Ozenfant, *Foundations of Modern Art,* trans. John Rodker (New York: Brewer, Warren, and Putnam, 1931); F. L. Dimmick, "A Reinterpretation of the Color Pyramid," *Psychological Review* 36 (1929): 83–90; Christine Ladd-Franklin, *Colour and Colour Theories* (New York: Harcourt, Brace, and Co., 1929); Glen Fry, "Modulation of the Optic Nerve-Current as a Basis for Color-Vision," *American Journal of Psychology* 45 (1933): 488 ff.; and James Ward, "Is 'Black' a Sensation?" *British Journal of Psychology* 1 (1908): 407–27.

13. See Ladd-Franklin, *Colour and Colour Theories.*

14. See Hospers, "Hartshorne's Aesthetics," 116–17.

15. On aesthetic contextualism, see Pepper, *Aesthetic Quality.* Also see Lewis Hahn, *A Contextualistic Theory of Perception* (Berkeley: University of California Press, 1942).

16. See Hospers, "Hartshorne's Aesthetics," 122–23.

17. See Whitehead, "Objects and Subjects," in *Adventures of Ideas,* chap. 11.

18. See n. 15.

19. See Hospers, "Hartshorne's Aesthetics," 124.

20. See Langer, *Feeling and Form,* chap. 7–9.

21. See the essays in Wallin, Merker, and Brown, *The Origins of Music.* Also see Mason Matthews, *Primer of Music* (Chicago: John Church, 1894); Max Schoen, ed., *The Effects of Music: A Series of Essays* (New York: Harcourt, Brace, 1927); Percy Scholes, *The Listener's Guide to Music with a Concert-Goer's Glossary* (1919; reprint, Oxford: Oxford University Press, 1925); and Robert Ogden, *Hearing* (1924; reprint, London: Cape, 1925).

22. Hartshorne relies here on Valentine and Myers, "A Study of the Individual Differences in Attitude toward Tones." Also see C. W. Valentine, *The Experimental Psychology of Beauty* (London: Methuen, 1962); and Carroll Pratt, *The Meaning of Music: A Study in Psychological Aesthetics* (New York: McGraw-Hill, 1931).

23. See Gustav Fechner, *Religion of a Scientist,* ed. and trans. Walter Lowrie (New York: Pantheon, 1946). For a critique of Helmholtz compatible with Hartshorne's, see J. P. Nafe, "A Quantitative Theory of Feeling," *Journal of General Psychology* 3 (1929): 29; also H. H. Price, *Perception* (London: Methuen, 1932), 120 ff. On the body as a society of living cells, see C. K. Ogden, *The Meaning of Psychology* (New York: Harper, 1926), 36. On the intersensory continuum, see

Nathan Cohen, "Equivalence of Brightness across Modalities," *American Journal of Psychology* 46 (1934): 117–19.

24. Donald Viney, *Charles Hartshorne and the Existence of God,* 120–21.

25. Ibid.

26. Sherburne, *A Whiteheadian Aesthetic,* xxvi, 115. Also see Robert Woodworth, *Psychology: A Study of Mental Life* (New York: Holt, 1921); Charles Baudouin, *Psychoanalysis and Aesthetics* (New York: Dodd, Mead, 1924); and R. W. Church, *An Essay on Critical Appreciation* (Ithaca: Cornell University Press, 1938).

27. See Troland, *The Principles of Psychophysiology,* 1:131 and 2:352 ff.

28. See David Halliday et al., *Physics* (New York: John Wiley, 1992), 2:42–50.

Chapter Eight

1. Dale Jamieson, "Against Zoos," in *In Defense of Animals,* ed. Peter Singer (Oxford: Blackwell, 1985), 108–17; also see "Zoos Revisited," in *The Philosophy of the Environment,* ed. T. D. J. Chappell (Edinburgh: Edinburgh University Press, 1997), 180–92.

2. See, e.g., D. T. Suzuki, *An Introduction to Zen Buddhism* (New York: Grove, 1964).

3. Regarding Plato see, e.g., *Sophist* 237A. On Henri Bergson and absolute nothingness see his *Creative Evolution,* trans. Arthur Mitchell (Lanham, Md.: University Press of America, 1983). Also see Donald Viney, "The Varieties of Theism and the Openness of God: Charles Hartshorne and Free-Will Theism," *Personalist Forum* 14 (1998): 196–234.

4. On the anthropic principle see Errol Harris, *Cosmos and Anthropos: A Philosophical Interpretation of the Anthropic Cosmological Principle* (Atlantic Highlands, N.J.: Humanities Press, 1991). Also see Barry Whitney, "Divine Persuasion and the Anthropic Argument," *Personalist Forum* 14 (1998): 141–69. Finally, see my "Being *Is* Power," *American Journal of Theology and Philosophy* 16 (1995): 299–314.

5. See Barry Whitney, *What Are They Saying about God and Evil?* (New York: Paulist, 1989). On Hartshorne's global argument see Donald Viney, *Charles Hartshorne and the Existence of God.*

6. See my "Pacifism and Hartshorne's Dipolar Theism," *Encounter* 48 (1987): 337–50, and *Christian Pacifism* (Philadelphia: Temple University Press, 1991). Also see Mark Davies, "The Pacifism Debate in the Correspondence," in HB (121–31).

7. See John Moskop's fine study *Divine Omniscience and Human Freedom: Thomas Aquinas and Charles Hartshorne* (Macon, Ga.: Mercer University Press, 1984) on the relationship between divine omniscience and organic inclusion.

8. See Eugene Peters, *Hartshorne and Neoclassical Metaphysics: An Interpretation* (Lincoln: University of Nebraska Press, 1970), especially chap. 6–7.

9. See note 5 above.

10. See Aldrich, *Philosophy of Art,* 56, 103. Also see Viladesau, *Theological Aesthetics,* 30–31. Finally, see Hans Urs von Balthasar, *Theo-Drama,* 5 vols., trans. Graham Harrison (San Francisco: Ignatius Press, 1988–98).

11. See Joseph Bracken and Marjorie Suchocki, eds., *Trinity in Process: A Relational Theology of God* (New York: Continuum, 1997).

12. See Whitehead, *Process and Reality,* 342.

13. See Alfred North Whitehead, *Science and the Modern World,* 276.

14. See my *St. John of the Cross* on the relationship between mystical experience and problems with classical theism.

15. See Frank Lloyd Wright, *The Future of Architecture* (New York: Horizon Press, 1953). Also see Paul Tillich, *On Art and Architecture,* ed. John Dillenberger and Jane Dillenberger, trans. Robert P. Scharlemann (New York: Crossroad, 1989).

16. See Edgar Brightman, *The Problem of God* (New York: Abington, 1930), for a related view that influenced Hartshorne.

17. See Alfred North Whitehead, *The Concept of Nature: Tarner Lectures in Trinity College* (Cambridge: Cambridge University Press, 1920), 163.

18. See Aldrich, *Philosophy of Art,* 99–100.

19. Ibid., 45–46, 72, regarding reluctance to bring metaphysical issues to bear on aesthetics. Also see J. W. N. Sullivan, *Beethoven: His Spiritual Development* (New York: Knopf, 1927).

20. See John Richmond, "Reconsidering Aesthetics and Religious Experience: A Companion View," *Journal of Aesthetic Education* 33 (1999): 29–47. Richmond relies on Bennett Reimer, *A Philosophy of Music Education* (Englewood Cliffs, N.J.: Prentice-Hall, 1970). Also see Nicholas Wolterstorff, *Works and Worlds of Art* (Oxford: Clarendon Press, 1980).

21. See Viladesau, *Theological Aesthetics,* 95, and *Theology and the Arts: Encountering God through Music, Art, and Rhetoric* (New York: Paulist Press, 2000), 11–12, 14, 154, 158, 167. He relies on Whitehead, *Religion in the Making,* 21–23, 33. See also James Waddell and F. W. Dillistone, eds., *Art and Religion as Communication* (Atlanta: John Knox, 1974); M. A. Couturier, *Sacred Art,* trans. Granger Ryan (Austin: University of Texas Press, 1989); and Jean-Luc Marion, *God without Being: Hors-Texte,* trans. Thomas A. Carlson (Chicago: University of Chicago Press, 1991).

22. See my *St. John of the Cross,* chap. 5, on language. Also see William Elton, ed., *Aesthetics and Language* (New York: Philosophical Library, 1954); Edward Caird, *Essays on Literature and Philosophy* (New York: Macmillan, 1892); and A. Maude Rayden, *Beauty in Religion* (New York: Putnam's, 1923).

23. See Schubert Ogden, "The Experience of God: Critical Reflections on Hartshorne's Theory of Analogy," in EA (16–37).

24. William Alston, *Perceiving God: The Epistemology of Religious Experience* (Ithaca: Cornell University Press, 1991).

25. Sherburne, *A Whiteheadian Aesthetic,* 160, 162–64, 172–73, 175–76, 178, 182–83.

Chapter Nine

1.   See my *Analytic Theism, Hartshorne, and the Concept of God* (Albany: State University of New York Press, 1996). On inde-sponses see Richard Creel, *Divine Impassibility: An Essay in Philosophical Theology* (Cambridge: Cambridge University Press, 1986).

2.   See an excellent study by Thomas McFarland, *Romanticism and the Forms of Ruin: Wordsworth, Coleridge, and Modalities of Fragmentation* (Princeton: Princeton University Press, 1981). I have relied heavily on McFarland regarding the idea of a flickering candle of hope held against mechanistic materialism.

3.   See Henry Simoni-Wastila, "Is Divine Relativity Possible: Charles Hartshorne on God's Sympathy with the World," *Process Studies* 28 (1999): 98–116; and Donald Viney's response to this and other articles by Simoni-Wastila in "What Is Wrong with the Mirror Image? A Brief Reply to Simoni-Wastila on the Problem of Radical Particularity," *Process Studies* 29 (2000): 365–67, 390–91.

4.   See Donald Viney, *Charles Hartshorne and the Existence of God.*

5.   See my "Taking the World Soul Seriously," *Modern Schoolman* 69 (1991): 33–57; "An Anticipation of Hartshorne: Plotinus on *Daktylos* and the World Soul," *Heythrop Journal* 29 (1988) 462–67; and my forthcoming *A Platonic Philosophy of Religion.*

6.   See my "Hartshorne and Plato," in Hahn, *The Philosophy of Charles Hartshorne.*

7.   See David Ray Griffin's classic study *God, Power, and Evil: A Process Theodicy* (Philadelphia: Westminster, 1976); and *Evil Revisited: Responses and Reconsiderations* (Albany: State University of New York Press, 1991).

8.   Hartshorne thinks that Henri Bergson's two worst books were *Introduction to Metaphysics* (Indianapolis: Bobbs-Merrill, 1955) and *Time and Free Will,* trans. F. L. Pogson (1910; reprint, New York: Harper, 1960), where the denigration of abstract logical thought, the criticism of intersensory continuum, and flirtation with dualism can all be found. However, Hartshorne shows admiration for Bergson's *Comedy,* even if this work does not capture all of the incongruities that make up comedy, and for Bergson's essay on dreaming (zF, chap. 11).

9.   See Sherburne, *A Whiteheadian Aesthetic,* 52, 181.

10. See an excellent study by Andrew Bjelland, "Durational Succession and Proto-Mental Agency," in *Bergson and Modern Thought: Towards a Unified Science,* ed. Andrew Papanicolaou and Pete Gunter, 19–28.

11. See Charles Darwin, *The Origin of Species* (Chicago: Encyclopaedia Britannica, 1952), 243.

12. See J. N. Findlay's famous "Can God's Existence be Disproved?" in *New Essays*

in Philosophical Theology, ed. Anthony Flew and Alasdair MacIntyre (London: SCM Press, 1955), 47–56; Norman Malcolm, "Anselm's Ontological Arguments," *Philosophical Review* 69 (1960): 41–62; and Alvin Plantinga, ed. *The Ontological Argument, From St. Anselm to Contemporary Philosophers* (Garden City, N.Y.: Anchor Books, 1965).

13. See Ilya Prigogine, *From Being to Becoming: Time and Complexity in the Physical Sciences* (San Francisco: Freeman, 1980); and Henry Stapp, "Quantum Mechanics, Local Causality, and Process Philosophy," *Process Studies* 7 (1977): 173–82.

14. Sherburne, *A Whiteheadian Aesthetic,* 185–91. Also see John Hospers, *Meaning and Truth in the Arts* (Chapel Hill: University of North Carolina Press, 1947).

Chapter Ten

1. On this and other matters surrounding the levels of religious discourse in Hartshorne, see Schubert Ogden, "The Experience of God: Critical Reflections on Hartshorne's Theory of Analogy."

2. See Evander Bradley McGilvary, "Space-Time, Location, and Prehension," in *The Philosophy of Alfred North Whitehead,* ed. P. A. Schilpp (LaSalle, Ill.: Open Court, 1941), 231.

3. See William Myers, "Hartshorne, Whitehead, and the Religious Availability of God."

4. Again, see Schubert Ogden, "The Experience of God: Critical Reflections on Hartshorne's Theory of Analogy."

5. See Mohammed Valady, Introduction to ZF, xxvi.

6. See Nelson Pike, ed., *God and Evil: Readings on the Theological Problem of Evil* (Englewood Cliffs, N.J.: Prentice-Hall, 1964),1–5, 85–102.

7. See William James, "The Dilemma of Determinism," in *The Will to Believe and Other Essays in Popular Philosophy,* ed. Frederick H. Burkhardt, Fredson Bowers, and Ignas Skrupskelis (Cambridge: Harvard University Press, 1979),114–40.

8. Wallace Stevens, "Sunday Morning," in *The Collected Poems of Wallace Stevens* (1954; reprint, New York: Knopf, 1978).

9. Darwin, *The Origin of Species,* 243.

10. See Whitehead, *Process and Reality,*29, 60, 81, 128, 146–47, 210, 340.

11. See John Keats, "Ode on a Grecian Urn," in *Fine Frenzy: Enduring Themes in Poetry,* ed. Robert Baylor and Brenda Stokes (New York: McGraw-Hill, 1972).

12. See my *Rawls and Religion: The Case for Political Liberalism* (Albany: State University of New York Press, 2001).

13. See G. E. H. Palmer et al., trans. and eds., *The Philokalia* (London: Faber and Faber, 1979–1995).

14. Marjorie Hewitt Suchocki, "Charles Hartshorne and Subjective Immortality," *Process Studies* 21 (1992): 118–22; quotation on p. 118. Also see Norris Clarke, *The Philosophical Approach to God: A Contemporary Neo-Thomist Perspective* (Win-

ston-Salem: Wake Forest University Press, 1979), and "Death and the Meaning of Life in the Christian Tradition," in *Sixth International Conference on Unity of Science* (New York: International Cultural Foundation, 1977), 493–504.

15. See William Wordsworth, "The Tables Turned," in *Poetical Works* (Oxford: Oxford University Press, 1981).

16. Randall Auxier, "Why One Hundred Years Is Forever: Hartshorne's Theory of Immortality," *Personalist Forum* 14 (1998): 109–32; quotation on p. 117.

17. Barry Whitney and J. Norman King are like Suchocki and Auxier at least in that they deal with the issue of subjective immortality more from the perspective of ethics (justice) than from the perspective of aesthetics. See their comparative essay, "Rahner and Hartshorne on Death and Eternal Life," *Horizons* 15 (1988): 239–61.

18. On the inseparability of the mental and physical poles, see Whitehead, *Process and Reality,* 108. Also see Griffin, *Reenchantment without Supernaturalism,* pp. 230–46, where the author argues that the need for a "physical pole" is not the same as the need for a physical body. According to Griffin, objective immortality or contributionism is necessary for a satisfactory solution to the problem of death, but not sufficient. A sufficient solution, he thinks, involves the idea that the physical prehensions required by each occasion of the soul's existence need not require a brain. However, it is hard for me to see how this involves only a "numerical distinction" between soul and body and not an ontological dualism as well. In any event, Griffin, Auxier, Suchocki, and Donald Viney are to be thanked for pointing out that although Hartshorne himself did not believe in subjective immortality, and although Whitehead did not affirm it, there are other options regarding this issue that are open to process thinkers. I have a lingering doubt, however, that I share with David Pailin: if subjective immortality is an emergent property, as Griffin alleges, then why not say the same regarding experience, thereby destroying the basis for panexperientialism?

19. William Wordsworth, "Ode: Intimations of Immortality from Recollections of Early Childhood," in *Poetical Works.* It is not clear that Wordsworth's view of immortality is necessarily subjective immortality, as I hope to show in a future essay.

20. See John Hick, *Death and Eternal Life* (New York: Harper and Row, 1976), 217–21. Also see LP, 258, where Hartshorne says that if "I can inspire multitudes who will never see me in the flesh, then the incense I send up to God will continue to rise anew for many generations."

21. See Barry Whitney, "An Aesthetic Solution to the Problem of Evil," *International Journal for Philosophy of Religion* 35 (1994), 21–37.

22. On St. Paul, see Acts 17:28 and 1 Corinthians 12:12. As Brian Henning likes to put the point, if contributionism is to make sense, then the values we contribute to God must include the intrinsic values of our own experiences as well as the values that we have contributed to other creatures' experiences.

Bibliography

Works by Charles Hartshorne (in chronological order)

"An Outline and Defense of the Argument for the Unity of Being in the Absolute or Divine Good." Ph.D. diss., Harvard University, 1923.

"Sense Quality and Feeling Tone." *Proceedings of the Seventh International Congress of Philosophy,* ed. Gilbert Ryle (1931): 168–72.

"The Intelligibility of Sensations." *Monist* 44 (1934): 161–85.

Philosophy and Psychology of Sensation. Chicago: University of Chicago Press, 1934.

Beyond Humanism: Essays in the Philosophy of Nature. Lincoln: University of Nebraska Press, 1968. Originally published in 1937.

Review of *Arts and the Man,* by Irwin Edman. *Ethics* 50 (1940): 369–70.

Review of *The Arts and the Art of Criticism,* by Theodore Greene. *Ethics* 51 (1940): 116–17.

Man's Vision of God. New York: Harper and Brothers, 1941.

The Divine Relativity. New Haven: Yale University Press, 1948.

"Time, Death, and Eternal Life." *Journal of Religion* 32 (1952): 97–107.

Philosophers Speak of God. Ed. Charles Hartshorne and William L. Reese. Chicago: University of Chicago Press, 1953.

Reality as Social Process: Studies in Metaphysics and Religion. Boston: Beacon Press, 1953.

The Logic of Perfection , and Other Essays in Neoclassical Metaphysics. LaSalle, Ill. .: Open Court, 1962.

"Is God's Existence a State of Affairs?" In *Faith and the Philosophers,* ed. John Hick, 6–33. New York: St. Martin's, 1964.

Anselm's Discovery. LaSalle, Ill.: Open Court, 1965.

"The Social Theory of Feelings." *Southern Journal of Philosophy* 3 (1965): 87–93.

A Natural Theology for Our Time. LaSalle, Ill.: Open Court, 1967.

"Psychology and the Unity of Knowledge." *Southern Journal of Philosophy* 5 (1967): 81–90.

"The Aesthetics of Birdsong." *Journal of Aesthetics and Art Criticism* 26 (1968): 311–15.

Creative Synthesis and Philosophic Method. LaSalle, Ill.: Open Court, 1970.

"Why Study Birds?" *Virginia Quarterly Review* 46 (1970): 133–40.

Whitehead's Philosophy: Selected Essays, 1935–1970. Lincoln: University of Nebraska Press, 1972.

Born to Sing: An Interpretation and World Survey of Bird Song. Bloomington: Indiana University Press, 1973.

"The Environmental Results of Technology." In *Philosophy and Environmental Crisis,* ed. William Blackstone, 69–78. Athens: University of Georgia Press, 1974.

"Why Psychicalism? Comments on Keeling's and Shepherd's Criticisms." *Process Studies* 6 (1976): 67–72.

"The Acceptance of Death." In *Philosophical Aspects of Thanatology,* ed. Florence Hetzler and Austin Kutscher, 1:83–87. New York: Arno, 1978.

"A Philosophy of Death." In *Philosophical Aspects of Thanatology,* ed. Florence Hetzler and Austin Kutscher, 2:81–89. New York: Arno, 1978.

"The Rights of the Subhuman World." *Environmental Ethics* 1 (1979): 49–60.

"In Defense of Wordsworth's View of Nature." *Philosophy and Literature* 4 (1980): 80–91.

"Science as the Search for the Hidden Beauty of the World." In *The Aesthetic Dimension of Science : 1980 Nobel Conference,* ed. Deane Curtin, 85–106. New York: Philosophical Library, 1982.

Insights and Oversights of Great Thinkers: An Evaluation of Western Philosophy. Albany: State University of New York Press, 1983.

Creativity in American Philosophy. Albany: State University of New York Press, 1984.

Existence and Actuality: Conversations with Charles Hartshorne. Ed. John B. Cobb Jr. and Franklin I. Gamwell. Chicago: University of Chicago Press, 1984.

Omnipotence and Other Theological Mistakes. Albany: State University of New York Press, 1984.

"An Anglo-American Phenomenology: Method and Some Results." In *Pragmatism Considers Phenomenology,* ed. Robert Corrington, Carl Hausman, and Thomas M. Seebohm, 59–71. Washington, D.C.: University Press of America, 1987.

"Bergson's Aesthetic Creationism Compared to Whitehead's." In *Bergson and Modern Thought: Towards a Unified Science,* ed. Andrew C. Papanicolaou and Pete A. Y. Gunter, 369–82. London: Harwood Academic, 1987.

"Mind and Body: A Special Case of Mind and Mind." In *A Process Theory of Medicine: Interdisciplinary Essays,* ed. Marcus Ford, 77–88. Lewiston, N.Y.: Edwin Mellen Press, 1987.

"Some Theological Mistakes and Their Effects on Modern Literature." *Journal of Speculative Philosophy* 1 (1987): 55–72.

Wisdom as Moderation: A Philosophy of the Middle Way. Albany: State University of New York Press, 1987.

The Darkness and the Light: A Philosopher Reflects upon His Fortunate Career and Those Who Made It Possible. Albany: State University of New York Press, 1990.

The Philosophy of Charles Hartshorne. Ed. Lewis Hahn. LaSalle, Ill.: Open Court, 1991.

"The Aesthetic Dimensions of Religious Experience." In *Logic, God, and Metaphysics,* ed. James Franklin Harris, 9–18. Boston: Kluwer, 1992.

"Reminiscences." *Journal of Aesthetics and Art Criticism* 51 (1993): 286–89.

"Three Important Scientists on Mind, Matter, and the Metaphysics of Religion." *Journal of Speculative Philosophy* 8 (1994): 211–27.

The Zero Fallacy and Other Essays in Neoclassical Philosophy. Ed. Mohammed Valady. LaSalle, Ill.: Open Court, 1997.

"Charles Hartshorne's Letters to a Young Philosopher: 1979–1995." *Logos-Sophia* 11 (2001): 1–66.

"Darwin and Some Philosophers." *Process Studies* 30 (2001): 276–88.

"God as Composer-Director, Enjoyer, and, in a Sense, Player of the Cosmic Drama." *Process Studies* 30 (2001): 242–60.

Hartshorne and Brightman on God, Process, and Persons: The Correspondence, 1922–1945. Ed. Randall E. Auxier and Mark Y. A. Davies. Nashville: Vanderbilt University Press, 2001.

"A Psychologist's Philosophy Evaluated after Fifty Years: Troland's Psychical Monism." *Process Studies* 30 (2001): 237–41.

"Thomas Aquinas and Three Poets Who Do Not Agree with Him." *Process Studies* 30 (2001): 261–75.

Secondary Sources

Adler, Julius, and Wing-Wai Tsi. "Decision-Making in Bacteria." *Science* 184 (June 21, 1974): 1292–94.

Aldrich, Virgil C. *Philosophy of Art.* Englewood Cliffs, N.J.: Prentice-Hall, 1963.

Alston, William P. *Perceiving God: The Epistemology of Religious Experience.* Ithaca: Cornell University Press, 1991.

Anselm, St. *Basic Writings: Proslogium; Monologium; Gaunilon's in Behalf of the Fool; Cur Deus Homo.* Trans. S. W. Deane. 2d ed. LaSalle, Ill.: Open Court, 1962.

Auxier, Randall E. "Susanne Langer on Symbols and Analogy: A Case of Misplaced Concreteness?" *Process Studies* 26 (1997): 86–106.

———. "Why One Hundred Years Is Forever: Hartshorne's Theory of Immortality." *Personalist Forum* 14 (1998): 109–32.

Auxier, Randall E., and Mark Y. A. Davies, eds. *Hartshorne and Brightman on God, Process, and Persons: The Correspondence, 1922–1945.* Nashville: Vanderbilt University Press, 2001.

Balthasar, Hans Urs von. *The Glory of the Lord: A Theological Aesthetics.* 7 vols. Ed. Joseph Fessio and John Riches. San Francisco: Ignatius Press, 1983–1991.

———. *Theo-Drama.* 5 vols. Trans. Graham Harrison. San Francisco: Ignatius Press, 1988–1998.

Baudouin, Charles. *Psychoanalysis and Aesthetics.* Trans. Eden Paul and Cedar Paul. New York: Dodd, Mead, 1924.

Baylor, Robert, and Brenda Stokes, comps. *Fine Frenzy: Enduring Themes in Poetry.* New York: McGraw-Hill, 1972.

Begbie, Jeremy. *Voicing Creation's Praise: Towards a Theology of the Arts.* Edinburgh: T. and T. Clark, 1991.

Bell, Clive. *Art.* New York: Capricorn, 1958.

Bergson, Henri. *Time and Free Will.* Trans. F. L. Pogson. 1910. Reprint, New York: Harper, 1960.

————. *Introduction to Metaphysics.* Indianapolis: Bobbs-Merrill, 1955.

————. "Laughter." In *Comedy: An Essay on Comedy* [by] George Meredith. *Laughter* [by] Henri Bergson. *Introduction and Appendix: The Meanings of Comedy,* by Wylie Sypher. 1st ed. Ed. Wylie Sypher. Garden City, N.Y.: Doubleday, 1956.

————. *Creative Evolution.* Trans. Arthur Mitchell. Lanham, Md.: University Press of America, 1984.

Birch, Charles. "Chance, Purpose, and Darwinism." In *The Philosophy of Charles Hartshorne,* ed. Lewis Hahn, 51–63, 584–86. LaSalle, Ill.: Open Court, 1991.

Birren, Faber. *Color Psychology and Color Therapy: A Factual Study of the Influence of Color on Human Life.* 1950. Reprint, New Hyde Park, New York: University Books, 1961.

Bjelland, Andrew. "Durational Succession and Proto-Mental Agency." In *Bergson and Modern Thought: Towards a Unified Science,* ed. Andrew C. Papanicolaou and Pete A. Y. Gunter, 19–28. London: Harwood Academic, 1987.

Bode, Wilhelm von. *Die Meister der Holländischen und vlämischen Malerschulen.* Leipzig: Verlag von E. A. Seemann, 1917.

Bohm, David, and B. J. Hiley. *The Undivided Universe: An Ontological Interpretation of Quantum Theory.* London: Routledge, 1993.

Bosanquet, Bernard. *A History of Aesthetic.* 1892. Reprint, New York: Macmillan, 1904.

Bracken, Joseph A., and Marjorie Hewitt Suchocki, eds. *Trinity in Process: A Relational Theology of God.* New York: Continuum, 1997.

Brightman, Edgar Sheffield. *The Problem of God.* New York: Abington, 1930.

Brimblecombe, Mark. "Dipolarity and God." Ph.D. diss., University of Auckland, 2000.

Bronowski, Jacob. *The Ascent of Man.* 1973. Boston: Little, Brown, and Co., 1974.

Brown, Frank Burch. *Religious Aesthetics: A Theological Study of Making and Meaning.* Princeton: Princeton University Press, 1989.

————. *Good Taste, Bad Taste, and Christian Taste: Aesthetics in Religious Life.* Oxford: Oxford University Press, 2000.

Brown, J. Daniel. *Masks of Mystery: Explorations in Christian Faith and the Arts.* Lanham, Md.: University Press of America, 1997.

Bulloch, Edward. "'Psychical Distance' as a Factor in Art and an Esthetic Principle." In *Problems in Aesthetics: An Introductory Book of Readings,* ed. Morris Weitz, 646–56. New York: Macmillan, 1959.

Bullough, Edward. "The Perceptive Problem in the Aesthetic Appreciation of Single Colors." *British Journal of Psychology* 1 (1908): 443–48.

———. "The Apparent Heaviness of Colors." *British Journal of Psychology* 2 (1909): 111–15.

Byron, Robert, and David Talbot Rice. *The Birth of Western Painting: A History of Colour, Form, and Iconography, Illustrated from the Paintings of Mistra and Mount Athos, of Giotto and Duccio, and El Greco.* New York: Knopf, 1931.

Cabanac, Michel. "Sensory Pleasure." *Quarterly Review of Biology* 54 (1979): 1–25.

Caird, Edward. *Essays on Literature and Philosophy.* New York: Macmillan, 1892.

Cappon, Alexander P. *About Wordsworth and Whitehead: A Prelude to Philosophy.* New York: Philosophical Library, 1982.

Carritt, E. F. *The Theory of Beauty.* London: Methuen, 1914.

———, ed. *Philosophies of Beauty from Socrates to Robert Bridges.* Oxford: Oxford University Press, 1931.

Cassirer, Ernst. *Substance and Function and Einstein's Theory of Relativity.* Trans. William Curtis Swabey and Marie Collins Swabey. Chicago: Dover, 1923.

———. *The Philosophy of Symbolic Forms.* 4 vols. Trans. Ralph Manheim. New Haven: Yale University Press, 1953–1996.

Chandler, Albert R. *Beauty and Human Nature: Elements of Psychological Aesthetics.* New York: Appleton, 1934.

Chiaraviglio, Lucio. "Hartshorne's Aesthetic Theory of Intelligence." In *The Philosophy of Charles Hartshorne,* ed. Lewis Hahn, 77–90, 589–98. LaSalle, Ill.: Open Court, 1991.

Church, R. W. *An Essay on Critical Appreciation.* Ithaca: Cornell University Press, 1938.

Churchland, Paul M. *Matter and Consciousness: A Contemporary Introduction to the Philosophy of Mind.* Cambridge: MIT Press, 1984.

Clarke, Norris. "Death and the Meaning of Life in the Christian Tradition." In *Sixth International Conference on Unity of Science,* 493–504. New York: International Cultural Foundation, 1977.

———. *The Philosophical Approach to God: A Contemporary Neo-Thomist Perspective.* Winston-Salem: Wake Forest University Press, 1979.

Cobb, John. "Toward Clarity in Aesthetics." *Philosophy and Phenomenological Research* 18 (1957): 169–89.

Cohen, Nathan. "Equivalence of Brightness across Modalities." *American Journal of Psychology* 46 (1934): 117–19.

Collingwood, R. G. *The Principles of Art.* Oxford: Oxford University Press, 1958.

Coomaraswamy, Ananda. *Christian and Oriental Philosophy of Art.* New York: Dover, 1956.

Couturier, M. A. *Sacred Art.* Trans. Granger Ryan. Austin: University of Texas Press, 1989.

Creel, Richard E. *Divine Impassibility: An Essay in Philosophical Theology.* Cambridge: Cambridge University Press, 1986.

Croce, Benedetto. *Brevario di estetica.* Bari: Laterza, 1928.

———. *Aesthetic as Science of Expression and General Linguistic.* Trans. Douglas Ainslie. London: Macmillan, 1922.

Cross, Richard. *Duns Scotus.* Oxford: Oxford University Press, 1999.

Danto, Arthur. *The Abuse of Beauty.* LaSalle, Ill.: Open Court, 2003.

Darwin, Charles. *The Origin of Species.* Chicago: Encyclopaedia Britannica, 1952.

Davies, Mark. "The Pacifism Debate in the Correspondence." In *Hartshorne and Brightman on God, Process, and Persons: The Correspondence, 1922–1945.* Ed. Randall E. Auxier and Mark Y. A. Davies. Nashville: Vanderbilt University Press, 2001.

Dean, William. *Coming To: A Theology of Beauty.* Philadelphia: Westminster, 1972.

———. "Whitehead's Other Aesthetic." *Process Studies* 13 (1983): 104–12.

Dewey, John. *Art as Experience.* New York: Minton, Balch, and Co., 1934.

———. *The Essential Dewey.* Ed. Larry A. Hickman and Thomas M. Alexander. Bloomington: Indiana University Press, 1998.

Dillenberger, John. *A Theology of Artistic Sensibilities: The Visual Arts and the Church.* New York: Crossroad, 1986.

Dimmick, F. L. "A Reinterpretation of the Color Pyramid." *Psychological Review* 36 (1929): 83–90.

Dombrowski, Daniel A. "Pacifism and Hartshorne's Dipolar Theism." *Encounter* 48 (1987): 337–50.

———. "An Anticipation of Hartshorne: Plotinus on *Daktylos* and the World Soul." *Heythrop Journal* 29 (1988): 462–67.

———. *Hartshorne and the Metaphysics of Animal Rights.* Albany: State University of New York Press, 1988.

———. *Christian Pacifism.* Philadelphia: Temple University Press, 1991.

———. "Hartshorne and Plato." In *The Philosophy of Charles Hartshorne,* ed. Lewis Hahn, 465–88, 703–4. LaSalle, Ill.: Open Court, 1991.

———. "Taking the World Soul Seriously." *Modern Schoolman* 69 (1991): 33–57.

———. *St. John of the Cross: An Appreciation.* Albany: State University of New York Press, 1992.

———. "Being *Is* Power." *American Journal of Theology and Philosophy* 16 (1995): 299–314.

———. *Analytic Theism, Hartshorne, and the Concept of God.* Albany: State University of New York Press, 1996.

———. "Hartshorne and Heidegger." *Process Studies* 25 (1996): 19–33.

———. *Kazantzakis and God.* Albany: State University of New York Press, 1997.

———. *Rawls and Religion: The Case for Political Liberalism.* Albany: State University of New York Press, 2001.

———. *A Platonic Philosophy of Religion.* Forthcoming.

Drake, Durant. *Mind and Its Place in Nature.* New York: Macmillan, 1925.

Dryden, Donald. "Whitehead's Influence on Susanne Langer's Conception of Living Form." *Process Studies* 26 (1997): 62–85.

Ducasse, Curt. *The Philosophy of Art.* New York: Dial, 1929.

Eco, Umberto. *Art and Beauty in the Middle Ages.* Trans. Hugh Bredin. New Haven: Yale University Press, 1986.

Edelman, Gerald M. *The Remembered Present: A Biological Theory of Consciousness.* New York: Basic Books, 1989.

Edman, Irwin. *Arts and the Man: A Short Introduction to Aesthetics.* New York: W. W. Norton, 1939.

Ellis, Havelock. "The Psychology of Red." *Popular Science Monthly* 57 (1900): 365–75.

———. "The Psychology of Yellow." *Popular Science Monthly* 68 (1906): 456–63.

Ellis, Ralph. *Questioning Consciousness: The Interplay of Imagery, Cognition, and Emotion in the Human Brain.* Philadelphia: John Benjamins, 1995.

Elton, William R., ed. *Aesthetics and Language.* New York: Philosophical Library, 1954.

Eslick, Leonard. "Bergson, Whitehead, and Psychical Research." In *Bergson and Modern Thought: Towards a Unified Science,* ed. Andrew C. Papanicolaou and Pete A. Y. Gunter, 353–68. London: Harwood Academic, 1987.

Eysenck, Hans. "A Critical and Experimental Study of Colour Preferences." *American Journal of Psychology* 54 (1941): 385–94.

Fechner, Gustav. *Religion of a Scientist.* Ed. and trans. Walter Lowrie. New York: Pantheon, 1946.

Ferré, Frederick. *Living and Value: Toward a Constructive Postmodern Ethics.* Albany: State University of New York Press, 2001.

Findlay, J. N. "Can God's Existence be Disproved?" In *New Essays in Philosophical Theology,* ed. Anthony Flew and Alasdair MacIntyre, 47–56. London: SCM Press, 1955.

Ford, Lewis, ed. *Two Process Philosophers: Hartshorne's Encounter with Whitehead.* Tallahassee, Fla.: American Academy of Religion, 1973.

Ford, Marcus P., ed. *A Process Theory of Medicine: Interdisciplinary Essays.* Lewiston, New York: Edwin Mellen, 1987.

Frank, Jerome. "Mind-Body Relationships in Illness and Healing." *Journal of International Academy of Preventive Medicine* 2 (1975): 46–59.

Fry, Glen. "Modulation of the Optic Nerve-Current as a Basis for Color-Vision." *American Journal of Psychology* 45 (1933): 488–92.

Fry, Roger. *Vision and Design.* New York: Brentano's, 1924.

Gerard, Robert. "Color and Emotional Arousal." *American Psychologist* 13 (1958): 340.

Gilbert, Katharine Everett, and Helmut Kuhn. *A History of Esthetics.* New York: Macmillan, 1939.

Godlovitch, Stan. "Creativity in Nature." *Journal of Aesthetic Education* 33 (1999): 17–26.

Gray, Jeffrey. "Brain Systems that Mediate Both Emotion and Cognition." *Cognition and Emotion* 4 (1990): 269–88.

Green, Garrett. *Imagining God: Theology and the Religious Imagination.* San Francisco: Harper and Row, 1989.

Greene, Theodore Meyer. *The Arts and the Art of Criticism.* Princeton: Princeton University Press, 1940.

Griffin, David Ray. *God, Power, and Evil: A Process Theodicy.* Philadelphia: Westminster, 1976.

———. *Evil Revisited: Responses and Reconsiderations.* Albany: State University of New York Press, 1991.

———. *Parapsychology, Philosophy, and Spirituality: A Postmodern Exploration.* Albany: State University of New York Press, 1997.

———. *Reenchantment without Supernaturalism: A Process Philosophy of Religion.* Ithaca: Cornell University Press, 2001.

Grosse, Ernst. *The Beginnings of Art.* New York: Appleton, 1897.

Grudin, Louis. *A Primer of Aesthetics: Logical Approaches to a Philosophy of Art.* New York: Covici, Friede, 1930.

Hahn, Lewis Edwin. *A Contextualistic Theory of Perception.* Berkeley: University of California Press, 1942.

Halliday, David, et al. *Physics.* New York: John Wiley, 1992.

Harries, Richard. *Art and the Beauty of God.* London: Mobray, 1993.

Harris, Errol E. *Cosmos and Anthropos: A Philosophical Interpretation of the Anthropic Cosmological Principle.* Atlantic Highlands, N.J.: Humanities Press, 1991.

Harrison, Hazel. *How to Paint and Draw.* New York: Anness Publishing, 1994.

Haught, John. *God after Darwin: A Theology of Evolution.* Boulder, Colo.: Westview, 2000.

Henning, Brian. "A Genuine Ethical Universe: Beauty, Morality, and Nature in a Processive Cosmos." Ph.D. diss., Fordham University, 2002.

Hick, John. *Death and Eternal Life.* New York: Harper and Row, 1976.

Hodges, Myrtis. *Life Interpreted through Color.* Holyoke, Mass.: Towne, 1926.

Hospers, John. *Meaning and Truth in the Arts.* Chapel Hill: University of North Carolina Press, 1946.

———. "Hartshorne's Aesthetics." In *The Philosophy of Charles Hartshorne,* ed. Lewis Hahn, 113–34, 600–606. LaSalle, Ill.: Open Court, 1991.

James, William. *Some Problems of Philosophy: A Beginning of an Introduction to Philosophy.* 1911. Reprint, New York: Greenwood, 1968.

———. *The Will to Believe and Other Essays in Popular Philosophy.* Ed. Frederick H. Burkhardt, Fredson Bowers, and Ignas K. Skrupskelis. Cambridge: Harvard University Press, 1979.

Jamieson, Dale. "Against Zoos." In *In Defense of Animals,* ed. Peter Singer, 108–17. Oxford: Blackwell, 1985.

———. "Zoos Revisited." In *The Philosophy of the Environment,* ed. T. D. J. Chappell, 180–92. Edinburgh: Edinburgh University Press, 1997.

Johnson, James. "The Unknown Langer." *Journal of Aesthetic Education* 27 (1993): 63–73.

Jones, Judith. *Intensity: An Essay in Whiteheadian Ontology.* Nashville: Vanderbilt University Press, 1998.

Kandel, Eric R., James H. Schwartz, and Thomas M. Jessell, eds. *Principles of Neural Science.* 4th ed. New York: McGraw-Hill, 2000.

Kandinsky, Wassily. *Concerning the Spiritual in Art.* Trans. and with an introduction by M. T. H. Sadler. New York: Dover, 1977.

Keeling, L. Bryant. "Feeling as a Metaphysical Category: Hartshorne from an Analytic View." *Process Studies* 6 (1976): 51–66.

Kohák, Erazim. *The Embers and the Stars: A Philosophical Inquiry into the Moral Sense of Nature.* Chicago: University of Chicago Press, 1985.

Köhler, Wolfgang. *Gestalt Psychology.* New York: Liveright, 1929.

Kovach, Francis J. *Philosophy of Beauty.* Norman: University of Oklahoma Press, 1974.

Kuntz, Paul. "Whitehead's Category of Harmony." *Process Studies* 29 (2000): 43–65.

Lachmann, Rolf. "From Metaphysics to Art and Back: The Relevance of Susanne K. Langer's Philosophy for Process Metaphysics." *Process Studies* 26 (1997): 107–25.

Ladd-Franklin, Christine. *Colour and Colour Theories.* New York: Harcourt, Brace, and Co., 1929.

Langer, Susanne K. *Philosophy in a New Key: A Study in the Symbolism of Reason, Rite, and Art.* Cambridge: Harvard University Press, 1942.

———. *Feeling and Form: A Theory of Art.* New York: Scribner's, 1953.

———. *Mind: An Essay on Human Feeling.* Baltimore: Johns Hopkins University Press, 1967.

Leclerc, Ivor. "Whitehead and the Dichotomy of Rationalism and Empiricism." In *Whitehead's Metaphysics of Creativity,* ed. Friedrich Rapp and Reiner Wiehl, 1–20. Albany: State University of New York Press, 1990.

Lee, Vernon. "Empathy." In *A Modern Book of Esthetics: An Anthology,* ed. Melvin Rader, 370–82. 1952. Reprint, New York: Holt, Rinehart, and Winston, 1960.

Leeuw, Gerardus van der. *Sacred and Profane Beauty: The Holy in Art.* Trans. David E. Green. New York: Holt, Rinehart, and Winston, 1963.

Leopold, Aldo. *A Sand County Almanac.* New York: Oxford University Press, 1966.

Malcolm, Norman. "Anselm's Ontological Arguments." *Philosophical Review* 69 (1960): 41–62.

Marion, Jean-Luc. *God without Being: Hors-Texte.* Trans. Thomas A. Carlson. Chicago: University of Chicago Press, 1991.

Maritain, Jacques. *Art and Scholasticism, With Other Essays.* New York: Scribner's, 1930.

Martin, F. David. *Art and the Religious Experience: The "Language" of the Sacred.* Lewisburg, Pa.: Bucknell University Press, 1972.

Martin, Isolde. "Universal v. Learned Emotional Responses to Colors." *Arts in Psychotherapy* 9 (1982): 245–47.

Matthews, Mason. *Primer of Music.* Chicago: John Church, 1894.

McFarland, Thomas. *Coleridge and the Pantheist Tradition.* Oxford: Clarendon Press, 1969.

———. *Romanticism and the Forms of Ruin: Wordsworth, Coleridge, and Modalities of Fragmentation.* Princeton: Princeton University Press, 1981.

McGilvary, Evander Bradley. "Space-Time, Location, and Prehension." In *The Philosophy of Alfred North Whitehead,* ed. Paul A. Schilpp, 209–39. LaSalle, Ill.: Open Court, 1941.

McManus, I. C., et al. "The Aesthetics of Colour." *Perception* 10 (1981): 651–66.

Menta, Timothy. "The Origin and Development of Moral Sensibility." Ph.D. diss., Boston University, 1996.

Middleton, Darren J. N., ed. *God, Literature, and Process Thought.* Burlington, Vt.: Ashgate, 2002.

Moskop, John. "Mill and Hartshorne." *Process Studies* 10 (1980): 18–33.

———. *Divine Omniscience and Human Freedom: Thomas Aquinas and Charles Hartshorne.* Macon, Ga.: Mercer University Press, 1984.

Munro, Thomas. *Toward Science in Aesthetics: Selected Essays.* New York: Liberal Arts, 1956.

Myers, William. "Hartshorne, Whitehead, and the Religious Availability of God." *Personalist Forum* 14 (1998): 170–95.

Nafe, J. P. "Psychology of Felt Experience." *American Journal of Psychology* 39 (1927): 367–89.

———. "A Quantitative Theory of Feeling." *Journal of General Psychology* 3 (1929): 29.

Nagel, Thomas. *Mortal Questions.* Cambridge: Cambridge University Press, 1979.

Nairn, Thomas. "Hartshorne and Utilitarianism." *Process Studies* 17 (1988): 170–80.

Navone, John. *Toward a Theology of Beauty.* Collegeville, Minn.: Liturgical Press, 1996.

Neville, Robert C. *Creativity and God: A Challenge to Process Theology.* New York: Seabury, 1980.

Newton, Natika. *Foundations of Understanding.* Philadelphia: John Benjamins, 1996.

Nichols, Aidan. *The Art of God Incarnate: Theology and Image in Christian Tradition.* New York: Paulist Press, 1980.

Nikkel, David H. *Panentheism in Hartshorne and Tillich: A Creative Synthesis.* New York: Peter Lang, 1995.

Nolte, John. *The Human Brain: An Introduction to Its Functional Anatomy.* St. Louis: Mosby, 1999.

Ogden, Charles Kay. *The Meaning of Psychology.* New York: Harper, 1926.

Ogden, Charles Kay, I. A. Richards, and James Wood. *The Foundations of Aesthetics.* 1922. Reprint, New York: International Publishers, 1925.

Ogden, Robert. *Hearing. 1924.* Reprint, London: Cape, 1925.

Ortega y Gasset, José. "The Dehumanization of Art." In *A Modern Book of Esthetics: An Anthology,* ed. Melvin Rader, 411–19. 1952. Reprint, New York: Holt, Rinehart, and Winston, 1960.

Ozenfant, Amédée. *Foundations of Modern Art.* Trans. John Rodker. New York: Brewer, Warren, and Putnam, 1931.

Pailin, David. "Review of David Ray Griffin, *Reenchantment Without Supernaturalism.*" *Religious Studies* 38 (2002): 225–31.

Palmer, Clare. *Environmental Ethics and Process Thinking.* Oxford: Clarendon Press, 1998.

Palmer, G. E. H., et al., trans. and eds. *The Philokalia.* 4 vols. London: Faber and Faber, 1979–1995.

Parker, De Witt H. *The Principles of Aesthetics.* New York: Silver, Burdett, and Co. 1920.

———. *The Analysis of Art.* New Haven: Yale University Press, 1926.

Parker, G. H. *Smell, Taste, and Allied Senses in the Vertebrates.* Philadelphia: Lippincott, 1922.

Pepper, Stephen. *Aesthetic Quality: A Contextualistic Theory of Beauty.* New York: Scribner's, 1937.

Peters, Eugene H. *Hartshorne and Neoclassical Metaphysics: An Interpretation.* Lincoln: University of Nebraska Press, 1970.

Piaget, Jean. *The Child's Conception of the World.* London: Routledge and Kegan Paul, 1929.

Pike, Nelson, ed. *God and Evil: Readings on the Theological Problem of Evil.* Englewood Cliffs, N.J.: Prentice-Hall, 1964.

Plantinga, Alvin, ed. *The Ontological Argument , From St. Anselm to Contemporary Philosophers.* Garden City, N.Y.: Anchor Books, 1965.

Popper, Karl R. *Objective Knowledge: An Evolutionary Approach.* 1972. Reprint, Oxford: Clarendon Press, 1979.

Pratt, Carroll C. *The Meaning of Music: A Study in Psychological Aesthetics.* New York: McGraw-Hill, 1931.

Price, H. H. *Perception.* London: Methuen, 1932.

Prigogine, Ilya. *From Being to Becoming: Time and Complexity in the Physical Sciences.* San Francisco: Freeman, 1980.

Rayden, A. Maude. *Beauty in Religion.* New York: Putnam's, 1923.

Reck, Andrew. "Hartshorne's Place in the History of Philosophy." *Tulane Studies in Philosophy* 34 (1986): 5–19.

Regan, Tom. *The Case for Animal Rights.* Berkeley: University of California Press, 1983.

Reimer, Bennett. *A Philosophy of Music Education.* Englewood Cliffs, N.J.: Prentice-Hall, 1970.

Richards, I. A. "Science and Poetry." In *A Modern Book of Esthetics: An Anthology,* ed. Melvin Rader, 270–85. 1952. Reprint, New York: Holt, Rinehart, and Winston, 1960.

Richmond, John. "Reconsidering Aesthetics and Religious Experience: A Companion View." *Journal of Aesthetic Education* 33 (1999): 29–47.

Roberts, Louis. *The Theological Aesthetics of Hans Urs von Balthasar.* Washington, D.C.: Catholic University of America Press, 1987.

Santayana, George. *The Sense of Beauty; Being the Outline of Aesthetic Theory.* 1896. Reprint, New York: Modern Library, 1955.

Scheler, Max. *On Feeling, Knowing, and Valuing: Selected Writings.* Ed. Harold J. Breshady. Chicago: University of Chicago Press, 1992.

Schoen, Max, ed. *The Effects of Music: A Series of Essays.* New York: Harcourt, Brace, 1927.

Scholes, Percy. *The Listener's Guide to Music with a Concert-Goer's Glossary.* 1919. Reprint, Oxford: Oxford University Press, 1925.

Seager, William. "Consciousness, Information, and Panpsychism." *Journal of Consciousness Studies* 2 (1995): 272–88.

Sherburne, Donald W. *A Whiteheadian Aesthetic.* New Haven: Yale University Press, 1961.

———. "Whitehead without God." *Christian Scholar* 40 (1967): 251–72.

Sherry, Patrick. *Spirit and Beauty: An Introduction to Theological Aesthetics.* Oxford: Clarendon Press, 1992.

Shields, George W. "Physicalist Panexperientialism and the Mind-Body Problem." *American Journal of Theology and Philosophy* 22 (2001): 133–54.

———. "Omniscience and Radical Particularity: A Reply to Simoni." *Religious Studies* 39 (2003): 225–33.

———, ed. *Process and Analysis: Whitehead, Hartshorne, and the Analytic Tradition.* Albany: State University of New York Press, 2003.

Shurley, Jay. "Profound Experimental Sensory Isolation." *American Journal of Psychiatry* 117 (1960): 539–45.

Simoni-Wastila, Henry. "Is Divine Relativity Possible: Charles Hartshorne on God's Sympathy with the World." *Process Studies* 28 (1999): 98–116.

Skutch, Alexander. "Bird Song and Philosophy." In *The Philosophy of Charles Hartshorne,* ed. Lewis Hahn, 65–76, 586–89. LaSalle, Ill.: Open Court, 1991.

Slater, Peter. "Birdsong Repertoires: Their Origins and Use." In *The Origins of Music,* ed. Nils Wallin, Björn Merker, and Steven Brown, 49–64. Cambridge: MIT Press, 2000.

Spinoza, Benedictus de. *Ethics.* London: Dent, 1913.

Stapp, Henry. "Quantum Mechanics, Local Causality, and Process Philosophy." *Process Studies* 7 (1977): 173–82.

Stein, Edith. *On the Problem of Empathy.* Trans. Waltraut Stein. The Hague: Martinus Nijhoff, 1964.

Stevens, Wallace. *The Collected Poems of Wallace Stevens.* 1954. Reprint, New York: Knopf, 1978.

Strong, C. A. *The Origins of Consciousness.* London: Macmillan, 1918.

Suchocki, Marjorie Hewitt. "Charles Hartshorne and Subjective Immortality." *Process Studies* 21 (1992): 118–22.

Sullivan, J. W. N. *Beethoven: His Spiritual Development.* New York: Knopf, 1927.

Suzuki, D. T. *An Introduction to Zen Buddhism.* New York: Grove, 1964.

Taylor, C. D. "Visual Perception versus Visual plus Kinaesthetic Perception in Judging Colored Weights." *Journal of General Psychology* 4 (1930): 229–46.

Thorpe, W. H. "The Learning of Song Patterns by Birds." *Ibis* 100 (1958): 553–70.

———. *Bird-Song: The Biology of Vocal Communication and Expression in Birds.* Cambridge: Cambridge University Press, 1961.

Tillich, Paul. *On Art and Architecture.* Ed. John Dillenberger and Jane Dillenberger. Trans. Robert P. Scharlemann. New York: Crossroad, 1987.

Toulmin, Stephen Edelston. *Foresight and Understanding: An Enquiry into the Aims of Science.* New York: Harper, 1961.

Towne, Edgar. *Two Types of New Theism: Knowledge of God in the Thought of Paul Tillich and Charles Hartshorne.* New York: Peter Lang, 1997.

———. "The New Physics and Hartshorne's Dipolar Theism." *American Journal of Theology and Philosophy* 22 (2001): 114–32.

Troland, Leonard Thompson. *The Principles of Psychophysiology.* 3 vols. New York: Van Nostrand, 1929–1932.

Turner, W. J. *Orpheus; or, The Music of the Future.* New York: Dutton, 1926.

Valady, Mohammed. Introduction to *The Zero Fallacy and Other Essays in Neoclassical Metaphysics,* by Charles Hartshorne, xiii–xxxii. LaSalle, Ill.: Open Court, 1997.

Valentine, C. W. *The Experimental Psychology of Beauty.* London: Methuen, 1962.

Valentine, C. W., and C. Meyers. "A Study of Individual Differences in Attitude toward Tones." *British Journal of Psychology* 7 (1914): 68–72.

Valenza, Robert. "Aesthetic Priority in Science and Religion." *Process Studies* 31 (2002): 49–76.

Vaske, Martin. *An Introduction to Metaphysics.* New York: McGraw-Hill, 1963.

Viladesau, Richard. *Theological Aesthetics: God in Imagination, Beauty, and Art.* Oxford: Oxford University Press, 1999.

———. *Theology and the Arts: Encountering God through Music, Art, and Rhetoric.* New York: Paulist Press, 2000.

Viney, Donald. *Charles Hartshorne and the Existence of God.* Albany: State University of New York Press, 1985.

———. "Jules Lequyer and the Openness of God." *Faith and Philosophy* 14 (1997): 212–35.

———. *The Life and Thought of Charles Hartshorne.* Pittsburg, Kans.: Logos-Sophia Press, 1997.

———. "The Varieties of Theism and the Openness of God: Charles Hartshorne and Free-Will Theism." *Personalist Forum* 14 (1998): 196–234.

———. "What Is Wrong with the Mirror Image? A Brief Reply to Simoni-Wastila on the Problem of Radical Particularity." *Process Studies* 29 (2000): 365–67, 390–91.

Viney, Donald, and Rebecca Viney. "For the Beauty of the Earth: A Hartshornian Ecological Aesthetic." *Proceedings of the Institute for Liberal Studies* 4 (1993): 38–44.

Viney, Wayne. "Charles Hartshorne's Philosophy and Psychology of Sensation." In *The Philosophy of Charles Hartshorne,* ed. Lewis Hahn, 91–112, 598–600. LaSalle, Ill.: Open Court, 1991.

Vivas, Eliseo, and Murray Kreiger. *The Problems of Aesthetics: A Book of Readings.* New York: Rinehart, 1953.

Waddell, James, and F. W. Dillistone, eds. *Art and Religion as Communication.* Atlanta: John Knox, 1974.

Wallin, Nils, Björn Merker, and Steven Brown, eds. *The Origins of Music.* Cambridge: MIT Press, 2000.

Ward, James. "Is 'Black' a Sensation?" *British Journal of Psychology* 1 (1908): 407–27.

Warren, Richard M. and Roslyn Warren. *Helmholtz on Perception, Its Physiology, and Development.* New York: John Wiley, 1968.

Weinberg, Steven. *Dreams of a Final Theory.* 1992. Reprint, New York: Vintage Books, 1994.

Wellek, René, and Austin Warren. *Theory of Literature.* New York: Harcourt Brace, 1949.

Whaling, Carol. "What's behind a Song: The Natural Basis of Song Learning in Birds." In *The Origins of Music,* ed. Nils Wallin, Björn Merker, and Steven Brown, 65–76. Cambridge: MIT Press, 2000.

Wheeler, J. A. and W. H. Zurek, eds. *Quantum Theory and Measurement.* Princeton: Princeton University Press, 1983.

Whitehead, Alfred North. *The Concept of Nature: Tarner Lectures Delivered in Trinity College.* Cambridge: Cambridge University Press, 1920.

———. *Science and the Modern World.* New York: Macmillan, 1925.

———. *Religion in the Making.* New York: Macmillan, 1926.

———. *Adventures of Ideas.* New York: Macmillan, 1933.

———. *Modes of Thought.* New York: Macmillan, 1938.

———. *The Function of Reason.* Boston: Beacon Press, 1958.

———. *Process and Reality: An Essay in Cosmology.* Corrected ed. Ed. David Ray Griffin and Donald Sherburne. New York: Macmillan, 1978.

Whitney, Barry L. *What Are They Saying about God and Evil?* New York: Paulist Press, 1989.

————. "An Aesthetic Solution to the Problem of Evil." *International Journal for Philosophy of Religion* 35 (1994): 21–37.

————. "Divine Persuasion and the Anthropic Argument." *Personalist Forum* 14 (1998): 141–69.

Whitney, Barry L., and J. Norman King. "Rahner and Hartshorne on Death and Eternal Life." *Horizons* 15 (1998): 239–61.

Wickiser, Ralph Lewanda. *An Introduction to Art Education*. New York: World Book Co., 1957.

Wolterstorff, Nicholas. *Art in Action: Toward a Christian Aesthetic*. Grand Rapids, Mich.: Eerdmans, 1980.

————. *Works and Worlds of Art*. Oxford: Clarendon Press, 1980.

Woodworth, Robert Sessions. *Psychology: A Study of Mental Life*. New York: Holt, 1921.

Wordsworth, William. *Poetical Works*. Oxford: Oxford University Press, 1981.

Wright, Frank Lloyd. *The Future of Architecture*. New York: Horizon Press, 1953.

Zangwill, Nick. *The Metaphysics of Beauty*. Ithaca: Cornell University Press, 2001.

Name Index